OPEN ACCESS AND THE HUMANITIES

G000136757

If you work in a university, you are almost certain to have heard the term 'open access' in the past couple of years. You may also have heard either that it is the utopian answer to all the problems of research dissemination or perhaps that it marks the beginning of an apocalyptic new era of 'pay-to-say' publishing. In this book, Martin Paul Eve sets out the histories, contexts and controversies for open access, specifically in the humanities. Broaching practical elements alongside economic histories, open licensing, monographs and funder policies, this book is a must-read for both those new to ideas about open-access scholarly communications and those with an already keen interest in the latest developments for the humanities. This title is available as open access via Cambridge Books Online.

MARTIN PAUL EVE is a lecturer in English at the University of Lincoln and is the author of *Pynchon and Philosophy* (2014) and editor of the open-access journal of Pynchon scholarship, *Orbit*. Eve is well known for his work on open access, which includes appearing as an expert witness before the UK House of Commons Select Committee BIS Inquiry into Open Access, being a steering-group member of the OAPEN-UK project and a member of the HEFCE Open Access Monographs Expert Reference Panel, and founding the *Open Library of Humanities*.

OPEN ACCESS AND THE HUMANITIES

Contexts, Controversies and the Future

MARTIN PAUL EVE

CAMBRIDGE
UNIVERSITY PRESS

CAMBRIDGE
UNIVERSITY PRESS

University Printing House, Cambridge CB2 8BS, United Kingdom

Cambridge University Press is part of the University of Cambridge.

It furthers the University's mission by disseminating knowledge in the pursuit of education, learning and research at the highest international levels of excellence.

www.cambridge.org
Information on this title: www.cambridge.org/9781107484016

© Martin Paul Eve 2014
Preface © Peter Suber 2014

First published 2014

A catalogue record for this publication is available from the British Library

ISBN 978-1-107-09789-6 Hardback
ISBN 978-1-107-48401-6 Paperback

For Helen

Contents

vii

To begin with such a practical self-criticism would make a
real difference in the way we do our work.

Jerome McGann, 'Information Technology and the Troubled Humanities', p. 110

Preface

Open access benefits the sciences and humanities about equally, but has been growing faster in the sciences. That may seem odd until we realise that benefits aren't the only factors affecting growth. Sunlight benefits all plants about equally, but some plants live in dry climates, some at high altitudes, some in rocky soil.

Open access (OA) helps readers find, retrieve, read and use the research they need. At the same time, it helps authors enlarge their audience and amplify their impact. Those are the main benefits. But these benefits lead to others. If OA helps readers and authors of research, then it helps advance research itself and all the benefits that depend on research. In the case of the sciences, that can mean new medicines and useful technologies, and in the case of the humanities it can mean enriched education, politics, compassion, imagination and understanding.

One of the most compelling arguments for legislated OA policies is that governments should assure public access to the results of publicly funded research. This argument is widely effective because it aims to accelerate the research we've already decided to fund with public money, increase the return on the public's large investment in research, and improve fairness to taxpayers. There's no downside for the public interest, only an incomplete upside. There is more public funding for scientific research than for humanities research. Far more. Call this a dry climate for the humanities.

Journals in the humanities have higher rejection rates than journals in the sciences. This is not because they are more rigorous, but because they cover wider topics and receive correspondingly more submissions per published paper. In any case, their higher rejection rates affect their ability to charge fees to cover the costs of production. (Charging these fees is the best-known but not the most common business model for OA journals.) If someone on the author side of the transaction, such as the author's employer or funder, pays an article processing charge, then no one needs to pay on the reader side, and the work may become OA. But the fee for an article must cover the costs of vetting all the articles rejected for every one accepted. Hence, fee-based OA journals with high rejection rates must charge higher fees than other journals. The fee-based model works best in well-funded fields with relatively low rejection rates, and worst in fields like the humanities. This is a dry climate combined with the difficulty of transplanting a misty-climate crop to a dry climate.

Journal articles tend to be primary literature in the sciences and secondary literature in the humanities. In the sciences, books tend to synthesise research published in articles, while in the humanities articles tend to report on the history and interpretation of books. Tenure in the sciences depends more on published articles than on books, while tenure in the humanities depends more on published books than on articles. This would just be an observation about disciplinary differences if it weren't for the inconvenient fact that OA for books is objectively harder than OA for articles. The production costs of a book are significantly higher than the production costs of an article. Hence, it's significantly harder to find the business models or subsidies to pay for OA books than those to pay for OA journals. To top it off, academic monographs can pay royalties, in theory, even if they seldom do so in practice. By contrast, scholarly articles never pay royalties, which is the main reason why the worldwide OA movement has focused on articles. Hence, author consent for OA is easier to win for articles than for books.

Despite these obstacles, OA for books is feasible and growing, thanks to many innovative start-ups including the Open Library of Humanities, founded by Martin Eve and Caroline Edwards. However, even progress for OA books doesn't change the fact that scholars in the humanities have reasons to publish in genres where OA is more difficult, like farmers with reasons to plant higher up the mountainside.

I'll add one more difference between the disciplines and then stop. Certain myths and misunderstandings about OA are more tenacious and widespread in the humanities than in the sciences. This adds needless obstacles to the growth of OA. For example, by percentages more humanists than scientists believe that publishing in a high-prestige non-OA journal rules out making the same work OA through an online repository, that even well-implemented OA risks copyright infringement, that most OA journals charge author-side fees, that most fees at fee-based OA journals are paid by authors out of pocket, that most non-profit society publishers fear and shun OA, and that most OA publishers are lax with quality control.

I'd like to think that these myths and misunderstandings are more common in the humanities merely because humanists have had less time than scientists to catch up with the relatively recent advent of OA. But that's not true. They've had exactly as much time. Nor is the explanation that humanists are more careless readers of contracts, policies, statutes, or studies of OA itself. I suspect the true explanation is that humanists have had fewer working examples of OA to prove the concept and prove that the sky does not fall. They've had fewer working examples to dispel misunderstandings, generate enthusiasm and inspire commitment. If so, then the humanities labour within a vicious circle in which the slower growth of OA causes a slower growth of good understanding, and vice versa. By contrast the sciences enjoy a virtuous circle in which the faster growth of OA causes a faster growth of good understanding, and vice versa. This is rocky soil for the humanities.

But the same explanation contains a ground for hope. There was a time when the growth of OA in the sciences was also slow, and kept slow by a vicious circle. In fewer than twenty years, however – long in internet time, short in the history of scholarship – the vicious circle in the sciences became a virtuous circle. This reversal is not logically impossible. It requires steady growth in working examples, to feed understanding, and steady growth in understanding, to feed working examples.

The good news is that we see this growth today in the humanities. Martin Eve is among the leaders in making this happen. He's a leader in providing working examples, and a leader in correcting myths and misunderstandings, without underestimating genuine difficulties, through his articles, blog posts, public speaking and now through this book.

PETER SUBER
DIRECTOR, OFFICE FOR SCHOLARLY COMMUNICATION
HARVARD UNIVERSITY

Acknowledgements

There are many individuals and groups who have positively contributed not only to this book, but to my discovery of and immersion in open access. Although it may be clichéd and/or trite, I would like to thank all those who have participated in the discussions around and practical implementations of open access.

There are also, however, some figures from whom I have received individual assistance and I would like to acknowledge them more specifically here, with apologies to those I have no doubt omitted. Firstly, I thank Caroline Edwards for being my co-conspirator on the OLH project and with whom I planned this volume. She is not only a rigorous, sharp and quick thinker but a kind friend and an excellent colleague. I also, of course, thank Peter Suber for his generous preface to this book but also for his untiring efforts to make open access a reality.

I would furthermore like to acknowledge the help of Ellen Collins for the contribution that her literature review into OA monographs made to this book and for her comments on my write-up of the OAPEN-UK project. Likewise with respect to OAPEN-NL and OAPEN-UK, I owe a debt to Eelco Ferwerda, Caren Milloy and Graham Stone. With regard to the sections on the commodity form of open-access articles, I thank Joss Winn, an astute thinker in the Marxist tradition. For invitations to other various panels, projects and discussions that have informed this book, I would like to thank Geoff Crossick, Ben Johnson, Chris Wickham, Nigel Vincent, Ben Showers, Kitty Ingliss, Jane Harvell, Ann Rossiter, Neil Jacobs and Michael Bhaskar.

Elsewhere, in no particular order, I would like to thank the following for conversations, ideas and projects: John Willinsky, Alex Garnett, Juan Pablo Alperin, Don Waters, Kathleen Fitzpatrick, Cameron Neylon, Adam Hyde, Mike Taylor, Jane Winters, Tim Hitchcock, Liz Sage, Joe Brooker, Martin McQuillan, Roger Luckhurst, Hilary Fraser, James Baker and Ernesto Priego. For reading early drafts of this book, I thank Ruth Charnock and James Emmott.

I thank all my friends and colleagues at Lincoln who have put up with me banging on about open access, but especially Siân Adiseshiah, Christopher Marlow, Rebecca Styler, Amy Culley, Owen Clayton, Hannah Field and Agnes Woolley.

I am immensely grateful to Cambridge University Press for their support of this volume and particularly to Richard Fisher, Linda Bree, Anna Bond, Jessica Murphy and Frances Brown. It is, of course, difficult to write about or criticise scholarly publishing within the confines and power structures of that very system. I am a believer, however, that the amplificatory power of good presses is real and that through this route this book will reach readers who would otherwise remain in the dark. While, therefore, it was a condition of this book that it be written as close to neutrality as possible, it was nonetheless brave of Cambridge University Press to let me go ahead with the project. The Press have also extremely kindly agreed to make this book open access at launch (including a form of open licensing) while selling electronic and physical copies. I was offered a royalty, but have instead chosen to donate any authorial proceeds to Arthritis Research UK, without whose work I could neither live nor work. Please do support the project by buying a copy if you are reading this online. If you are reading in print, thank you but please don't forget that there is also a searchable electronic version available to you freely.

Some portions of the writing here have appeared before in other forms, either on my personal website or elsewhere. Most notably, the meditations on peer review in Chapter 5 appeared in a significantly altered form, yet clearly enough for the genesis to be seen, as 'Before the Law: Open Access, Quality Control and the Future of Peer Review', in *Debating Open Access*, edited by Nigel Vincent and Chris Wickham (London: British Academy), pp. 68–81. Some of the remarks on collective/collaborative funding initiatives appeared within my 'All That Glisters: Investigating Collective Funding Mechanisms for Gold Open Access in Humanities Disciplines', *Journal of Librarianship and Scholarly Communication*, 2, 3 (2014).

Finally, I would like to thank my wife, Helen Eve, for her spark, patience and love and without whom I almost certainly would not have become an academic. This book is dedicated to her.

Citing this work

As per the provisions of section 3.a.1.A.i of the CC BY-SA license, when attributing this work, I request that you reproduce the following elements in your citation: Martin Paul Eve, *Open Access and the Humanities: Contexts, Controversies and the Future* (Cambridge: Cambridge University Press, 2014) and the URL http://dx.doi.org/10.1017/CBO9781316161012. If a derivative, you should acknowledge this fact. Although I cannot legally enforce it under the license, I would be grateful if you would summarise any changes made in a derivative.

CHAPTER I

Introduction, or why open access?

WHAT IS OPEN ACCESS?

In the first decade and a half of the twenty-first century, the words 'open access' have been uttered with increasing frequency in universities around the world.[1] Beginning as little more than a quiet murmur in niche scientific sub-disciplines but developing towards a globally mandated revolution in scholarly communication, the ascent of open access looks set to continue. Despite this rapid, worldwide rise, however, many misunderstandings about the phenomenon remain. At the most basic level, this includes the key question: what exactly is 'open access'?[2] Regardless of the nuances and complexities that will be discussed in this book, 'open access' can be clearly and succinctly defined. The term 'open access' refers to the removal of price and permission barriers to scholarly research.[3] Open access means peer-reviewed academic research work that is free to read online and that anybody may redistribute and reuse, with some restrictions.

For a piece of academic research to be called 'open access', it must be available digitally for anybody to read at no financial cost beyond those intrinsic to using the internet; the removal of price barriers. This is similar to the majority of content on the world wide web but it is not the basis on which scholarly publication has historically relied. After all, most websites do not charge readers to access their content while, by contrast, most academic publications are currently bought by libraries as either one-off purchases or ongoing subscriptions. Open access means implementing a new system that allows free access to peer-reviewed scholarly research on the world wide web. The term also means, perhaps more contentiously, that people should be able to reuse this material beyond the provisions of fair use enshrined in copyright law, as long as the author is credited. This is the removal of permission barriers that advocates claim is necessary to facilitate activities such as assembling a course pack of lengthy extracts for teaching. The removal of these two 'barriers' alters the current model of scholarly communications because, at present, access to research is only allowed when content has been purchased from a publisher and because, at the moment, one may only redistribute and use works in accordance with the fair dealings provisions of copyright.

The possibility of open access to scholarly research rests on several technological and economic bases, the contexts of which are all more complex than this introduction alone can suggest. That said, there are some key prerequisites that can be identified with ease. Firstly, open access relies upon the potential of the internet to disseminate work almost indefinitely at a near-infinitesimal cost-per-copy. This is because, in the digital world, the majority of costs lie in the labour to reach the point of dissemination rather than in the transmission of each copy. Open access was not, therefore, truly feasible in times before this technology; OA requires the digital environment and the internet.[4] The second aspect that makes open access possible, according to Stevan Harnad – one of the leading figures of the Open Access movement – is that the economic situation of the academy is different from other spheres of cultural production. Academics are, in Harnad's view, 'esoteric' authors whose primary motivation is to be read by peers and the public, rather than to sell their work.[5] While the labour of *publishing* still needs to be covered (and these costs cannot be denied), this situation potentially enables academics employed at universities to give their work to readers for free; this specific subset of researchers are paid a salary, rather than earning a living by selling their specialist outputs.

Stemming from the possibilities of these intertwined economic and technological roots, advocates of open access believe that the broadest global exposure to research outputs would be achieved through a system that did not require the reader to pay. These benefits are claimed to extend, among other groups, to academics whose libraries cannot meet the price of subscriptions and to the general public for whom much research material remains unaffordable. As George Veletsianos and Royce Kimmons put it, 'Many scholars hope and anticipate that open practices will broaden access to education and knowledge, reduce costs, enhance the impact and reach of scholarship and education, and foster the development of more equitable, effective, efficient, and transparent scholarly and educational processes.'[6] As will be seen, however, some forms of open access have also proved highly controversial both for the inversion of the economic model that they might engender and for the more permissive reuse rights that they could bestow. In both cases, these objections have been prominently raised in the humanities disciplines in particular. The degrees of 'disruption' and objection to the current ecosystem are, though, tiered according to the ways in which OA is implemented. While, therefore, some forms of open access require new economic models to sustain the labour of publishing, other mechanisms seem to co-exist peacefully with a subscription ecosystem, at least at present.[7] Nonetheless, these potentially radical changes to the scholarly communications environment embroil OA uptake within a set of complexities, nuances and controversies, ranging from academic dissent through to corporate concerns over economics. In this light, it may be true that open access is a simple idea, in theory. In its real-world implementation and transition, however, it is proving to be messy and contentious.

*

This book is dedicated threefold to an exploration of the claimed potential benefits of open access for the humanities disciplines; to unravelling the problems that must be dealt with if these are desired; and to giving fair voice to the controversies that have arisen as a result. It is written for academics, policymakers, librarians, funders, curators, publishers and the generally interested public: in short, each of the groups for whom open access could be important. Although this work may serve as a primer for those unfamiliar with open access, it is designed less as a comprehensive introduction and more as a critical investigation into the effects that open digital dissemination and reuse might have upon humanities disciplines and academic publishing. Those looking for a more general introduction would do well to consult Peter Suber's *Open Access* (itself freely available online).

By way of cartography, with respect to this book's subtitle – 'contexts, controversies and the future' – this work is mapped thematically rather than chronologically. This book does not begin with 'contexts' for open access and the humanities, then move to 'controversies' and end with 'the future', but rather weaves these elements throughout its investigations. To this end, the remainder of this chapter is devoted to terminological basics; to unpacking the history of the Open Access movement; to addressing the problems of and potential lessons from the genesis of open access in the scientific field; and to exploring the objections from various stakeholders in outline. The first two of these areas may be superfluous to those already familiar with the basics of open access, while the latter two may present fresh angles for those coming with a scientific perspective.

Because any transition to open access must necessarily interact with the value systems of the academy and its publishing mechanisms, the second chapter unpacks the economics of scholarly publishing in the two interlinked senses of an 'economy' of academic prestige and of finance. Beginning with the ways in which ideas of academic symbolic capital ('prestige') intersect with real-world pricing, this chapter also examines the commodity form of research work; the contexts of humanities scholarship; and the rhetoric of 'crisis' that pervades these disciplines. Concluding that there are, paradoxically, both supply-side and demand-side 'crises' affecting scholarly publishing (itself a heterogeneous term with a great deal of international variance in practice), the chapter ends with an examination of the different economic models that have been proposed for OA in the humanities. This chapter will hold value for librarians, funders and researchers but also to anybody more broadly interested in the economics that shape the research activities of the humanities disciplines.

The third chapter focuses on the contentious issue of open licensing, explored most thoroughly through the Creative Commons licenses.[8] This chapter gives a historical background to open licensing and copyright before describing the reasons why it might be needed and the objections that have been mounted. There are also some observations, in this chapter, on the differing political rationales for desiring open licensing and the ways in which these merge with broader concerns about the future of the public university, which have been most notably voiced by John Holmwood. This chapter will be of interest to anybody who has ever signed a copyright assignment form, to those who are curious about the controversies of open licensing and to those who wish to understand why various factions differ politically on this aspect of OA.

The fourth chapter of this book examines the context of monographs and open access, which comes with higher barriers to entry than the journal sphere for a variety of reasons. This chapter begins by setting out what these differences are before detailing projects that have studied open-access monographs and the economic models that are emerging to support them. Some consideration is also given here to the nature of trade crossover books and the potential difficulties that appear in such a scenario. This chapter will be of interest to publishers, researchers, librarians and funders; in short, all the major stakeholders in the humanities' monograph production and consumption cycle.

The fifth and final chapter of this book unearths potential innovations that are possible with OA. Although, as I take pains to point out throughout, open access entails no more than the lowering of price and permission barriers, this historic juncture does also afford a space in which critically to reappraise several other practices. In this chapter, I provocatively think through just two such potential realms of change: peer-review and editorial work. The volume concludes with a glossary of terms that may prove useful to the newcomer.

The geographical scope of this book is international because open access is a worldwide phenomenon. However, the urgency of implementation has greater impetus in some nations because of strong OA mandates from large, centralised funders. While open access therefore has global histories and international implementations, particularly in South America, the current wave of controversies and scrambles for transition has taken place within the Anglophone academy. Nowhere is this embodied so clearly as in the anxieties surrounding the UK government's Finch Report into open access and the subsequent Select Committee inquiry in 2013, which will be discussed at length below. It is also the case that wherever greater degrees of funder centralisation can be found, there is more scope for mandates to trigger a full-scale transition. Once more, the UK is a good example here. With its state-sponsored research funding councils as the primary sources of research income for many in the humanities, it is clear that if these bodies require OA, as they now do, a greater degree of interest will emerge than in nations with more devolved and/or autonomous funders. To that end, deriving partly from these observations and partly from my own situation, this book may tend at times towards an Anglo- and/or Euro-centrism, despite the extensive discussion of international challenges and descriptions of global projects throughout. That said, the vast majority of the debates covered in this volume have re-emerged in every new location where OA has come to the fore. This seems to indicate that even when dilemmas appear local, they usually have global applicability.

Finally for this preamble, in the service of upfront disclosure, it is important to state that I have worked heavily on open access in the belief that it is a positive force that could transform scholarly communications for the better. I am not, however, so naïve as to think that this is a view shared universally and I also recognise the difficulties in practical implementations. This disclaimer is, therefore, necessary: this book aims to represent fairly, to the best of my ability, the arguments of those who dissent while laying out reasons why advocates remain in favour. This book is not meant as a pro-OA polemic, even if I do eventually side with OA, but attempts to give information and arguments conservatively from both sides; it is intended to open a space in which it is possible to think critically (and sometimes more abstractly) about the research and publication practices of the academy and to allow others to join these debates. Indeed, an account that did not critically consider all aspects of open access would '[limit] the validity and credibility of the field as a site of serious academic endeavour', as Neil Selwyn has put it with reference to the positivist bent in educational technology.[9] That said, total neutrality is, of course, practically impossible; even by selecting various sources I will advance an interpretation. I accept, therefore, that it is unlikely that all stakeholders will feel entirely content. *Caveat lector.*

*

Before beginning any work in earnest, it is worth highlighting the fact that open access is a deeply politicised issue. Indeed, given the number of stakeholders involved, it would be surprising if such a radical overhaul of the scholarly communications system were straightforward and universally accepted. That said, any alignment of OA with specific political positions is complex. As Nigel Vincent and Chris Wickham noted in the foreword to a British Academy volume on the topic, open access 'has a current force, however, which is not only moral but now political, with Conservative politicians in effect lined up with unequivocal egalitarians'.[10] This political ambivalence has been seconded by Cameron Neylon, a prominent figure in the OA world of the sciences, who recently likewise pointed out that to work on open-access projects is to find oneself accused one day of being a neoliberal sell-out and the next of being an anti-corporatist Marxist.[11] In reality, open access was born within various contexts of both corporate and radically anti-corporate politics in which one side proclaims the benefits for free-market business and the other believes 'in an ethical pursuit [of] democratization, fundamental human rights, equality, and justice'.[12] This means that it is extremely difficult to situate the entire phenomenon at such political polarities; different aspects of open access perform different functions that may align with different political agendas.[13]

Fundamentally, however, there is also an understanding of OA emerging that seems desirable to a large number of stakeholders, regardless of political position: open access would function simply to allow researchers and the general public to have access to academic research material when they otherwise could not. Broader motivational differences for desiring this, of course, remain. Some also think open access to be pragmatically impossible, particularly on the economic front. As an ideal goal, though, the proposition of OA is fairly well accepted by a range of figures, with a seeming tipping point of consensus reached in 2013, as can be seen in the section of Chapter 2 on international mandates for open access. It is now more often the practicalities of achieving such a goal that are the focus of disagreement: how should open access be implemented? How is the labour underpinning this operation to be subsidised and who will pay? Such questions are hardly tangential and, even if OA was deemed desirable across the majority of the stakeholder spectrum, without satisfactory answers, it may remain under-realised. In other words: while many different factions now agree that open access is a good idea in principle, there are a number of remaining real-world challenges to be overcome if it is to become the norm. Advocates of open access strive to work around these problems (or, on occasion, deny that the difficulties exist), while sceptics wonder whether the potential disruption is worth the claimed benefits (or whether these hurdles are insurmountable).

Furthermore, the danger of this political minefield is intensified by the fact that open access is a treacherous territory for the newcomer, despite the fundamental simplicity of the concept. As with many other aspects of policy, so it is also with OA: it can appear to the paranoid as though there might be a conspiracy to make the subject so dull and laden with jargon that people are unable to pay attention. Likewise, though, as it is with almost all policy elements that seem tedious and terminologically dense, to ignore these changes would be a catastrophic mistake for anybody who works within a university and a research context. In this light, in order to make this engagement as pain-free as possible, I will try to use as few jargon terms as possible throughout this book. However, there are certain base elements that are so taken for granted when thinking about open access that they are worth unravelling from the outset.

A BRIEF GLOSSARY OF AND INTRODUCTION TO OPEN ACCESS

While a more extensive glossary is available at the end of this book, by this point we already have definitions for 'open access' (the removal of price and permission barriers to research) and the title-case 'Open Access' (the movement to make this happen). There are, however, several ways in which open access can be implemented, each with its own terminology.

Gold open access is the most well known, but sometimes most sceptically viewed, of these 'flavours'. Gold open access refers to research being made available for free in its full, original form in the journal where it was published (or, in the case of a book, being made freely available by the publisher). Gold open access journals can either be entirely open access, or they can be 'hybrid', in which subscription publications carry a subset of articles that are free for all to read. For readers who encounter a gold open access article in a

journal or a gold open access book, there is no subscription or price
to pay and no institutional login form to complete; they can simply
access the material free of charge.
Clearly, this has implications for the economic models of publishers. If publishers cannot sell the work (because they are giving it away
for free), they must find remuneration elsewhere. Therefore, some
forms of gold open access require that the author or his/her institution pay a fee to the publisher, a move that constitutes an inversion
of the current subscription model. This is known as an 'article
processing charge' (APC) or a 'book processing charge' (BPC). It is
true that many publishers are adopting this model for gold open
access in which publishing becomes a service for which academics
and/or their institutions pay. It is also true that, faced with a new and
wholly disruptive proposition in which publishers are less sure of
their revenue forecasts, the current pricing level of processing charges
has sometimes been determined through a re-apportioning of the
status quo.[14] As will be seen, this has often led to levels of pricing
beyond the reach of humanities researchers who receive far less
funding than those working in the sciences.[15]
Gold open access does *not* intrinsically mean, however, that the
author pays and, indeed, this was not integral to the term as it was
coined by Stevan Harnad.[16] At the time of writing in mid 2014, the
majority of gold venues listed in the Directory of Open Access
Journals do not operate on the basis of article processing charges
and instead fund their operations through other means, covered in
Chapter 2.[17] To this end, in this book, whenever I refer to 'gold open
access', I mean open access delivered at source by journals, books or
other output format; open access *at the publisher*. I am not referring
to any particular kind of business model. It is exclusively in the
instances where I write 'article processing charges' or 'APCs', 'book
processing charges' or 'BPCs' that I will be talking about payment to
publishers.
The 'opposite', but also complement, to gold open access is called
green OA. Green open access is OA delivered by an *institutional* or *subject
repository*. An institutional repository is a website, normally administered
by a university library, that holds the metadata about and copies of
affiliated authors' works. For instance, the repository at the University
of Lincoln, UK can be found at http://eprints.lincoln.ac.uk/. Whenever

a staff member has published an article or book (even in a subscription journal or with a traditional, toll-access press) he or she is encouraged to add information about it to the repository and then to upload a copy of the work in accordance with publisher policies (which can stipulate a delay for the copy to be made open access: an 'embargo'). In instances where the publisher policy allows it, this work is then made publicly available, thereby achieving green open access. A surprising number of publishers allow authors to do this for journal articles and there are now a variety of tools to allow authors to check publisher policies, such as SHERPA/RoMEO, a project hosted at the University of Nottingham in the UK that aggregates information on journals.[18] Fewer publishers allow this for books, though, as covered in Chapter 4.

There are several ways, however, in which green open access on its own can be a poor substitute when compared to gold. Unlike gold open access, the version uploaded to a repository is not always the final publisher PDF, the 'version of record' (although some publishers do allow this). Furthermore, there is often (but not always and not by necessity) a delay period before the author is allowed to upload his or her work. This is usually stipulated to protect publisher revenues. In many humanities disciplines where there are strict normative citation standards to the version of record, green open access can also be problematic if the pagination/content differs in the green OA version. If there are lengthy embargoes, this can also reduce the value of green open access in some fields of contemporary study where the most current research is desired quickly.

A typical researcher workflow for a green open access deposit of a journal article would be one in which I, as an author, submit my article to a journal of my choice (including a traditional, toll-access journal). The journal carries out its usual peer-review, copyediting and typesetting procedures and publishes the article. At some time during the process, I check the publisher policies using SHERPA/ RoMEO and create records on my institutional repository that carry the information about the article. If allowed, I might also, at this stage, upload my author version of the paper (the Word document that was accepted by the journal), or even the publisher PDF, to the repository. If the publisher specifies that there is an embargo on the release of material, I set this up in the repository, telling the software the date on which it can make the file(s) public. At the point determined by the embargo, the copy of the document that I uploaded will be made public for everyone to view; it will be open access.

Green open access fulfils several important functions. One of the foremost of these is to address the challenges of *digital preservation*.[19] The impetus for this comes from the history of preservation in the print sphere. Indeed, while it is tempting to think that print is simply more enduring than digital material, this is often only true because sophisticated mechanisms for preserving print have been actively developed (distribution to multiple libraries with temperature- and humidity-controlled environments, for instance).[20] Taking this as a cue, there are now many systems designed to protect purely digital scholarly research. These take the same form as research libraries: if digital material is distributed to hundreds of computers at hundreds of libraries worldwide, then we militate against geographically local points of failure. One of the most well-known digital preservation mechanisms is called LOCKSS, which stands for 'Lots of Copies Keeps Stuff Safe', a name that embodies this principle. A green deposit of an article is just one further instance where that material is stored somewhere else, reducing the chance of a catastrophic single failure. This also explains why green is not just the opposite of gold. Greenly depositing gold articles further protects them through duplication.

The other function that green OA fulfils is to provide access when a gold option is not available. One of the substantial advantages (or disadvantages in some opinions) of green OA is that there is currently no evidence that it requires a reconfiguration of publishers' economic models, at least for journals.[21] When a publisher wishes to continue their subscription business model but still wants (or needs) to provide open access, green is currently a viable solution. The flip side of this is that, therefore, while green open access helps researchers, it does not help libraries with their costs.[22] Green open access is the form mandated by many funders, as shown in the international discussion in Chapter 2.

Green and gold open access constitute the delivery mechanisms for the removal of price barriers to research. On its own, this is called 'gratis' OA: material that is free to read but that comes with no lowering of permission barriers. The removal of permission barriers that enables so-called full 'libre' OA is usually achieved through a form of open licensing. Traditionally, academic authors sign copyright assignment agreements with publishers, who then hold the exclusive dissemination rights to the research material for the duration of that copyright. However, all the initial declarations on open access, to which I will turn shortly, also specify the lowering of permission barriers as a crucial part of OA. Open licenses are structures that sit on top of copyright and under which the author uses his or her legal intellectual property rights explicitly to allow others to redistribute and, in some cases, modify the work in question. In almost every case this retains the demand for attribution. The most commonly implemented licenses to achieve libre open access are the Creative Commons licenses, covered below in Chapter 3.

These, then, are the fundamental tenets of open access: 'green', 'gold', 'gratis' and 'libre'. With these definitions now covered, this initial chapter is designed to provide an overview of and background to the origins of the Open Access movement (which are important to consider when thinking about the humanities). The chapter is structured into three parts. The first examines the historical background to open access. The second interrogates whether, given its origins in science and technology, OA might be appropriate purely in the scientific disciplines. The third lays out the omnipresent voices of dissent.

OPEN ACCESS: A HISTORICAL BACKGROUND

It would be beyond the scope of this book to provide a complete history or a general theory of publishing, which others have more thoroughly already attempted.[23] Instead, in relation to the rise of open access and following the pioneering arguments of John Willinsky,[24] I propose a set of two different, alternative, converging histories: the history of the economics of recent academic journal publishing and the history of the free culture movement, which has its roots in the world of computer software. Although these histories are interlinked, in order to answer 'why open access?' it is necessary to know the history of the former and to inquire into the economic conditions of research publication. In order to answer 'why the Open Access movement?' the latter socio-cultural context is more pertinent.

Library budgets, the 'serials crisis' and over-supply

Various studies based on statistics from the Association of Research Libraries show that the cost to academic libraries of subscribing to journals has outstripped inflation by over 300% since 1986.[25] Meanwhile, total library expenditure (i.e. budget for staff, services, technology and books) has outpaced inflation by only 79% over the same period.[26] While the humanities' expenditure accounts for a smaller portion of this 'serials crisis' than the natural sciences in absolute terms, this rise is reflected proportionately in humanities journals.[27] This budgetary problem has been fuelled not only by price increases, but also by an explosion of research output over the past half-century. The effect of this serials crisis is one of the core motivators for academic open-access advocates: as their libraries are unable to afford the subscriptions, academic researchers and students at many institutions come up against paywalls that hinder their ability to conduct research and to teach/learn efficiently. This effect is not, of course, felt uniformly: those at top, prestigious and wealthy institutions may not suffer from or notice this compared with their colleagues at the poorer end of the financial scale. However, even Harvard University, one of the wealthiest institutions in the world, has claimed that it cannot afford the material that it needs.[28] Some, like me, believe that this demonstrates that the economics of the system are broken, while others think such a claim to be overstated.[29] However, what certainly is true is that those without access to a well-endowed library, such as independent researchers or those at poorer institutions, find themselves locked out of a pay-to-read system if they cannot afford the fees. There are, of course, mitigating aspects that help with this. Although slow (thereby disadvantaging those without direct access in terms of productivity), inter-library loans are one good way in which a greater number of people can read work. This seems, however, to be more of a patch that is designed to hold together a system of subscription and purchase access, rather than an attempt to address the underlying economic problems that prevent direct access.

As is detailed more thoroughly in Chapter 2, the economics of scholarly publishing are complex. For instance, it is worth considering whether true markets can exist in journal subscriptions or book sales to academic institutions and whether the profit motive stands in fundamental opposition to the goal of academic research. After all, because academic work must be original, there should be no comparable 'competition' to an article or book when a researcher needs it, a fact that makes it difficult to construe conventional economic markets.[30] When a particular article or book is necessary, nothing else will do and the researcher must acquire access to it. From this fact, in every instance the publisher has a 'mini-monopoly' on an article or book, as Peter Suber frames it,[31] an aspect made possible because, unlike many other commodities, books and journal articles 'differ in that they are not substitutes for each other'.[32]

Regardless of this, the demand-side system of subscriptions and sales was working relatively well until the late 1980s when a sudden mass expansion of higher education in the Anglophone academy (and elsewhere) triggered changes to the supply side of the ecosystem.[33] Combined with a growing credentialism in academia that focused on research output, the demand to be able to publish research in often niche areas overtook and outstripped the desire necessarily to read that same research.[34] This led to fierce competition to publish in prestigious journals or with respected publishers as they began to act as proxy measures for hiring committees, eventually replicating the scarcity in the job market and the high number of applicants for each post.

This is to say that, as much as there is a library budget crisis in being able to afford access to all research, there is also a supply-side crisis for all researchers to be able to publish their work; an aspect that becomes ever more crucial to holding a secure academic post.[35] This logic sounds callous when put in relation to academic research: humanities academics are, after all, most frequently used to viewing their niche work as holding esoteric, rather than popular or even utilitarian, value. It feels grimly utilitarian to specify that problems in library budgets could be driven by the presence of too much interesting work that should be published, but this is one way of viewing the problem.[36] To think firstly in terms of journals, as more researchers produce material in the ever more competitive quest for jobs, the need and desire to publish in top journals is increased. Because these journals will then have a continual supply of high-quality material, it is imperative that libraries subscribe to them. As this material over-flows through rejection and cascades down to the next level of 'mid-range' publications, libraries find that there are also far more venues to which they must subscribe, a fact triggered by over-supply (not to mention material published in niche journals that may also be necessary for research). In short, paradoxically, there are both supply-side crises (too much competition for top journal slots) and demand-side crises (institutions' inability to afford all material for students and researchers) in academic publishing. These are split across two forms of scholarly economics into which I delve in Chapter 2: the 'economics' of scholarly prestige and the economics of paying for the labour of publishing.

Similar phenomena exist in the monograph sphere and these are dealt with separately in Chapter 4 because of the importance of the book form to humanities disciplines. There are some differences, however, that are worth briefly highlighting here. Monographs are more clearly the gold standard for accreditation and reputation in the humanities. They also take an order of magnitude longer to write than their journal article counterparts, meaning that scholars expect a commensurate reputational return. The print runs for academic monographs in the humanities, though, are extremely low; around 200–250 is the figure that is usually cited. This means that presses often have returns on volumes and the margins are far lower than in scientific journal publishing, for instance. Presses then find them-selves caught in a double bind. On the one hand, they cannot afford to raise prices as they are competing for the same library resources that have been dented by the serials crisis. On the other hand, presses must therefore stringently limit their intake on the basis of quality control (peer review) so that their authors see a reputational gain through exclusivity (prestige) and so that they do not expend labour on titles that will not sell to their target audience. Of course, there are other models: lowering review standards (and perhaps production quality) while opting for a wider list is an alternative tactic that relies on successful titles carrying others through cross-subsidy. Broadly speaking though, there are also supply-side and demand-side 'crises' in the monograph world.

This is where open access plays a role, at least in one respect. OA rests on a specific economic form called 'nonrivalrous commodity exchange'.[37] This form, which requires digital dissemination, is one wherein the 'use' of a commodity does not entail somebody else's inability to use it, meaning that the costs no longer inhere in reproducing objects but instead in the labour required to create the first copy. This is the case for digital content. When one downloads a file this will not affect the next user's ability to likewise access that content in most normal circumstances because this is essentially an act of near-instantaneous copying in which the original remains.[38] This differs from the past systems of paper where, for example, printing a book again and again came with a material cost in each case because in selling a copy it was given away; one cannot re-sell the physical object that one has just sold (not to mention the costs of warehousing etc.). Under this new form of nonrivalrous commodity exchange in which replication costs almost disappear, if it were possible to allow anybody access to scholarly material at no charge, covering instead the labour costs to first copy, the demand-side problem would be eliminated. The 'if' in that sentence is somewhat large and the supply-side problem is far more difficult to broach without budget increases or cost reductions but, broadly speaking, the problem of demand-side economics and restricted access is one to which open access could be positioned as a partial solution, predicated upon nonrivalrous commodity exchange.

Free culture, copyright and an open ethos

Alongside the explosive growth of higher education and research output has been an enormous increase in technological capacity that it is also important to consider for an understanding of the emergence of open access. Indeed, the overwhelming assumption from the literature on open scholarship is that it has co-evolved with broader technological developments.[39] Although much of the recent history of computing technology is ensconced within commercial and military paradigms, it is also the birthplace of the free culture movement. Counter-intuitively, this stems from the fact that the historical rise of general-purpose computing to mainstream prominence took place within commercial paradigms. From Multics, through to Unix, Windows and Mac OS, there has been a raft of closed-source operating systems that are licensed to users for corporate profit and which have formed the basis of most people's interaction with computer systems. However, in response to this corporate practice, a counter-discourse of 'free culture' was also born. Free culture in this context does not exclusively mean monetarily free but more often refers to freedom of action; the freedom to reuse material. This movement finds its meeting point with academia in the proposed removal of reuse barriers under open access and the modifications to the practicalities of copyright that this would require.

One of the most important figures in the history of this movement is Richard M. Stallman who, in 1989, wrote a document called the GPL (the GNU Public License) that radically redefined thinking about copyright. Copyright is, in almost all global jurisdictions, an automatically conferred, time-limited, exclusive right to distribute an original work. Copyright, which is covered more thoroughly below in Chapter 3, is the legal mechanism through which any notion of control over one's academic or artistic work comes into being. Without copyright, anybody could do anything to anybody else's work, from redistributing to altering, and there would be no obligation to acknowledge the original source. While most software licenses are designed to use copyright to restrict the end-user's freedom to modify the underlying source code and/or redistribute the program, Stallman's license reverses this, using the authority of copyright to stipulate, explicitly, that the source code for applications must be made public to allow anybody else to view, redistribute and, most importantly, modify the program. The license further specifies that anybody else's modifications to the software must be redistributed under the same terms, thereby ensuring that this freedom is extended to future users. In other words, the GPL license is 'viral', sticking to future works, a phenomenon which is called CopyLeft.[40]

Of perhaps more direct interest to those in the humanities, Stallman argues that in the past thirty years or so a tacit understanding of copyright has been adopted that sits badly with its original intent and that is now damaging the ability of others to create new, socially useful work. As Stallman notes from a 1932 Supreme Court case in the United States:

> The *sole interest* of the United States and the *primary object* in conferring the monopoly lie in *the general benefits derived by the public* from the labors of authors.[41]

While authors generally think of copyright as protecting their intellectual property, Stallman disputes such a stance.[42] This is not, he would argue, the original goal of legislation, which instead posits copyright as 'a balance between a public goal and market forces' in which 'the government spends our freedom instead of our money'. For Stallman, '[f]reedom is more important than money'[43] and so there is, in his reading of the history of copyright, the impetus for the state to get the best bargain for the public and not for the individual creator.

This is where the lowering of permission barriers under open access begins to intersect with a history of copyright, technology and economics. In Stallman's reading, the goal of the compromise of copyright is to give authors a limited time-period in which to sell their works to support themselves financially. Academics, however, are not generally understood to be economically dependent upon selling their research output (I will revisit this logic in more detail in Chapter 2). The question that arises for the Open Access movement from this, taking Stallman as a starting point, is: why should academics retain the economic protections of copyright if they are not dependent upon the system of remuneration that this is supposed to uphold?[44] As is clear, this mirrors the arguments for free access that I explored above: if authors are not required to sell their work, why can't they give it away? In parallel: if authors are not required to sell their work, why do they require all of the protections of copyright and specifically those protections that exist for financial benefit? Stallman's reading of the history of copyright is not ubiquitously held and it is not the sole reason why advocates argue for (and sceptics argue against) the lowering of permission barriers to scholarly research, but it does form one cornerstone in the movement's history.

While it is wholly possible to dispute the health of the subscription-/sales-based economic model – and it certainly contributes to the financial problems of the serials crisis outlined above – an important point to register is that even under this mode there is usually no financial disincentive to a *researcher* in giving away the copyright to his or her work.[45] The same is not true, under a subscription or sale system, for publishers. To demonstrate this, consider that, under the current conditions of scholarly publishing, be that books or journals, copyright is usually assigned by the academic creator to a publisher. In most cases of journal publishing this is done without financial remuneration but is traded by the academic for symbolic reputational capital and the services that the publisher can provide. In the realm of books, publishers do pay royalties to academics, but because the majority of these monographs are not runaway trade successes, it is the reputational return that is most frequently desired in this sphere also. The publisher then retains that exclusive copyright and sells the packaged commodity object (an article or book), most often back to university libraries. Under the subscription economic model, therefore, it is publishers who exercise the rights enshrined in the time-limited exclusivity of the copyright monopoly to recover their labour costs and, in some cases, to make a profit.

The labours that must be compensated in publishing and that are currently protected by such copyright arrangements are many and varied. Publishers make a living through the sale of either journal subscriptions or books, to which they claim they add value. As has been most recently framed by Michael Bhaskar, at least three of these value-adding functions are 'filtering', 'framing' and 'amplification'.[46] While it is impossible to recapitulate his entire argument here, one of the most potent examples of the types of labour involved in these processes lies in the age-old example of publishing as 'making public'. Is an article or a book 'published' if only one single copy exists and it is put on a park bench? What about the printing of hundreds of copies of an article or a book that, then, nobody reads? Truly to publish, in these cases, requires some kind of amplification so that readers will 'hear' the content over the proliferation of noisy demands on their time. This requires labour. The term 'publishing', then, hides a multiplicity of labour activities that will be covered below, in Chapter 2. It is a mistake to think that publishing is the simple placement of material online and/or to think that it is labour-free, even in the digital age.

To this end, publishers currently require the protections of copyright for their subscription and/or sale business models. Scholars do not usually require such economic protections (instead, they need reputational protections), but they do need the labour of publishers. For open access advocates who see twofold difficulties in access and restrictive permission barriers, this adds up to a chiastic economic mess. While there remains no economic disincentive to researchers in allowing others to read their work for free, access is denied to scholarly research through paywalls that are necessary to remunerate publishers. On the other hand, while there is no financial disincentive to researchers in allowing others to redistribute and, in some cases, to reuse their work with attribution, permissions remain restricted in order to protect the paywall model through time-limited copyright. Under mechanisms where publishers could claim their remuneration elsewhere, which are the economic reconfigurations implied by gold open access, advocates of this economic stance believe that problems of both access and permissions would be resolved by new business models. Sceptics, conversely, believe that the new models for such a reconfiguration are unproven and could result in irreparable damage both to the economics of scholarly publishing houses and, consequently, to the circulation and discovery of high-quality research material in a useful form.

These difficulties notwithstanding and to return to the history, Lawrence Lessig, a Harvard-based lawyer, saw this logic unfurling in the wake of Stallman's and others' successes with the GPL and began working on a series of licenses that would allow creators of any type of content (i.e. not just software) to extend such reuse rights to others. It was in this light that the Creative Commons (CC) licenses were unveiled. Coming in a variety of types corresponding to different levels of permissiveness, these licenses – although contentious, as I will explore in Chapter 3 – are designed to allow content creators to use their copyright protections to allow others to redistribute, modify, translate and computationally analyse works, among other activities. It is Lessig's Creative Commons licenses that are most frequently used to achieve the lowering of permission barriers to open-access material, predicated on the reasoning outlined above.

Creative Commons licensing for academic material, as with the GPL, is not a replacement of copyright, but a superstructure atop it that undoes many of the provisions that stop others from using work. Many aspects of Creative Commons licensing seem unproblematic if access to research is monetarily free. For instance, if work is freely available, it makes sense to allow others to redistribute it at will. Few also seem to have a problem with the insistence in almost all CC licenses on the necessity for attribution of the original author. However, as will be seen, it is the modification/derivatives clauses that have aggravated certain parties. Opponents of open licensing fear reputational damage, which is the core currency for academics, and the erosion of academic citation norms, let alone the potential economic consequences for publishers. Yet the core questions that I will address later are, from the advocate's perspective, whether the time-limited copyright monopoly, when free of financial gain, was ever intended to be used to protect the integrity of work.

Convergences

It is at the convergence point of these two narratives – problems of supply-/demand-side economics and the birth of the free culture movement (but certainly others, also) – that open access emerges. Open access was defined in three influential documents written around the turn of the millennium: the Budapest Open Access Initiative (2002), the Bethesda Statement on Open Access Publishing (2003) and the Berlin Declaration on Open Access to Knowledge in the Sciences and the Humanities (2003). Peter Suber refers to these documents collectively as the 'BBB definition of OA'.[47] All three of these definitions outline the need for 'user' freedom beyond simply being able to read (i.e. they specify the lowering of permission barriers) but all three also specifically enshrine attribution of the author at the heart of their principles.

Over the last decade, OA has grown exponentially. Open Journal Systems, the free software project started by John Willinsky that provides the software needed to set up an OA academic journal, has clocked up over 11,000 worldwide installs. Various institutional, funder and national-level mandates have also been put into effect.[48] There have been legislative hearings in the UK, the States and elsewhere on open access. There are current panels around the world trying to ascertain strategies for OA monographs and projects working on new experimental business models for OA publication. Whatever else can be said of OA: governments want it, a portion of the research community wants it, some members of the public want it, funders want it, and it seems extremely probable that it will meet with widespread global adoption in some form over the next few years. What I hope this brief history has shown, though, is that the conditions of contemporary scholarly communication/publishing have been shaped by both legislative and financial mechanisms but that, from technological origins, a way of thinking arose that countered these norms. It is also clear that these technological and scientific origins pose a seemingly obvious follow-on question: if open access was born in the sciences and amid technologies, is OA, then, just for scientists? There are clear advantages for scientists in quickly and openly disseminating research and it has certainly been mooted that the humanities are being led to open access as part of a worldwide science-driven policy agenda. As will be seen, the answer to the question of whether OA is specific to the sciences is more complex than a simple 'yes' or 'no'.

THE TWO CULTURES: IS OA JUST FOR SCIENTISTS?

In order to answer the question of whether open access is applicable wholly or mainly to science, two more fundamental questions have first to be addressed: (1) what are the roles of research in the humanities and the sciences respectively and (2) what is the function of OA with respect to these roles? It is certainly notable that many critiques of the university are born within humanities disciplines. It is also the case that critique of research publication practices sometimes forms a part of that ecosystem of criticism. This criticism is often limited, though, and does not rejoin with practice. For instance, how many Anglo-American postcolonial critiques have been outsourced for typesetting to the Indian subcontinent and are typesetters remunerated at a fair rate under acceptable labour conditions? How has the popular reputation of the humanities – a frequent topic of lament – suffered from an inability of the public easily to read research work (in both the sense of impeded access and the sense of the unreadable complexity of the language of research)? At the risk of introducing some of that very complexity, and as I cover below in Chapter 5, I consider this type of thinking about academic publishing to be an instantiation of the history of critique; that is, a crucial part of a systematic examination of our practices, the aim of which is a more complete knowledge of the forces that define and shape our thinking and research production. Such critique does not have to conclude that 'open access' is the logical answer but it is certainly worth introducing the publishing and dissemination process into discussions of research practice in the humanities.

Open access: scientific origins

When the origin of the Free Culture movement within technological disciplines is coupled with the exponentially more challenging economic situation for scientific journals, a history of open access emerges that is firmly situated within the sciences. This is sometimes taken by sceptics to mean that the humanities should be excluded from funder requirements for open access because there are fundamental differences between these disciplines and the natural sciences. Disciplinary differences cannot be elided but, at the same time, there are ways in which open access could benefit, or at least alter, research practice for the humanities. To investigate this further, I want now to look at the differences a little more in terms of origins and policies to ascertain the exact points of tension.

It is true that a substantial degree of the development of open access has taken shape in the sciences. In fact, high-energy physics seems to be one of the strongest disciplines for OA. It is also wise to be cautious of the fact that the motivation of many governments pursuing open access is to allow industry to take the fruits of (often public) scientific research and to re-enclose it for commercial benefit. Depending upon your degree of market-orientation, this may or may not be a negative phenomenon. One's appraisal may also depend upon the type of enterprise appropriating the work; some would be happy with charities, for instance, using their work but not large corporations. Truly libre open access does not discriminate, however, on the type of activity undertaken by the reuser. This is a topic that will be explored in more detail in Chapter 3.

Despite the seemingly science-centric history of OA, however, open access also has both formal and impromptu roles and histories in the humanities. In terms of formality, the already-mentioned Peter Suber, a philosopher specialising in law, epistemology and ethics, was a principal drafter of the Budapest Open Access Initiative statement (the first formal statement on OA). Likewise, Jean-Claude Guédon, a professor of comparative literature at the University of Montreal, joined Suber in signing one of the other crucial formative documents of the Open Access movement, the 2003 Bethesda Statement on Open Access Publishing.[49] In this way, those working in the humanities were represented, even if under-represented, at the birth of the OA movement. That this representation of the humanities disciplines was proportionately minimal can be accounted for through two potential explanations: (1) that humanities disciplines are so distant from the sciences in the way in which they communicate research as to obviate the need for, or possibility of, open access – a line taken by some sceptics; or (2) that those working in the humanities have been less engaged in a critique of their own publication practices than the sciences and simply lag behind – the advocates' stance. These are, of course, merely the most extreme poles. In reality, responses sit on a spectrum between these points.

Even if the majority were not part of these formal histories, however, this does not mean that people working in the humanities have not, in smaller clusters, just 'done' open access. In fact, excluding publisher-initiated moves, for those academics who opt for a Do It Yourself approach to starting new digital initiatives and journals, open access seems to be the default. Take, for the basis of an utterly non-systematic and far-from-inclusive survey, *19: Interdisciplinary Studies in the Long Nineteenth Century*, an OA journal running since 2005; the NINES (Networked Infrastructure for Nineteenth-Century Electronic Scholarship) system; the *Journal of Ethics & Social Philosophy* (since 2005); *Gamut: Online Journal of the Music Theory Society of the Mid-Atlantic* (since 2008); *Foucault Studies* (since 2004); *Culture Machine* (since 1999) and other Open Humanities Press journals and books; *Digital Humanities Quarterly* (since 2007); *Journal of Neo-Victorian Studies* (since 2008); Open Book Publishers (since 2008, an open-access book publisher founded by scholars at Clare Hall and Trinity College, Cambridge); Punctum Books (since 2011, another scholar-led book project founded by Eileen Joy and Nicola Masciandaro); the list goes on. While such efforts are clearly significant, it is also evident that these scholar-led initiatives have not come to dominate the publishing landscape. There are also, on occasion, problems with their lack of publisher expertise. For instance, sometimes these venues do not have adequate digital preservation mechanisms to militate against disaster or do not adhere to commonly agreed upon standards for discoverability.

What these projects seem to indicate, more precisely, though, in their very existence, is that when academics design systems for communication from the ground up, independently, the idea of creating a subscription or sale model often doesn't seem to enter the equation (although it is more common as a form of supplementary income for OA book initiatives). Sceptics might point out that this is indicative of a fundamental unsustainability of these online academic resources; a lack of business sense. To my mind, however, it also signals that there cannot be an irreconcilable difference between the communication practices of the humanities and open dissemination on the internet – 'open access' – but that differences in research dissemination practice to the sciences must be found somewhere else, especially (but not only) in the journal sphere.

*

Even if, then, there is no fundamental tension between open online dissemination and the form of much humanities work, it is nonetheless no simple task to define precisely the role of research in the humanities subjects, as apart from the sciences. As Helen Small puts it, isolating distinctive traits of specific intellectual cultures is surprisingly difficult and even seemingly basic definitions very quickly become convoluted.[50] In Jerome McGann's formulation, however, the role of the humanities disciplines is 'to preserve, to monitor, to investigate, and to augment our cultural life and inheritance' and, in straightforward parlance, it is clear that those employed in universities' humanities departments conduct 'research' in the service of these goals.[51] It is also clear, though, that a single definition of research will likely be too loose to cover adequately the diversity of activities found within even this narrowed disciplinary spectrum. With that warning in mind, what does 'research' mean in broad strokes, what is its function and what does open access do to research activities in these disciplines?

Fundamentally, research – as opposed to 'scholarship', at least in some definitions – can be specified as the practice of either (1) discovering new aspects or interpretations of reality/cultures and communicating these findings; or (2) refuting previously communicated findings. This definition remains true across the sciences and the humanities and seems unaffected by methodological differences.[52] In terms of differences, it is certainly the case that in the practice of literary criticism, for just one example, it is rare to work on the model of a hypothesis followed by a controlled experiment. It is also true that few scientists would adopt the practice-based research methodologies seen among live-art researchers, for instance. That said, although different methodologies in the humanities and sciences may be thought of as respectively more subjective or objective, each is also concerned with fostering intersubjective understandings through repetition, whether that be through persuasive argument or hypothesis-driven experimentation. As Hannah Arendt put it, 'The reality of the public realm relies on the simultaneous presence of innumerable perspectives and aspects . . . Only where things can be seen by many in a variety of aspects without changing their identity can worldly reality truly and reliably appear.'[53] It is also worth noting that the interpretation of data in many parts of scientific practice relies on mediated subjective thinking and interpretation: the data do not speak for themselves.

None of this is to elide the very real differences in practice between the humanities and the sciences; the problem has not been referred to as the 'Two Cultures' for no reason.[54] It is instead, however, to note that the fundamental bases of conducting research are the same: the discovery and communication of new findings or interpretations. Furthermore, the ways in which such research is 'used' by others also has many overlapping characteristics between disciplinary fields, despite the problematic rhetoric of 'utility'. For instance, the uses of preceding work through citation in both the humanities and the sciences remain broadly the same: (1) to inform the reader of the existing body of work upon which the new research rests, along with its applicability to or difference from the new material; (2) to refute existing work when inaccuracies of fact are alleged or disagreements over interpretation have arisen; (3) to credit the preceding work and author(s) with value and novelty or to discredit through dissent;

(4) to create a chain of verification whereby the claims upon which the new work rests can be checked. It is worth unpacking these statements so that some of the purposes of scholarly communication and 'publication' of research can be defined for this discussion. The first of these points is, essentially, informational about the extant literature. Those new to a field, if presented with no preceding research, would be likely simply to replicate existing findings and arguments; their work would not be novel. By requiring reference to existing literature, a network of citations is slowly built that acts as a map of the field. The newcomer can quickly gauge the central points of a particular field by cross-correlating citations. Furthermore, the importance of an author's works within particular niche sub-areas is revealed when a work is more frequently cited within such an area (although caution towards such a quantified 'citation counting' approach should be urged as measuring worth in such numerical terms is of dubious applicability to the educational enrichment provided by the humanities). In those disciplines where artistic practice forms a part of research and the output is, therefore, more akin to (or even *is*) art itself, reference to others serves to contextualise the work; it provides a constellation of other work within which the piece under discussion can be situated, read and understood.

The second point, of criticism and refutation, is one of public communication. As arguments or facts come under scrutiny, debate between scholars is committed to record and new understandings emerge from communication. While arguments in academia can often seem petty, the amount of research effort that goes into verifying findings (in archival work, for instance) and constructing viable arguments is substantial, so it is of little surprise that a lot is at stake for academics in these debates (Sayre's law notwithstanding).[55] Few would dispute, though, that the majority are motivated by intellectual curiosity and truth rather than malice in publicly refuting another's work.

The third point is one of reputation and novelty.[56] While this is not strictly necessary within a totally idealistic system under which people might work solely for the benefit of truth with no personal, ulterior motive, this is not the world that exists. Scholars' reputations are positively founded and can negatively founder upon the basis of an idea that does or does not gain currency. This forms a crucial part of individualist contemporary systems of motivation and career accreditation and is enshrined in the legal and academic enforcement systems surrounding plagiarism (see Chapter 3 for more on this).[57]

The final of these points, of verification, is the most important. In order to check the truth of a particular piece of work, when it is built on the foundation of others, one must be able to go back to appraise the current use of existing academic source material. As Anthony Grafton has put it in his history of the footnote, 'the culturally contingent and eminently fallible footnote offers the only guarantee we have that statements about the past derive from identifiable sources. And that is the only ground we have to trust them.'[58] Without such an ability, one must simply place faith in the author not to have misrepresented, misattributed, misread or even misunderstood the piece that he or she is citing. With the best generosity in the world towards the character of fellow scholars, it is simply uncritical not to follow such practice in checking the assertions of others.

There are undoubtedly other areas of practice, but these seem to constitute at least some of the essence, and use values, of research in the humanities. Some of these are directly shared with the sciences. Of course, it is also clear that research in the humanities may not be purely 'used' in a practical sense and frequently exists to inform without a clear applicable use, at least in the sense of a market economy. However, within the spheres where use can be identified, it is important to consider how open access impinges upon each of these areas.

Taking these four points as a starting guide, it becomes possible to identify some of the ways in which open access interacts with research principles in the humanities. The first three of these notions – reporting upon preceding literature; refuting existing work; and crediting the preceding work and author(s) with novelty and value or discrediting through dissent – remain relatively unchanged in an open-access environment, although it is worth noting that various studies show that OA papers may be more widely cited, thus enhancing the citation map.[59] It may also be easier for researchers to undertake these activities (reporting on preceding literature etc.) if they have immediate, online, free access to work. In terms of value and credit, it is also important to remember that just because research is openly available to all (like the majority of websites on the world wide web) this does not mean that there are no quality controls (unlike the majority of the web).[60] Likewise, the need to cite the work of others remains in place.

The fourth of these points, however, the idea of creating a chain of verification whereby the claims upon which the new work rests can be checked, is potentially significantly enhanced in an open-access world. Although checking others' use of sources is currently a far less common practice than might be hoped, if all research were open access and the necessary technological infrastructure was put into place, an environment could exist in which this kind of checking could be instantaneous: a linked click. Of course, much humanities writing requires a more totalised understanding of the work than just a link to a single paragraph – it requires the argument, the aesthetic and the context – but this does not impinge upon the potential supplementary benefits of such a system. This could be available not only to those established within universities, though, but rather to anybody with access to the internet. This could range from independent researchers through to those fresh out of their degree. In much the same way as it becomes easy to spend hours following links that look interesting on Wikipedia, a world could be possible where the same is true of an interlinked network of high-quality scholarly papers. Of course, just because OA might offer the possibility of such a system existing does not mean that it would spontaneously burst into existence; new publisher labour would be required to implement the linking, format migration and any supplemental technologies that might facilitate this.

Beyond the broader goal of access to research, such thinking as this represents the kind of benefits that advocates believe would enhance research practice and is among the reasons why OA is not purely applicable to the sciences. However, not all scholars and commentators feel that these changes are positive and they often point out that current research practices have evolved over a long timeframe while, by contrast, the switch to digital is happening (too) rapidly. The same critics also often feel that, even if these types of benefits were acknowledged (on top of the more general principles of broader access, equality etc.), the damage of a transition period is too economically dangerous to be practical.

To that end, the next section of this chapter turns towards the reasons for dissent, especially in the humanities.

I have taken pains over the course of this chapter, and the rest of this book, to indicate that there is not a complete consensus on open access in the humanities. Indeed, there are prominent disagreements between members of different communities that are often heated. In this section I set out some of the more pronounced objections and weigh up the arguments. For pragmatic reasons, the scheme that I will follow in this discussion of dissenting voices will broadly be structured by stakeholder, divided into academics; commercial publishers; learned society and university press publishers; and dissenting librarians. In reality, such a division is artificial, of course, and there are clear overlaps between the groups. Broadly speaking, however, this division facilitates a sketch of the variety of motivations and rationales for dissent. I will cover the range of objections briefly and in outline here, with more concerted readings presented at relevant points throughout this volume.

Academics' oppositions to open access

As in every other stakeholder group, and as has already been seen, there are a number of academics in the humanities who totally support OA, even in its most liberal forms. There are also, however, two dissenting camps. The first group of academic dissenters support the principles of OA but object to the specific implementations that have been proposed, including concerns for the continued viability of humanities' academic research labour as an activity. Those in this group might support only the green route, for example, or require more restrictive licensing. The second group object to the principle of open access in its entirety.

The latter standpoint – a seemingly complete objection to open access – was most explicitly set out in recent times by Robin Osborne, a Cambridge-based Professor of Ancient History, who argued that:

Academic research is not something to which free access is possible. Academic research is a process – a process which universities teach (at a fee). It is neither a database, nor the ways and techniques by which the database is manipulated. Just as my database is useless to you without your having the skills to manipulate it, so those skills are useless to you without the database ... academic research publication is a form of teaching that assumes some prior knowledge. For those who wish to have access, there is an admission cost.[61]

Osborne's basic arguments are: that '[i]f there are fees for access to teaching there should be fees for access to research';[62] that the publications that result from a research project 'are only trivially a result of the research-funding' provided by the broader public (and hence should not be subject to funder requirements to make this work available to taxpayers);[63] and that OA makes no sense because those who wish to have access 'must invest in the education pre-requisite to enable them to understand the language used'.[64]

This book chapter, written by Osborne for the British Academy, caused some furore among OA advocates on its publication for obvious reasons. On the one hand, the thrust of Osborne's argument is clear: humanities research must be seen as more than simple Gradgrind-esque facticity and the provision of utilitarian databases for consult-ation. Osborne is correct that this is not the purpose of work in the humanities. On the other hand, though, this particular argument raises three specific questions in opposition: why should fees to access teaching (which is not the situation in every country, anyway) entail fees to access research, when teaching is that which provides the prerequisite to understanding research? If (taxpayer[65]) funding only contributes such a small amount to the overall gain in knowledge and efforts of a project, should those in the humanities receive it?[66] Finally, are there not a large number of humanities graduates who do not work in the university but who would be able to understand this work? Osborne's argument is among the more extreme of objections to open access, even if rooted in a fairly accepted view of the function of humanities research; most arguments, as I will go on to discuss, take issue with specific aspects of open access implementation.

In the more moderate camps, there are several groups of academics who have objected, not to the basic principle of open access, but rather to the way in which it is to be implemented through article or book processing charges (for the removal of price barriers) and the various aspects of reuse permitted by the Creative Commons Attribution ('CC BY') license (the removal of permission barriers). I will try to give a flavour of these here.

One of the clearest statements with regard to the former stance was voiced by the editors of the *Review of African Political Economy*, who believe that 'The potential gains of OA are fundamentally undermined by the "pay to publish" principle.'[67] Likewise, the Editors of History Journals' written submission to the UK's Business Innovation and Skills (BIS) Select Committee Inquiry in 2013 noted that they were 'concerned that the international reputation of UK journals is likely to suffer if scholars abroad begin to believe that they will have to pay to publish in UK journals'.[68] For now, I will let these statements stand on their own as concerns but will also note that in Chapter 2 below I address alternative business models for gold OA that may mitigate these problems. I will also note that there are no barriers of this sort to green OA which comes with no cost to authors. In other words, these objections were specifically addressed to the article/book processing charge implementation of gold open access. In turn, there is also concern that the pay-to-publish principle compromises academic freedom by tying finance to publication.[69] These economic worries are compounded by concerns that the destabilisation engendered by a switch to new models may hinder the ability of publishers to continue to operate as venues for the promulgation of research.

Academic objections to the lowering of permission barriers to humanities research have taken two different forms, which are explored much more thoroughly in Chapter 3. The first of these is an authorial worry over the potential corruption of scholarly integrity. In late 2013 this was aired by the Cambridge historian Peter Mandler in an article for the *Journal of Victorian Culture*. Mandler noted that, in the humanities, 'Our form of words is unique to us and it cannot be dismembered and mixed with the words of others – which CC BY [the Creative Commons Attribution license] facilitates – without yielding what we tell our students is plagiarism: the mixing of their words and our words without specifying (through quotation) which is which.'[70]

The second set of objections over permissive licensing of humanities work is made most forcefully by John Holmwood, whose concerns come in the wake of the UK government's decision to confer degree-awarding powers to entities that conduct no teaching, such as Pearson.[71] The worry here is that, at present, academics have established a system of legitimation based upon community validation of standards. External bodies that seek to set examinations for higher education while not teaching themselves could financially undercut the research university by providing high-quality research material free of charge (through open access), followed by an examination of students upon that material. This would present a severe challenge not only to academic autonomy but to the continued financial viability of the research university.[72] These concerns echo the political split that I outlined at the very outset of this book. Holmwood argues that:

One of the main drivers of open access is to make academic research more easily available for commercial exploitation, especially by small and medium enterprises. In this context, it is significant that the licence under which open access should function is CC BY which enables commercial exploitation and reuse in any form. The consequence, for the natural sciences, or any other research with a directly exploitable commercial idea, is to bring the underlying research under the protection of Intellectual Property Rights.

Furthermore, according to Holmwood, the humanities and social sciences are also at risk:

First, let it be noted that the very commercialisation of the university itself will have the consequence of dividing the higher education system between a small number of elite universities and others subject to the pressures from for-profit providers ... In this context, open access – especially MOOCS [Massive Open Online Courses] (and the online curriculum of Pearson) – provided by 'elite' universities is the means of undermining the conditions at other institutions and providing a tiered educational system that reinforces social selection to elite positions.

Equally significant, is that the argument for unbundling (some) universities [in which research and teaching are separated] is the claim that research is increasingly taking place outside universities ... It is here that access to 'big data' provides commercial opportunities. Open access is an opportunity to amalgamate data from different sources, develop techniques of analysis under patent, and re-present data, and the means of checking any analysis using it, behind a new paywall.[73]

Concerns such as these, centred in UK policy, cannot be wholly dismissed out of hand. They also have global consequences as the worldwide move to a financialised university continues. The most probable solution to this, in my mind, is to append a 'share-alike' clause to the license, as I outline below in Chapter 3.

Commercial publishers' oppositions to open access

As has been noted, a substantial portion of the most recent wave of controversies surrounding open access arose in response to the national-level mandates enacted in the UK in 2013, and the prominent representation of commercial publishers in this debate gives some good evidence of the core concerns of this group. Although these are not solely related to the humanities, the issues that were raised at this point, even in a scientific context, form an important backdrop to an understanding of the different camps. This is because some of the clashes aired at various moments in this inquiry were between OA advocates, a market-orientated government panel and selected traditional scholarly publishers. Broadly speaking, as business entities, the primary concern of many commercial scholarly publishers pertains to the sustainability (or profitability) of their activities under new, untested, economic models for open access.

One of the oft-touted arguments by left-spectrum OA advocates is that commercial publishers extort their captive library clients.[74] At the parliamentary hearings, this was most explicit in the questioning of Alicia Wise, representing Reed Elsevier, a scientific publishing company known for its vocal opposition to, and legal lobbying against, OA in the States.[75] Wise confirmed that Reed Elsevier reported a 37% profit with 'a revenue stream of £2.06 billion and a profit level of £780 million' in 2012.[76] In the face of such evidence, it seems difficult to fault the argument of advocates that at least some resistance from these entities must come from the fact that they fare extremely well under the current subscription model. Advocates point out that the profit margins of major oil companies, for comparison, sit at around 6.5%. Big Pharma usually manages about 16%.[77] It was, in fact, specifically Elsevier's profit margins that triggered the Cambridge mathematician Timothy Gowers' call for open access through a boycott of the publisher.[78]

However, it is important to stress that not all commercial publishers are alike, particularly when speaking of the humanities. Indeed, there are many small, independent humanities presses with no profit-driven agenda who can only dream of Elsevier's margins. University presses, covered below, are also 'commercial' in some senses but often have different mission statements and levels of profitability; specifically, an obligation to publish on the basis of quality. Many commercial presses also doubtlessly act out of a motivation to facilitate scholarly communication. Some of these publishers, therefore, dissent from open access not because they will lose massive profits, but rather because they fear that their business model will collapse under OA and that the labour needed to support their mission will no longer be viable.

This important point aside, there are also, though, both mega-publishers who operate in the humanities sphere and ongoing campaigns of top-loading acquisitions of smaller publishers by large conglomerates that span the humanities and the sciences (take for instance the fact that Palgrave Macmillan is a sister company of Nature publishing group). One of these latter types seems to be Taylor & Francis/Routledge. This publisher, known to humanities scholars for its range of journals and book publications, has, in recent times, begun seeking the views of its scholar-base on open access. However, advocates have charged that the methodology of their surveys betrays an implicit bias against OA through leading poll statements on topics such as: 'Open access journals are lower quality than subscription journals.'[79] Certainly, this publisher has a vested commercial interest in the subscription system. In terms of turnover, Informa Group, which owns Taylor & Francis and Routledge, posted a 'record' adjusted operating margin of 28.4% in 2012 with a £349.7m adjusted operating profit;[80] 38% of this came from Informa's publishing revenue, including their humanities division, which was, in the words of their annual shareholder report, 'dominated by subscription assets with high renewal rates, where customers generally pay us twelve months in advance. This provides strong visibility on revenue and allows the businesses to essentially fund themselves, with minimal external capital required.' For publishers thriving in this environment, regardless of whether this limits those who can read research work, to use their own words: 'It is a uniquely attractive mode.'[81] With statements like these, it is hardly surprising that there is opposition to new models that might make it harder to achieve those margins and to continue a year-on-year 10% increase of dividends to shareholders.[82]

The list goes on. Bloomsbury Academic is a humanities and social science publisher that seems to be using its trade success to buy up other academic publishers who are in the black, such as Continuum, an organisation that had itself previously acquired Cassell, and also T&T Clark, Berg Publishers, Methuen Drama, Arden Shakespeare, Bristol Classical Press, Fairchild Books and AVA.[83] In its 2012 financial report, the company noted an adjusted continuing profit of £12.1m on a continuing margin of 12.4%.[84] Of Bloomsbury's activities, 'The Academic & Professional division grew the most year on year with a £2.9 million increase in continuing adjusted operating profit, due to both the acquisition of Continuum [a solely humanities-orientated publisher] and a significant increase in income from content licensing deals.'[85] Interestingly, the original intention of the Bloomsbury Academic imprint, when it was launched in 1998 under the stewardship of Frances Pinter (whose Knowledge Unlatched project is covered below), was one in which the 'new publishing model [would consist] of releasing works for free online through a Creative Commons or other open license, and then offering print-on-demand (POD) copies at reasonable prices'.[86] This never came to long-term, mass-scale fruition, possibly because of fears for ongoing revenue. However, the publisher does continue to publish some books in an open-access form.

Now, it must be noted that there are advantages to having such financially healthy publishers. For one, especially in book markets, it allows commissioning editors to take risks with the list that would be untenable were they wholly reliant on a financial return on every single volume published. While, in a post-Friedman world, it seems that shareholder return must always be a chief concern of these entities, publishing is not a science and it is often impossible to know which volumes will succeed, thereby entailing the need for calculated risk.[87] Secondly, as John Thompson notes, good non-academic editors with strong disciplinary knowledge are valued by the academics they are serving.[88] It is only through having corporate entities with sufficient capital to retain staff that this remains possible, which, albeit in the university press sector, was the driving logic behind the accumulated surpluses of Cambridge and Oxford University Presses in the 1980s and 1990s, according to Thompson.[89] In another sense, though, it is problematic to have this tie to profit/ surplus margins. It firstly discredits legitimate oppositions to aspects of open access when voiced by entities with (sometimes large) financial stakes in the current model. Secondly, there is the problematic nature of competition (the 'mini-monopoly') in scholarly publishing that seems oddly placed to function within a competition-centred, free-market environment. Thirdly and finally, there is the additional difficulty, at present, of the way in which academics are shielded from the economic consequences of their publishing decisions and how this benefits commercial organisations. In fact, advocate publishers in the sciences (such as PLOS – the Public Library of Science – originally a scientist-led enterprise that now runs the largest journal in the sciences) describe the present subscription scenario as a 'systemic market failure' because 'authors have no price sensitivity when they choose a journal in which to publish'.[90] By this they mean that the price of the library subscription to a journal, or cost of a book, is usually not considered by researchers in their choice of where to publish. Of course, if one is to accuse subscription/sale-based publishers of having an economic motivation for perpetuating one model, PLOS has a similarly strong motivation from the obverse, open-access perspective.

This lack of researcher awareness of the price of journals is, though, a type of academic freedom: it is freedom from price impinging on the selection of where to publish. Whether this liberty is a positive force could be debated. How important is it for the communication of research (rather than for the career of the researcher) in the digital age that academics have the ability to choose exactly where to publish with limited financial awareness? Even if it remains important now, is it possible to foresee a time when it might not be? This phenomenon also represents, however, the way in which academics do not necessarily make for good rational market actors in this scenario. In the same way as students may not be rational agents in their choice of a university where they pay fees (what are their comparators if they've never been before and may never go again?), academics choose to publish on the basis of prestige (a form of symbolic capital) and often do not know (or care), in a subscription/sale environment, how much their choice of journal or book venue costs.[91] This is due not just to publisher bundling practices and non-disclosure agreements, although these contribute, but rather to the fact that academics *publish* and *consume* but it is libraries that *purchase*. As non-rational actors will not get the best deal for themselves under market logic, this type of academic freedom – the freedom from knowing/directly bearing the financial consequences of one's actions – happens also to benefit commercial entities. Conversely, though, even the supposedly rational actors – libraries, that is – cannot get a good result out of this situation. Indeed, at least in the sciences, it has been shown that price does not correlate with quality but rather that 'libraries typically must pay 4 to 6 times as much per page for journals owned by commercial publishers as for journals owned by non-profit societies'.[92] Of course, commercial publishers are not always the stereotypical villains that some OA advocates make them out to be and so some of the arguments set out below on the oppositions of university presses, learned societies and even academics will also apply to commercial publishers. That said, at least a few of the oppositions of commercial publishers to OA, where they have been voiced, must be on grounds of finance, whether that be profit or sustainability.

University press and learned society publishers'
oppositions to open access

That this certainty of income stream has benefits can be seen in a different group of publishers: those of learned societies and university presses (UPs). While both can technically also be called 'commercial' in various senses, they often have very different agendas and histories and, where they object to open access, it can be for very different reasons. It is worth noting, upfront, that there are UPs and learned societies who have wholeheartedly embraced open access. The Linguistic Society of America (LSA), for instance, launched the open-access journal *Semantics and Pragmatics* in 2007. This journal does not levy article processing charges and instead receives sponsorship from the MIT Library, the MIT Department of Linguistics & Philosophy, the MIT School of Humanities, Arts, and Social

Sciences and the University of Texas at Austin, Department of Linguistics.[93] In fact, as of April 2014, the 'Societies and Open Access Research' catalogue run by Caroline Sutton, Peter Suber and Amanda Page gives a list of 868 societies publishing 827 full-OA (i.e. not hybrid) journals.[94] Likewise, several smaller US-based academic presses have embraced OA. Amherst, Michigan, National Academies, Australian National University and Penn State all have affiliated presses who have expressed support for open access. In the case of Amherst's new enterprise, this is due to the belief that 'when some presses ... disseminate free literature, everybody (including those who run libraries) will enjoy access to that literature'.[95] Likewise, Patrick Alexander of Penn State UP notes that 'Penn State University Press is philosophically and practically in favor of open access.'[96] Most interestingly, National Academies Press has provided free, full-text copies of its books online (open access) alongside priced print editions since 1994.[97]

This positive stance on OA is not one that is universally shared among these entities and related university presses. Although there has been a shift of opinion in favour since 2013,[98] there have been objections from learned societies to the removal of both price and permission barriers.[99] The most frequently reiterated argument made by learned societies is that they depend on journal subscription revenue to fund their other activities. Indeed, a recent survey of thirty-three learned societies, across all disciplines, concluded that 'Learned societies overwhelmingly agree that Open Access will inevitably place some learned societies' journals into financial jeopardy.'[100] This is clearly a recognised problem as Jisc (formerly the UK's Joint Infrastructure and Services Council) commissioned research into the impact that a change to an open-access model would have upon learned societies' business models. This report – which was commissioned in 2005 and is, therefore, somewhat out of sync with more recent developments – noted that while learned societies were interested in open-access models, at that point none of the publishers could see substantial cost advantages in the move to an OA publishing model and the majority highlighted the extra costs incurred in administering and collecting article processing charges.[101] Although this report is now nine years old and suggested investigations of 'pay for print' and 'freemium' models that will be covered below, the arguments remain mostly unchanged today. This can be seen in the fact that Dame Janet Finch, who chaired the UK parliamentary report on OA that bears her name, warned of the implications of her own policy recommendation in early 2013, stating that there is 'no doubt' that some learned societies will face 'some difficulty finding a business model that will work'.[102] While a series of new business models are outlined below that might be applicable to learned societies, I will close these remarks only by noting that advocates feel that, in most cases, OA seems directly in line with the mission statements of societies to further and spread knowledge. If open access is to become widespread, however, those societies who do exist off subscription revenues have a potentially difficult road ahead to transition to alternative sources of revenue.

University presses are, again, another distinct group, but also one that has different sub-groupings. While there is, therefore, a need to speak broadly, it is also important that these differences should not be elided. That said, a good indication of UP interest to date has come from membership of the OAPEN-NL and OAPEN-UK projects. These projects, covered in more detail in the chapter on monographs below, have been investigating the effects of, and business models for, making monographs open access. While OAPEN-NL was proposed by Amsterdam University Press, OAPEN-UK has had Liverpool University Press and University of Wales Press as long-standing participants since its inception in 2011, with Oxford University Press joining in 2013.[103] From this involvement, especially in the monograph sphere, UP objections to open access can broadly be inferred as a conjoined worry about business models, concerns over unknown side effects and a lack of author demand for the mode. While noting that certain university presses are compelled to return their surpluses to their affiliated institution (particularly in the case of Oxford), on the whole, university presses are less vocally opposed to OA on profit (as opposed to sustainability) grounds as they do not have shareholders but rather exist to serve the academic community in the further-ance of their mission statements. As with learned societies, objec-tions from university presses are, as a result, more often aligned with academic concerns concurrent with some clear worries about sustainability.

Librarians' oppositions to open access

Finally, there is a substantial movement within the library community that favours open access. After all, librarians bear the brunt of frustration when researchers cannot access material, an aspect potentially solved by OA. Where objections exist, the primary anxieties raised by librarians with regard to OA concern the future status of the library. If a library no longer owns a collection, then what is its function? What is the role of a librarian in this new world? The answer that has been circulating at most recent library conferences has been a suggested move from 'collecting to connecting'[104] – meaning that the library becomes a place that helps curate and find material. In some senses this is a return of the subject librarian, with an additional fresh role in digital preservation and access via institutional repositories. Of course, it is unclear whether these aspects might also be subjected to disintermediation by commercial entities in the future; what is to say that Google might not feel itself better placed to take this role?

There is a contingent of librarians whose constituents remain sceptical, however. The foremost of these figures is Jeffrey Beall. Beall is most widely known for his curation of a list ('Beall's List') that is designed to expose predatory open-access 'publishers'. These predatory entities have disreputable review procedures and solicit material solely to collect article processing charges (thereby failing to filter material adequately for their supposed audience). While his curation of such a list is a valuable service, detractors feel that Beall should have done more to point out that the same is true of some types of 'predatory' publishers who work on the sale/subscription model, an aspect most clearly demonstrated by mass emails sent after conferences to solicit material for edited collections.[105] This finally spilled over into a full-scale revision of Beall's motivations when, in late 2013, he published an article that accused the OA movement of being an 'anti-corporatist', extreme-Leftist outfit 'that wants to deny the freedom of the press to companies it disagrees with', a radical opinion that separated Beall even from the usually conservative Scholarly Kitchen site (a popular weblog on scholarly communications known for its general scepticism towards the viability of open access).[106] Beall's article was not well received and sparked a series of responses that both decried the lack of evidence in his piece and noted that such a stance was unusual among librarians. One article even suggested that a 'Randian worldview' was the most plausible explanation for his stance.[107] That said, there are, of course, anti-corporatists who support OA (and, naturally, 'anti-corporatist' need not be a McCarthyite pejorative term) but there are also a large number of corporate publishers who do likewise. Where there are library-rooted objections to OA, then, they can intersect with concerns about quality and finance, but are also usually also related to anxieties surrounding the future role of the library and Beall remains a marginal, albeit loud, voice.

*

These form the core points of dissent with respect to open access in the humanities: fundamental objections to the principle; objections to specific implementations (including article or book processing charges and open licensing); objections on corporate-economic grounds; and objections around the future of the library. More broadly, this chapter has covered three specific background elements to open access: the history of the movement; the exceptionality (or otherwise) of the humanities; and the aforementioned objections. It should be apparent, I hope, to all readers that while open access is a theoretically simple idea, that simplicity hides a multitude of complexities. Whether these be financial, scholarly or even political, it is clear that OA is caught between stakeholders with a variety of motivations and levels of power. While these debates continue to rage, they can only be understood in totality through detailed examinations of the contexts within which they take place. In order to do so, over the next three chapters – on economics, open licensing and monographs – I further explore the terrain in the hope of more accurately charting the phenomenon of open access.

Digital economics

In light of the discussion in the previous chapter it is clear that open access is a phenomenon embroiled in the fields of economics and value. However, systems of economics and value in scholarly communication/publishing are determined not solely in financial terms but also in the exchange of symbolic capital. There are, in fact, many different complex and intersecting social and financial economies of value that make up the landscape. Although interdependent, these systems can be broken down into questions of quality and value as socially ascribed and questions of finance in terms of labour value and capital (even if the latter are, also, social at their core). The first of these modes covers the aspects that make a journal or publisher prestigious and the economics that regulate this symbolic field. The second encroaches upon questions of finance, including, but not limited to, asking who pays how much for the labour of academic publishing.

In this chapter, I devote time to each of these issues in turn, beginning with a dissection of academic prestige, followed by a more thorough discussion of the assertion that scholars are well placed to give away their work. Given that humanities research is sometimes thought of outside the sphere of monetary exchange, often with no clear practical use-value, this entails an analysis of the commodity form of open-access research work, including the question of whether work that is given away for free assists in a decommodification of the research production of the contemporary university. I then move to examine the practical business models for gold OA and the evidence for a model of green in parallel to subscriptions. Finally, I look at the international contexts within which this discussion sits, given that the fear of isolationism exists alongside concerns over the repercussions of national-level actions within global contexts. The purpose of this chapter is to address the problems of supply-side economics (academic prestige) and also the pragmatics of the demand-side crisis (affordability) so that, when I later approach the monograph in Chapter 4 and innovations to peer review in Chapter 5, the confluence of quality control and economics is explicit.

CULTURAL AND SYMBOLIC CAPITAL IN ACADEMIC PUBLISHING

Any academic in the twenty-first century knows that publication is important. It is important to communicate findings to other interested parties but it is also crucial for career progression. Indeed, in both the humanities and the sciences, publication forms the core unit of currency in the hiring, firing and promotion ladder. This has now reached the point where the executive editor for the humanities at Harvard University Press is united with a former editor of the *British Medical Journal* in the opinion that universities have 'effectively outsourced to journals and publishers the function of assessing academic quality'.[1] However, regardless of whether one feels this to be over-stated, it is also clear to all concerned that this currency comes in different denominations and that these value units are not purely related to the size of the object. A single, smaller journal article in a top venue will be valued more highly by this process than a two-volume mega-tome put out through a notorious vanity publisher. Furthermore, as Michael Jensen notes, there are some slender signs of changes to the systems of authority, in which new forms that exist outside of the traditional publishing circuit, such as blogs, appear to be gaining some momentum, triggered threefold by technology, economics and academic culture.[2] It is to systems of prestige, quality and authority – sites of symbolic economic interchange for both cultural and material capital – that this first section is dedicated.

While, superficially, 'prestige' seems like an unproblematic concept, the fact that it can be made to sit so tightly with metaphors of economics – 'outsourcing', 'currency' and 'value' – betrays the fact that it is actually the front for a series of often unchallenged assumptions about academic publishing. This is because prestige and quality are not synonymous. Prestige is a proxy measure for quality that is gained through an economic rationing of material. The accumulation of prestige then affects the material economics and pricing of scholarly research. In truth, it is difficult to think through the economics of open access, or even of scholarly communications, without first understanding quality control mechanisms and the means by which they are appraised. This is because the economics of scholarly publication are concerned with scarcity, supply and demand, which are all aspects mirrored in the processes of quality control that condition the flow of academic material.

For those versed in Pierre Bourdieu's theories of material, social, cultural and symbolic capital, whereby financial and reputational forms become interchangeable, this link between prestige and material economics will not come as a surprise. In fact, in his *Outline of a Theory of Practice*, Bourdieu writes of a 'conversion of material capital into symbolic capital itself reconvertible into material capital'.[3] In this particular instance, a piece of research work is a demonstration of an author's cultural capital; it is the product of the skill, knowledge and ability of the author(s). The acceptance of such research by publishers who possess both material capital (needed to undertake the labour and effectively disseminate the work) and cultural capital (knowledge of publishing and academic systems) constitutes a payoff in the form of social capital (endorsement and support) for the author that can be re-converted back into the symbolic capital (prestige/reputation) that is needed for peer respect and a job/promotion (material capital). Acquiring authors with high levels of cultural, social or symbolic capital for their list improves a press's own social, symbolic and material capital (in the ability to sell research).

However, Bourdieu also notes that this very phenomenon of interchangeability is often denied by participating societies. In the case of scholarly communication this stems from the conjoined facts that prestige is useful to academics but also that the academy and especially the humanities often wish to distance themselves from market economics. Indeed, as Bourdieu puts it, 'The endless reconversion of economic capital into symbolic capital, at the cost of a wastage of social energy which is the condition for the permanence of domination, cannot succeed without the complicity of the whole group: the work of denial which is the source of social alchemy is, like magic, a collective undertaking.'[4] Concurrently, it has been argued in other fields that 'over time, economic and political domination become inseparable from prestige, cultural expertise, and ideological dominance'.[5] From this argument, it seems imperative that notions of prestige be critically interrogated within the field of scholarly communication. The primary question that I suggest should be asked is: what are the effects of prestige (which nonetheless has many practical benefits) within various economic spheres and in the context of a transition to open access? As I will show, these systems of prestige contribute to the behaviour of academics towards the implementation of open access, to the economics of scholarly communications and also to the external perception of the academy.

In order to begin this analysis of the intersection of symbolic reputational exchanges and real-world finance, it is worth posing a set of critical, rhetorical questions along with some hypothetical reasoning that, in each case, implicitly views the *function* of journal/publisher prestige as more than a direct correlative of quality. In opening up this space, it should then become possible to gain a broader understanding of the way in which the economics of scholarly communication are bound up in a series of symbolic exchanges that are engendered by institutional (academic) practices.

1. **What does prestige do to the economics of scholarly publishing?** There is perceived pressure from assessment mechanisms to publish articles in high-prestige journals and books with high-prestige presses. Such journals and presses, therefore, are highly sought after by authors, creating a high level of supply. If good authors appear in prestigious journals or with presses, libraries must subscribe to their journals or purchase their books so that their researchers can read the material. If libraries must subscribe or buy, demand and perceived value is higher for such venues, which justifies a price increase. Journals and presses that hold prestige, however, are subject to the same series of transfers and buyouts as other forms of publishing, as seen in Chapter 1. This potentially concentrates ever more expensive venues in ever fewer hands, which could make competition on price more difficult.

2. **What does prestige do for dissemination and how does it fit with OA?** If academics know where to find top-quality material, then the brand name of a journal or a press serves as a

discoverability mechanism; they can *find* good material by knowing where it will be. However, if academics and/or the public are unable to *access* this material because of pricing, then did prestige help with dissemination? While it is absolutely true that the highest-prestige journals and presses might offer brilliantly targeted discoverability and dissemination, is it the case that a prestigious pay-for-access version could *always* and *intrinsically* be better disseminated than an open-access equivalent? Furthermore, in theory, should not targeted amplification and dissemination also be possible with an open-access version? Access to academic materials is wider than ever before, particularly through partnership schemes with public libraries. For the specific question of whether prestige is causally connected to accessibility in the context of OA, however, this can be viewed as an issue of dissemination against discoverability.

3. **How do prestige and quality interact?** Using a branded proxy measure (a journal/publisher) to evaluate whether material is good (well selected by peer review) comes with advantages. It reduces the labour time in finding excellent research and makes the effort of hiring panels viable. However, if good research is determined by the academic community and through peer review, how does the publisher or journal brand correspond to that determination? Especially in smaller fields, the same reviewers often work for different journals and publishers, so the choice of where a piece was submitted could potentially have no bearing upon the reviewer pool. Under what circumstances do quality and prestige, therefore, diverge?

These critical questions are designed to make it possible to reconsider prestige as an economic force that is both constituted by and affects the academic community. The critical framing of these questions is certainly not designed to deny the pragmatic benefits that come with prestige. As I outlined above, the over-supply of qualified individuals for a small number of posts attests to the need for proxy measures that accurately denote quality. Publishers' and journals' 'brand-name' prestige is one such proxy measure. It seems important, however, to explore these questions if an understanding of scholarly economics with regard to open access is to emerge.

*

To expand upon the above introduction to the symbolic capital of reputation in academia, prestige, in terms of publication venue, is accumulated through an economy of scarcity. It is definitively gained through exclusivity, in which one decides to publish only the best material. The definition of 'best' is formulated through a negotiated process of peer review to ascertain likely future winners in terms of content. The process is 'negotiated' because review is mediated, in all cases, by an editor. This can be an academic editor who may choose to apply different criteria, or a commissioning editor of a monograph who may also have to balance the marketability of an individual book against a set of glowing reader reports while also taking into account the overall list coherence (both in terms of the intellectual coherence of a publisher's offerings and in terms of the economic sense in taking on a title).

Prestige, however, is a proxy measure for quality. It economically mirrors academic labour scarcity because it stands as a surrogate in order to avoid the labour-intensive practices of constantly reappraising academic material in every situation. A journal's or publisher's prestige, then, can be considered as a labour-saving shorthand that, in theory, should denote a venue in which top experts deemed other material to be first rate. If the experts in a field can only be asked to review a certain quantity of material and if those producing top-quality research can only submit a certain amount of work to a limited number of venues, the argument goes, then a prestigious journal or publisher will only take scholarship from the academics reviewed and favoured by those experts. However, because prestige is a proxy measure tied to labour scarcity, acting as a substitute for quality, it is not, therefore, right to think of quality and prestige as the same. In fact, it is possible that they can drift apart, which is where problems can occur. As Peter Suber puts it, primarily in relation to journals:

Quality and prestige overlap significantly. Because quality feeds prestige and prestige feeds quality, this is no accident. But sometimes they diverge, for at least three reasons: because some journals are new and prestige takes time to cultivate, because prestige is a zero-sum game and quality is not, and because prestige can be based on inaccurate or outdated judgments of quality. It's always convenient, and usually irresistible, to use prestige as a surrogate for quality. When quality and prestige overlap, that's entirely legitimate. But when they diverge, favoring prestige harms university hiring practices, research funding practices, and the growth [of] every kind of science and scholarship represented by new journals (which always lack prestige). Universities have a responsibility to notice when prestige and quality diverge, resist the almost irresistible temptation to favor prestige in those cases, do their best to recognize and reward quality, and give faculty an incentive to put quality first as well.[6]

Because prestige is used as a surrogate for quality that acts to compensate for labour scarcity, it also rests upon particular financial considerations pertaining to labour. The first and most important of these observations is that the model of traditional review, in which material is pre-screened for worthiness, relies upon academic labour. Validation is performed through a process whereby academics confer value upon the piece in question. The system that is erected here is one wherein humanities academics cyclically confer prestige upon a journal or publisher twofold by submitting their pieces to the venue that they believe to be the most prestigious and by reviewing with strict (even if unquantifiable) standards for those same destinations. Reviewer selection is often the task of an academic or commissioning editor who knows the field. In short: many of the major elements of authority and value that constitute the selection process and that therefore build prestige are undertaken by academics.

However, there are at least three reasons why academic labour is a necessary but insufficient condition for prestige accumulation in scholarly communications. Firstly, this is because there is a coordination role in which publisher labour and expertise is deployed; cultural and material capitals. Secondly, there is a negotiated and mediated process of selection in which the publisher also participates to preserve its own necessary interests in the market and quality; another intersection of cultural and material capitals. Thirdly and finally, the existing possession of social, cultural, material and symbolic capital allows publishers to confer prestige; the various forms of capital historically acquired by publishers are bestowed, in turn, upon authors in a mutually re-enforcing cycle. Thus, while academic quality may be determined entirely by academics conducting peer review, the economics of prestige work very differently.

In terms of open access, there is, theoretically, no reason why a new gold open access venue could not accumulate substantial academic credibility and prestige over time, should it attract the prerequisite submissions and reviewers. Indeed, there are many reasons why a gold open access venue may fare better on prestige in the long run. For example, the fact that there is no need to fill an issue in order to give subscribers value for money should make it possible to be more exclusive, if one desired.[7] This is undercut, however, by a strongly conservative disciplinary mechanism. The hiring, firing and promotion committees for which prestige serves as a useful proxy measure also fuel the need for academics to publish in existing venues that hold prestige. This same disciplinary mechanism, itself, partly restricts the ability for academics to publish whereseoever they might like with impunity; researchers sometimes select to publish in the venue that they feel will do the most for their research assessment return rankings or employ-ability (its prestige) as a primary criterion. In many cases, fledgling (OA) journals are not believed to fulfil these criteria. Prestige takes a long time to accumulate because the proxy measure requires a signifi-cant sample to prove its worth and because new venues are competing within an economically regulated field of symbolic capital.

From this logic, a partial answer to the first of my questions can emerge: the accumulation of prestige, as a form of symbolic capital, is difficult as the system is heavily weighted towards the normative. The use of prestige as a proxy measure by research exercises and hiring procedures has, to some extent, a disciplinary function that encourages publication in known venues. Likewise, publishers have an incentive to seek out academics who are known quantities (pos-sessing social and symbolic capital), particularly in the monograph sphere, to preserve their own prestige. These factors increase the number of high-quality micro-monopolies (published articles/books) held by such publishers and through this cycle the prices of top venues can go up. Although it could be possible for such publishing entities to use this privileged position (when they hold much quality material) to lower costs across the subscriber and/or purchaser base (simply by dint of a larger number of subscriptions and purchases), and although some publishers would probably say that they do so, this is against the market logics of profit, scarcity and perceived-value pricing. At the same time, as these disciplinary measures make it harder for new venues to gain prestige, the market logic that compe-tition could force prices down is not particularly efficacious.

Conversely, however, in the absence of other proxy measures, it could be the case that prestige saves departmental time and money in hiring and assessment processes. This could mean that prestige would offset its own potential economic disadvantages through an obviation of the need to reappraise work constantly. It would be incredibly hard to determine empirically what the costs would look like if labour time were needed to compensate for an absence of prestige. However, the situation is serious enough that there are now a number of projects investigating alternative metric systems to appraise quality ('altmetrics').[8] Such 'altmetrics' attempt to shift the focus of quality assessment away from the use of journal or publisher brand name as a signifier of quality. Sometimes these metrics are flawed, though, in that they can be easily gamed. For example, if one uses social media mentions of a work as a measure then there is an extreme risk of populism playing too strong a role and authors can also artificially inflate their reputations through technological cheating (such as creating many fake Twitter accounts etc.).[9] As with all quantifying bibliometrics, technological altmetrics are also only adept at measuring downloads and not so good at determining actual use (i.e. reading, assimilation and value). This is to say that, as much as there are problems with prestige as a measure, there are difficulties with all proxy measures. This is because if a proxy measure directly indicated the thing itself, it would not be a proxy.

One such alternative metric that could work – although it is notably also bound to a measure of 'prestige' for an academic – is the name of an academic editor. This is already more frequently the case for edited collections where far greater emphasis is placed upon the status of the academic editor. A measure of value based upon the academic editor would not only partially militate against some of the economic problems outlined above but also assist with the discoverability and dissemination issues touched upon in my second question. This is because such a shift from journal brand to editor brand would disentangle the proxy measure from a specific (subscription/sales-based) economic model. Researchers would still have a proxy measure to find material (the name of the editor) but issues of access might be more easily resolved through lowered barriers to entry for new journals or publishers. This could, of course, also have its problems. Respected academic editors might find themselves being offered substantial (financial) incentives to edit specific publications, as just one example, so the system is hardly flawless.

Furthermore, continuing this sketch, which forms a part-response to my third question of how quality and prestige interact, peer reviewers are the other important signal of quality that the current system in the humanities somewhat disregards in favour of an accumulation of prestige. Peer review is, in the most basic terms, an expression of endorsement: which academics said that a piece of work was good and worthy of publication. Given that academic reputation is all-important, the fact that this information is very rarely made public leaves much to be desired in terms of a proxy measure for value. There are, of course, practical problems with revealing reviewer identity to which I will return in the pragmatic path that I suggest in Chapter 5, but there is something to be said for a system in which people publicly endorse others' work, as is done in the marketing blurbs of monographs.[10] Going even further, it is curious to think that the pages upon pages of feedback that academics write for one another as part of the review process are discarded after use every year. It is difficult fully to know the bounds that structure a field and that determine the forms of knowledge that are producible and valued when so much of the process that shapes that crafting is hidden. It is also extremely hard to map the correlation between quality and prestige when the determinants that built this form of symbolic capital are not available.

Finally, moving away from internal prestige now to think a little about external value conferral (the 'prestige' of the university), it also seems plausible to posit that the current sphere of circulation, based on the subscription or commodity-purchase mode, could bear upon the external perception of the university and research in the humanities. It is true that, at present, successful academic publishers are adept at amplifying research in specific ways.[11] The target audience that they can usually help academics reach, however, is other researchers, admittedly the primary group for whom academic research is important. In an overloaded online environment where discovery is a bigger challenge, this function should not be overlooked. That said, compared with the mooted lofty purposes of research in the humanities, this vision is fairly limited, constrained as it is by the subscription/sale model. Indeed, if these disciplines are historically situated within the tradition of liberal humanism, in which the humanities help to create an informed and critical populace, then should not the amplification of scholarship go beyond those circles? Could such a broader base, through open access, help to cement the public reputation of the academic humanities?

This has been billed by advocates as one of the more pragmatic arguments for open access: by allowing the general public access, a far better case is made for the value of academic research activities. Two criticisms could be mounted against this stance. Firstly, this already plays into a specific notion and rhetoric of 'value' that could be problematic. Secondly, following on from this, it could be argued that the general public are not equipped to understand this work and that the misreading of its purpose could further damage the credibility of these disciplines. Indeed, arguments that the public will not always understand humanities research may, in some instances, be true.[12] However, a growing proportion of the global population now receive a degree-level education, in which they are taught the skills to read humanities material critically. If the process of a university education is one wherein access to such material is plentiful while one is inside but prohibitively expensive once flung into the wider world (academic books frequently cost £50+ and a single journal article can often fetch £40), it is clear that the academy may struggle to function efficaciously as a tool of social change. Social change, after all, must be executed immanently. It cannot be effected from an external, prestigious site that simply tells others what to do and think. Advocates argue that open access could enhance the ability of the university to change society for the better.

Of course, to some degree, the isolation of the academy is a historical function of professional specialisation and is inherent in notions of expertise and authority. As Samuel Weber notes, 'In order for the authority of the professional to be recognized as autonomous, the "field" of his "competence" had to be defined as essentially self-contained ... In general, the professional sought to *isolate* in order to control.'[13] As Weber goes on to note, 'The university, as it developed in the latter half of the nineteenth century, became the institutional expression and articulation of the culture of professionalism ... The "insulation" or "isolation" of the American academic community from other segments of society is the negative prerequisite of that demarcation that marks the professional perspective, above all that of the university professor.'[14] Such social demarcation, mirrored internally within academic institutions through disciplinarity, generates a dilemma for the humanities. On the one hand, the humanities form a study of difference, designed to explore and preserve plurality. As Weber notes, however, the moment that the specificity of this tolerance is defined in the service of expertise, it retreats to a stance of isolation in pursuit of authority. In other words, to be an expert *means* isolating a field of knowledge in which one becomes authoritative, an act of demarcation. It makes little sense to say, however, that the demarcating feature of the humanities is to pursue the erasure of demarcation.[15] While such anti-disciplinary thinking may be theoretically valuable (and could chime with the aims of the humanities), it is, of course, extremely difficult to implement within existing structures of the academy.

As Bill Readings accurately diagnoses, however, the 'internal legitimation struggle concerning the nature of the knowledge produced in the humanities ... would not take on crisis proportions were it not accompanied by an external legitimation crisis'.[16] Indeed, the state of constant emergency for the humanities through its external, public perception is only set to continue. Due to various legislative shifts, which are fundamentally bound up with governmental market-orientated transformations of the university, there is top-down demand for transparency in academic dealings and for a quantifiable legitimation of the academy's activities.[17] Although, as Thomas Docherty notes, this transparency agenda seems to have evolved simultaneously with 'the growth and distribution of higher education, with a watering down of class prejudices and Establishment certainties, and with an ostensibly democratic demand for an opening of the doors of opportunity to all', it also specifies the priority of accountability and transparency, with the seeming aim to produce the ultimate rational market actor: one who has access to all information and therefore behaves in a predictably self-interested fashion.[18] While, then, it is possible to identify potentially irresolvable paradoxes at the heart of humanities study (demarcation/legitimation/utility), it will be much more difficult to overcome the smaller, more soluble challenges to the 'value' of work in the humanities if a resolution to the problem of external institutional legitimation is totally resisted. It may simply be that the rhetoric of proven value is now too politically strong to be fully resisted without incurring the total destruction of the humanities by those with material capital.

In the face of such tactics, two roads are possible with respect to open access for those who wish to resist market-based, utilitarian evaluations of the humanities. The first is to retain current closed publication practices and to keep a monetary price for access to research outputs. This comes with the potential disadvantages of degrading the university's liberal humanist potential through isolationism, of dividing the research community into those who can pay and those who cannot, of limiting the audience for research work, of sometimes over-delegating hiring and promotion procedures to proxy measures, and of under-utilising the potential of the internet to gain instantaneous access to research and teaching materials. Conversely, if open access is adopted, these aspects could potentially be mitigated where desirable, but sometimes at the price of playing into a justification on the basis of transparency and appraisal, quantification and measurement, among the many other controversies. These arguments must be weighed individually by all members of our university communities.

In the first part of this chapter, I have begun to discuss the way in which considerations of the economics of scholarly publishing are bound to considerations of a parallel system of symbolic exchange. This is often manifest in the abstract notion of prestige, which is a proxy measure for quality, rationed through academic labour scarcity. The financial and research benefits of prestige for and of the academy are many. However, prestige as a proxy also hinders the development of new (economic) models for publishing because it is a system that tends towards re-enforcement of existing systems. Indeed, once prestige has been accumulated, it is harder to lose than it ever was to build, an aspect that erects higher barriers for new initiatives to hurdle if they are to gain social and economic traction. Finally, it seems clear that a greater public face for the humanities is necessary to overcome the problematic perception of a prestigious, lofty site of anti-utilitarian authority, with open access positioned awkwardly in response to this challenge.

ECONOMICS, 'ACADEMIC LABOUR' AND PUBLISHING

From the preceding observations on value-ascription and assessment in the humanities, it is clear that the finances of scholarly publishing are in part determined by a complex set of socio-academic factors. From such thinking, however, and now beginning to move towards the purely financial side of open access, a fresh set of questions emerge. Why is open access peculiar to the university? Why, uniquely, should the university be forced to give its work away for free? Beyond this, if there were satisfactory answers to the preceding two questions, if the academy were able to give away its work for free through open access, would this present a point of resistance to the commodification of higher education and research outputs, given that something that is monetarily free looks as though it has no exchange value?

To think through such questions, it is necessary to begin with an observation that the theoretical premise on which the labour of academic scholarship rests is one where the author is paid an academic salary, part of which covers the production of research work. While this is sometimes supplemented by external grant income, it is also important to note that a vast quantity of humanities research work is undertaken on institutional (and sometimes personal) time. As touched upon above, this theoretical model yields a very good rationale for why scholars should give away their work: they are happily divorced from the need to sell research for a financial return. While some scholars may wish to gain supplemental income from selling their work, in most cases such returns are too small to make a tangible difference. Instead, academics see a longer term payoff in the form of reputation, which leads to promotion and eventual material self-gain, on top of the anticipated benefit to society through academic research. This is a good model because it moves academic work beyond the realm of popular market appeal. This means that niche investigations into important, but unpopular, areas can be published. However, as with many theoretical models, it can be difficult to pair the rhetoric to the reality. Contingent faculty who exist on short-term contracts under precarious labour conditions with no guarantee of work on a term-by-term basis make a mockery of this ideal system. This is clearly demonstrated by the existence of books such as Keith Hoeller's *Equality for Contingent Faculty: Overcoming the Two-Tier System* in which he points out that there are over *one million* contingent faculty members in the United States – a whopping 75% of all university teachers – or even the fact that Bill Readings' *The University in Ruins* is dedicated to Ann Wordsworth, of whom Readings wrote that 'She taught me about something that Oxford called "Critical Theory" and she did so on a *short-term contract*, teaching *in a hut* in the garden of one of the brick mansions of North Oxford.'[19] In the UK, over half of universities and colleges use lecturers on zero-hour, precarious contracts that bring no guarantee of work.[20]

In this light, it becomes harder to justify the argument that all academics are paid to write and so can afford to give material away. A substantial portion of the academic community do not benefit from the security of the ideal model. However, the counterargument is that those who wish to succeed must be able to publish with reputable presses, as publication is the unit of accreditation, the validating branded proxy measure that can lead to a job. The bold claim that academic labour is different from other forms of work in some respects, with regard to the outcome of research material, is therefore only partly true. Scholarship *is* different from other forms of output, in theory, because academics are paid to give their work away. In the current implemented reality, however, it is a form of labour like any other. Nevertheless, given the discrepancy between the ideal and reality, it is important to ask at this point whether there are viable and preferable alternatives to a system in which publishers do not directly compensate writers.

To address this, it is worth hypothesising three different business models for academic publishing. The three models that I will venture are: (1) a system under which academics are paid for their publications; (2) a system under which publishers are paid individually for their services; (3) a cooperative system. This list does not constitute a systematic overview but is rather an examination of a range of options that exemplify each type and that allow us to think about the historical emergence of the subscription/commodity-purchase model.

The first of these models, an 'academic pay for publication system', is a hypothetical one wherein academics would be paid by publishers for the work that they produce. Publishers would then recoup their costs and make a profit by selling the work back to academic libraries and a limited number of other interested parties. This already happens in reality with research monographs. In most cases of books, however, the royalties paid to authors are extremely small because of the low print runs of such volumes, a changing and increasingly competitive market space and the assumption that academics are already paid by institutions to write the works.[21] With this in mind, let us consider instead the case of journals.

If journals paid academics for their articles, the system would be altered in several ways. For one, journals would more directly weigh every contribution made by authors for return value. Secondly, new journals would have to find significant sources of funding to compete on any level. Thirdly, a hierarchy of payout would emerge that would further top-load the system as those who have capital would be able to offer the greatest monetary rewards. Fourthly, academic salaries would come under more intense scrutiny if a lucrative additional income source were available. Fifthly, institutions might desire to take a share of this and, in the process, require academics to obtain the highest return, thereby curtailing the ability to publish in some venues. Sixthly, presses might begin to favour authors whose names will bring them a better reputational return, thereby making entry to an academic post even harder for early career researchers. The list goes on. In fact, a model for journals that financially rewarded academics directly for their writing might well be disastrous. As Peter Suber writes, 'The academic custom to write research articles for impact rather than money may be a lucky accident that could have been otherwise. Or it may be a wise adaptation that would eventually evolve in any culture with a serious research subculture.'[22]

Assuming, then, that this 'academic pay for publication system' would be too damaging, what about a model in which publisher labour is considered as a service for authors? This is how many publishers already perceive their activities and it is the justification for not paying authors; academics are *clients* for whom publishers work (but, paradoxically, also *suppliers* and *customers* in various configurations). This model, which lies behind article and book processing charge setups, seems appealing. If authors, or their institutions, were to pay publishers for their work, which could then be made freely available, the economic burden would be transferred to the supply side and the demand-side library budgeting/access dilemma could be solved (although not the supply-side 'over-production' problem). This is a model that works on the basis of transferring financial risk towards academic institutions and away from publishers, who have traditionally needed capital surpluses to tide them over through long publication cycles in the hope of a payoff across their list.

In this inverted model, publishers are paid for the services they render and not in return for making sound judgements in a sales environment. As examples, in the natural and social sciences, two publishers, PLOS (a pure open-access publisher) and SAGE (a traditional publisher with open-access options), operate their gold journals on an article-processing-charge basis. Under this model, authors, their institutions or their research funders must pay a fee once an article is accepted. At the time of writing (mid 2014), for PLOS's journals this ranges from $1,350 to $2,900 per article but these charges may be waived in the case of the author not having the available funds. In the case of *SAGE Open*, the publisher currently charges $99, a discount from a launch price of $695, again with a waiver option that is judged on an individual basis (although in June 2014 SAGE sent a mass email cautioning of a potential price hike).[23] Traditional publishers are also now more frequently offering an open-access option, so-called 'hybrid' open access in which a combination of OA and subscription articles co-exist within an issue. For Taylor & Francis, the price of publishing an article in one of these venues is $2,950. Although there is a wide variance in APC levels, from £100 up to £5,000, according to Stuart Lawson the UK's Finch Report, acting on incorrect and outdated information, has now created a self-fulfilling prophecy whereby a more narrow range of £1,600–£2,000 has become the norm.[24]

This cost is multiplied when dealing with books. Commercial publishers such as Palgrave Macmillan have proposed a book processing charge of $17,500 (£11,000 GBP) per monograph-length title, which is simply unaffordable for scholars and departments in most humanities disciplines, even if this works out cheaper than the pro-rata equivalent for journals.[25] New born-OA academic publishers such as Ubiquity Press put the figure for books closer to $3,200 (£2,000 GBP). In light of the precarious labour models of the academy, however, it is clear that this is a seriously flawed model for the humanities and the outcry at APCs even *within* the university from tenured professors shows the kind of problems this could create for potential job applicants who cannot access fees. Indeed, this mode substantially worsens the situation for those at the bottom of the career ladder.[26]

It has also been argued, within the context of article and book processing charges, that this model for gold open access would impinge upon academic freedom, an aspect I have already briefly touched upon.[27] It is argued that funding mandates restrict academic freedom because they curtail the ability of academics without funding to publish in gold OA venues that have an article or book processing charge, or with other publishers without a policy on green archiving. While being sympathetic to such reasoning and also believing that APCs and BPCs at such rates are unaffordable for the humanities, I feel it is important to note that this argument requires a very specific reading of the formal term 'academic freedom'. There are different definitions of academic freedom in countries worldwide, with varying degrees of legal standing. Take, for instance, the 1940 *Statement of Principles on Academic Freedom and Tenure* by the American Association of University Professors which proclaims that 'Teachers are entitled to full freedom in research and in the publication of the results.'[28] As Benjamin Ginsberg points out, this US context is hardly legally binding at all because '[i]n recent years, the federal courts have decided that deanlets, not professors, are entitled to academic freedom' and that 'professors' ideas and utterances do not have any special constitutional status'.[29] In the UK, via the Education Reform Act of 1988, the wording is even more restricted, although it is enshrined in law: 'to ensure that academic staff have freedom within the law to question and test received wisdom, and to put forward new ideas and controversial or unpopular opinions, without placing themselves in jeopardy of losing their jobs or privileges they may have at their institutions'.[30] In one reading, these statements *could* be seen as endorsing free choice regarding where to publish one's research, in which case the arguments over academic freedom hold. In another take, though, one that situates academic freedom within a history of censorship, these doctrines refer to the full freedom *to publish* the work without fear of institutional or government reprisal, not to the choice of *where* to publish it, an aspect more strongly reflected in the wording of the UK's legislation. This can already be seen in the fact that journals and presses are allowed to reject academic work on grounds of quality (for both journals and books) and marketability (usually only for books), aspects that are not explicitly mentioned in these statements on academic freedom but which already limit the ability to publish wherever one would like.

In any case, the backlash against article and book processing charges has triggered investigations into a range of new models that seek to provide gold open access in a sustainable fashion without any author-facing charges, the third setup proposed above. Under such models – covered extensively below in 'How can open access be affordable for the humanities?' – many libraries each pay a small amount in order to sustain a large-scale infrastructure. It is thought by proponents that an extension of the service model in this way could prove less damaging and more amenable to the community, especially in the transition phase. Several projects, which often take the form of library consortial arrangements, including arXiv, SCOAP³, Knowledge Unlatched and the Open Library of Humanities, are currently investigating whether these models are favourable for libraries and/or feasible at scale.[31]

These consortial models are interesting because they operate, economically, less on the basis of competition and more on cooperation. When libraries cooperate to fund gold OA initiatives, the transition period and subsequent implementation could potentially look less damaging with the cost spread over a larger number of institutions. Such models, though, do not sit harmoniously within the present, dominant business context of free-market competition. As I have argued, however, the fact that there are inherent micromonopolies in scholarly publishing (i.e. the unique nature of each published artefact) means that it is difficult to construct marketplaces to which such notions of competition directly apply. Instead, I would argue, we need to understand the commodity character of research within market economies more fully, an aspect to which I will now turn.

Scholarship and the commodity form

In order to understand why market-orientated governments are keen on open access, which seems based on a more egalitarian premise than would usually be palatable to them, it is necessary to consider the economic use-values and sites of exchange of published research. As covered above in the section on objections to open access in the humanities, one core point of contention is the way in which open licensing could lead to reappropriation of university research by external commercial entities. It is true that this seems to be the goal of many government OA mandates: to ensure a link between university and industry. However, what happens when that link feeds companies and activities that pose a risk to the research university itself? In this part of this chapter I will look at the next point of value and economics in relation to humanities scholarship: the bundling of research work as a commodity object. This will not only enable an examination of some of the points where the use and exchange values of research are realised but also make it possible to think through the potential changes that open access might engender in this sphere. In other words: is open access a way in which the commodity form of research can be resisted since it is given away for free (the 'gift'), or is it complicit with deeper utilitarian, industrial exploitation ('use value')?

Given the nature of research production and remuneration in the university, it can *superficially appear* that the research work of the academy is different in its terms of production from other manufactured commodities. After all, as we have seen, in the ideal situation, academics are paid a salary in order to give their work away; a rare situation of patronage in contemporary economics. This can lead the more optimistic opponents of marketised higher education to deduce that open access might present a point of resistance to the commodification of knowledge. In fact, such an argument would run, what could better resist this process than work that is, in two senses, priceless? Sadly, as I will show, such a conclusion is flawed. Open-access research is not radically anti-corporate, as Jeffrey Beall's accusation against the movement suggests and, indeed, a Marxist analysis of the commodity form of open-access material will confirm this.[32] On top of this, while academic papers, whether open access or not, remain ensconced within the commodity form as objects that have both exchange- and use-value, it is also clear that the production of research/scholarship in the humanities is not simply an esoteric activity undertaken purely for its own sake. It is, instead, one of the many instruments through which academic labour is transformed into productive labour, especially when aligned with the historical provision of land grants (nineteenth century), research patenting (early twentieth century), mid-century war funding and late-twentieth-century venture capital, as Joss Winn notes.[33] As with open-source software, what can be seen as emerging around open access to scholarly research is the university as a service industry that can provide training in methods of reading, understanding and (re-)producing such material. When considering the role, function and exceptionality of scholarship, then, it is important not simply to fetishise a return to a form without value under capital. Instead, as Winn puts it, one must remember that 'the trajectory of higher education and its conceived role and purpose in public life over the last century can only be fully understood through a critique of capitalism as the historical mode of production which (re-)produces the university'.[34] It is this mode of thinking that will condition my remarks and situation of the economic landscape within which scholarship is produced and under which open access emerges.[35]

Thinking further about how open access intersects with contemporary academic labour, it is worth always remembering, as Amy Wendling notes, that 'Capitalism does not care if it produces quantities for use; it cares about producing profit.'[36] Even with this being the case, the fundamental aim of the labour of academic research in the humanities must be considered in terms of the use-values for various stakeholders, including those for the academics who write, who learn, who communicate and who are remunerated; for their readers, who are enriched and who learn to teach others; and for students, whose graduate prospects are improved (humanities graduates can get jobs because they can 'think critically', 'write well' etc.) and whose participation in democratic society, it is often claimed, is enhanced. Even these aspects, however, can prove somewhat too intangible for a materialist debate. Indeed, the question adeptly posed by Richard Hall – 'What is its [academic labour's] use-value for society, as opposed to its exchange-value or its price as a commodity?'[37] – is too broad to be covered here. That said, casting aside liberal humanism's ascribed democratic function, no matter how often the rhetoric of impact and use is foisted upon these disciplines, there are frequent discussions on whether the humanities hold materialist utility.[38]

Such efforts to disclaim economic or material utility appear somewhat fantastical because, in addition to the intangible benefits, it is clear that humanities research has exchange-value that is enmeshed in capital (a form of use-value where the only use is to generate surplus value). In other words, academic research, even that produced in the humanities, has an economic function.[39] This can be seen most prominently in the way in which the contemporary university uses research material for teaching, for which there is now often a charge to students.[40] This is the 'dominant narrative that conceives universities as educational "marketplaces" where faculty produce learning and student-consumers purchase a defined quantum of knowledge in the form of a degree'.[41] It can be seen wherever employers profit from the skills that their employees learned in a humanities degree. It can also be seen in publisher profits. It can be seen in the ticket prices for exhibitions at galleries, libraries, archives and museums (GLAMs). All of these sites extract surplus value over the academic labour that was necessary for the production of the research-commodity, even when the form looks as though it has no material value. Interestingly, though, under an open-access system, this research becomes even more adept at hiding its inherent labour – after all, for this object, nothing was paid by those directly acquiring the commodity.

It is important to emphasise this because many theorisations of university economics and commercial publication practices are masked behind the rhetoric of agency theory. Agency theories work on assumptions of calculated risk and bounded, rationally self-interested agents. For scholarship, as Raymond Hogler and Michael A. Gross set out in an important article, this means that:

First, the agency model demands that scholarship be commodified so as to play its part in the marketplace ... Second, agency theory posits that the exchange of commodities – publications for money – takes place under competitive market conditions akin to those in a commercial enterprise ... Third, the agency model features an idealized and discrete contractual bargain between a single faculty member and the university and necessarily ignores the institutional consequences of the marketplace conception of educational processes . . . Fourth, agency theory presents itself as a 'positive' methodology that claims to be superior in technique and result in the 'normative' kind of research that makes moral, philosophical, or emotional appeals to the academic community.[42]

The ubiquity of this model is problematic in many ways, but Hogler and Gross's argument reveals the core of this system: the dominant political and societal narrative (whether one wishes it so or otherwise) is that university research is a commodity from which surplus value is to be extracted. In this context, there is a potentially dangerous political risk that the monetarily free nature of open access might hide this economic presence and thereby sustain the illusion that research work is a liberated, esoteric activity (especially in the humanities) whose areas of inquiry are determined autonomously and free of market pressures. It seems unlikely that this is true at the present moment or that open access would change this in the future. The narrative of the commodity character of research work seems here to stay.

The other aspect of labour that is potentially hidden through the zero-price point of open-access research is publishing. While open access to research presents an object as free, this is not to say that academic publishing can ever be conceived of as a labour-free enterprise. Regardless of how the process is framed, even without any allowance for profit, publishers must be remunerated for their work. Indeed, publishing as it currently stands involves a value-chain of peer-review facilitation, typesetting (including XML or other formatting), copyediting, proofreading, design, printing, digital preservation, organisational membership (Committee on Publication Ethics, COUNTER [a body for the standardisation of usage metrics] and others), digital rights management and marketing, distribution, warehousing, as well as the more general costs of running a business (administration, accountancy, legal advice, trademark registration etc.).[43] Open access certainly eliminates some of these costs: there is no point in implementing digital rights management – which protects content from unauthorised copying – on material that is free to access and licensed for unlimited third-party dissemination. It could also be argued that, in a service-provision model, many of these costs could be optional and paid at the discretion of the author; for instance, if an author is confident that he or she does not require professional copyediting and/or proofreading, then this could be unbundled from the cost (although this particular aspect would certainly be a risky strategy for both the author and the brand of the publisher).

From this thinking about market agency approaches, gold open access throws into relief the anomalies of ascribing a monetary value for the purchase of a research article or book, given that the primary audience for its purchase is the same as its genesis. That said, eliminating this demand-side price and instead thinking of an OA article or book as 'free' (and labour-free) can lead to the fallacy that a gold open access work could resist the commodity form. If something is given away for free, such logic would run, is it a commodity? This originates from a simple oversight of the fact that cost does not equal value. As Winn puts it:

There may not be a direct relationship between the OA paper and money like there is for non-OA articles, but if the OA paper is used by someone to improve their labour, which is being paid for by a wage, then there is an equivalence between the wage which pays the worker to improve their labour power which makes them a better teacher, researcher, etc. which results in them writing more/better papers, reproducing better students, improving the reputation of the institution, attracting more external revenue of one kind or another. The point is that capital is a social relation and the creation of value is a dynamic social process that can be distilled down to the time it takes for labour to produce a commodity: 'socially necessary labour time'.[44]

Open-access articles and books retain an exchange-value because they are of use-value to people other than the creator, regardless of whether the object is purchased at a monetary sum. This, then, presents the opportunity for others to extract surplus value from the labour of academics, which explains, at least in part, why centre-right governments are so keen on OA. That said, even those who do not share such an agenda can nonetheless find themselves in sympathy with some forms of open access purely because they may create a level playing-field for access to research. Sceptics would say, however, that this egalitarian field is only one wherein academics are more equally free to be exploited and that supply-side payment models for gold will lead only to a less equal community wherein researchers without funds will be unable to publish.

Perhaps, then, this represents the compromise point for open access in terms of its political split: on the one hand, open access has the potential to eradicate the inability of academics to read the work of their peers. Conversely, all forms of OA under the BBB definitions allow a broader societal use-value (and that includes extending this to corporate entities).[45] While there are ways in which it would be possible to mitigate aspects of re-enclosure, if so desired – most notably through the addition of a clause to the license that means that any reuser must also make their derivatives available to the community under the same terms, covered below – these are harder to implement in political terms because of their anti-market connotations. What is clear, though, is that, under open access, the points of use- and exchange-value are decentred and deferred from the producer and even from the producer's employer (the university), rather than removed. Open access does not change this relationship to the commodity form of research. In other words: it is simply that the form of exchange-value *appears* differently under open access because there is no price. It is likewise clear that these topics require a more rigorous interrogation than might appear from a surface reading and also that the politics of OA must continue to be monitored for its potential dangers against its possible social good.

HOW CAN OPEN ACCESS BE AFFORDABLE FOR THE HUMANITIES?

In light of the need to compensate publisher labour, one of the most important components in Peter Suber's list of 'what open access is not' is that 'OA is not an attempt to deny the reality of costs'.[46] While some volunteer efforts have managed to operate on almost non-existent budgets, this does not seem a prudent idea when scaled to cover all research in the humanities. This then leads to the question of how it can be possible for the humanities to afford open access. Who, at the end of the day, pays?

The answers to these questions are multifaceted but the absolutely crucial point that should be made upfront is that no major reconfiguration of the current economic model is necessary with green open access. Under this system, where a subscription mechanism for journals co-exists with deposit in an institutional or subject repository, it is possible simply to continue with the existing economic model. This is because, at present, there is no evidence that green open access encourages institutions to cancel subscriptions, even in high-energy physics where the practice has been common since 1991.[47] Of course, this could change in the future (as posited by one much-criticised study[48]) and it may be that there is disciplinary variance, so caution is advisable. It is also unknown how this model could work in the monograph sphere, although this is covered more thoroughly below. A further study commissioned by the Association of Learned and Professional Society Publishers, however, also showed that there are many more important factors that determine subscription cancellation than green OA.[49] This study covered a broad range of subjects, including science and technology, medical and healthcare, humanities and social sciences, and business and management. However, the study found no discernible disciplinary differences for the reasons why librarians would cancel subscriptions; in all cases, green OA came well below pedagogical and research relevance, the level of usage and the price. As Peter Suber's analysis of this study puts it: 'toll-access journals have more to fear from their own price increases than from rising levels of green OA'.[50]

The reasons why green open access doesn't cause subscription cancellations are not wholly understood but must at least partially be attributed to the fact that green OA versions are often not on par with their version-of-record counterparts. Indeed, at the current permitted levels of deposit there would still be a hierarchy of access in which paginated, final versions of record, without embargo, could only be guaranteed to those at wealthier institutions. It is also true that the current rate of deposit, even when allowed by publishers, does not give substantial coverage due to the lack of institutional incentives (academics simply don't see the advantages of depositing to themselves).[51] Furthermore, green open-access versions often do not appear in traditional library discoverability search routes (although they may fare well in proprietary rankings, such as Google), which could contribute towards a continued perceived need among faculty for a subscription. Finally, the length of necessary embargo periods to maintain subscription rates is disputed. The UK's House of Commons Business, Innovation and Skills (BIS) Select Committee Inquiry concluded that there is no available evidence base to indicate that short or even zero embargoes cause cancellation of subscriptions. Evidence from the field of high-energy physics shows that despite nearly 100% immediate, unembargoed deposit (Green), subscriptions have not been damaged. The €4 million EU funded PEER (Publishing and the Ecology of European Research) project (2012) showed that traffic to journal websites increased when articles were made available through a publicly accessible repository, possibly because interest grew as articles were disseminated more widely.[52]

The field of high-energy physics is one that recurs in studies of open access because it is the discipline with the longest history of green self-archiving (open access). Although this presents problems of disciplinary specificity and especially the ease with which it can wrongly be assumed that all disciplines will follow the same route, the only real evidence that we have for existing models comes from the sciences. In this discipline, almost every journal allows green open access immediately with no embargo period. As the BIS inquiry noted, this has not resulted in cancellations. In fact, the PEER project showed, somewhat counter-intuitively, that making articles green open access (across a variety of disciplines) correlated to more visitors to the official publisher journal websites.

In terms of humanities disciplines, however, the committee also noted that 'Several submissions argued that short embargo periods were more harmful to HASS (humanities, arts and social sciences) than STEM (science, technology, engineering and medicine) disciplines. The most frequently deployed argument in HASS subjects is that since works in these disciplines have longer citation half-lives (i.e. are referred to over a longer period) a longer embargo is necessary.'[53] This is, in fact, the exact line of argument taken by Rebecca Darley, Daniel Reynolds and Chris Wickham in a recent report for the British Academy.[54] The BIS committee rejected this argument, however, noting that they did not receive any evidence to support this recommendation.[55]

Assuming, however, that a move beyond green to a gold route was desired, one in which publishing labour was remunerated from the supply side, one essential truth must always stand as a starting point: there is enough money within the total global system to cover the current rate of publication. Certainly, under the present arrangement, there is an insufficiently equitable distribution of capital among institutions to allow everyone to have access, an aspect that could just be reversed to the supply side through article or book processing charges for gold open access if care is not taken. However, the work is published and publishers are afloat, sometimes making healthy profits. This makes it possible to deduce some crucial information. Assuming that it is desirable to keep the volume of material published at the same level (i.e. the degree of pre-filtering/rejection would remain unchanged), any problems of unaffordability of gold open access must be attributed to one or more of three points. Firstly, this unaffordability could be the fault of a transition period to supply-side payments for gold open access in which there are the double costs of subscriptions and of open access (so-called 'double dipping'). Secondly, the difficulties of cost could be attributed to models for gold open access that rely on localised funding for authors (article/book processing charges), thereby replicating the existing problems of unequal access on the supply side and giving the impression of systemic budgetary crisis to authors who cannot publish. Thirdly and finally, publishers could fundamentally be charging more for gold open access.

The first of these issues – regarding transition costs and double dipping – is already being addressed. Publishers do not wish to seen to be charging twice for their work (i.e. charging both subscribers/purchasers for a subscription/book and authors/institutions for an article/book processing charge). To this end, many publishers have implemented arrangements whereby the amounts paid in processing charges are deducted from the costs paid by subscribers or purchasers. Taking an example of a journal, the problem here, of course, is that by reducing the amount paid across the whole range of subscribers, the cost to the individual institution that spent the APC is only marginally offset. This means that early adopters of APC-based gold open access pay more to support the transition. Taylor & Francis, for example, explain this thus for their journal model: 'We acknowledge that the worldwide benefit of an increase in open access content in subscription journals may initially be paid for by a small number of institutions at the forefront of funding open access. We are unable to offer these institutions direct substitution of OA charges for subscription fees, since our commitment to no "double dipping" means the reductions in cost need to be shared across all subscribers.'[56] Conversely, another way in which some open-access humanities publishers, such as OpenEdition, have avoided double dipping, while also taking a payment, is through selling add-on benefits to libraries who pay, even when an article is gold open access. This model is called 'freemium' and benefits can include better metadata and usage statistics. These two different systems for offsetting double dipping and costs do not necessarily result in equality. The results, however, are not necessarily unequitable if these institutions can afford to pay. It is instead a progressive transition mechanism in which those with the capital to do so carry forward those who do not, at least in theory.

Whether or not this leads to a fair outcome, however, is debatable. At the currently proposed levels of article/book processing charges for gold open access, even if some institutions were to switch to a wholly supply-side payment system, it is possible that they could still not afford to publish all the material produced and deemed worthy by their faculty. Current subscription budgets in some humanities departments in the UK, for example, would stretch to a mere three articles (and not even half a book) under currently proposed prices for gold open access.[57] This has led the green open access advocate Stevan Harnad to brand a switch to gold open access under such conditions as 'fools' gold'.[58] The reasons for this are clear. Firstly, publishers have to cover the cost of work that they perform upon rejected manuscripts (review coordination etc.) even though they receive no income from such works. Secondly, APCs and BPCs are sometimes being determined by publishers dividing their current list revenue by the number of desirable publications in the future.[59] While this tallies with remarks by David Sweeney of the Higher Education Funding Council for England that he does not think of open access as a cost-cutting exercise, there is a lack of disciplinary specificity in such remarks that causes some problems.[60] Foremost among these is that the library budgets for scientific disciplines are often magnitudes of order higher than their humanities counterparts, particularly in the case of journals at the top of the prestige scale.[61] Under article/book processing charge setups where pricing is either undifferentiated between disciplines or determined purely by emerging market levels set by such premises, the differences in financial circumstances between the humanities and the sciences are not adequately reflected.

However, the costs included are equal neither between disciplines nor even between individual articles/books.[62] For instance, while some costs remain the same regardless of the type of material under consideration (digital preservation, for example, unless considering big data [where custom applications must be written to ensure continued access to extremely large datasets]), other expenditures such as fact checking, peer review and typesetting vary enormously according to the type of publication. As an example, the fact checking and peer-review portions of an article proclaiming the safety or otherwise of a vaccine need to be conducted with greater rigour (and at greater labour time) than that of an article about the nineteenth-century novel. Likewise, if a piece of work features mathematical notation, complex chemical formulae, tables, associated data or any of a raft of other necessary formatting idiosyncrasies, the cost of labour and/or technology is necessarily higher. In other words, undifferentiated pricing of gold open access article processing charges leads to a system of cross-subsidy in which works that are easier to publish and that require less labour time effectively subsidise their counterparts. Why should a 1,500 word, plain-text book review cost the same in an APC model as an 8,000 word article with complex symbols and typesetting requirements?

Such a system of cross-subsidy may be desirable to ensure the continuation of those disciplines with more complex publishing requirements. However, gold open access charges set at a universal, undifferentiated rate have the potential to damage the credibility of a service-based, supply-side payment model of academic publishing. This is because undifferentiated pricing gives the impression of a black box into which money is thrown and out of which comes a product and sometimes profits, with insufficient justification to 'clients' for the resources. That said, there are also several clear factors that hinder the development of transparent, 'unbundled' pricing. The first factor is the difficulty of articulating and pricing the value-adding aspects of academic publishing. This should be easier than it appears given that this labour consists of, at least in the current age of the book: selective acquisition, financial investment/risk, content development, quality control, management/coordination and sales/marketing.[63] The second factor, however, is that it is often unclear which services can safely be 'unbundled' without losing other valued functions (i.e. many aspects of the publication workflow are not discrete but interlinked, such as 'quality control' and 'financial investment/risk'). Furthermore, this model could lead to painful job losses at publishers if the unbundled arrangement does not sustain their current staffing base. Of course, academic publishing as an industry exists to serve the needs of academic researchers, not to provide jobs and revenue for publishers. When dealing with real people's livelihoods, however, a greater degree of empathy and care may be necessary. Thirdly and finally, setting differentiated levels of pricing is a labour activity in itself that requires business sense and market research.

If the current problems of article and book processing charge pricing are a combined result, though, of inaction, a flawed hybrid environment and an unclear measure of costs, publishers also know that they cannot afford to sit idly by. As funders begin to insist on either green or gold for work they have funded, those publishers without open access options will find themselves unable to publish work that falls under the remit of these bodies.[64] Once this reaches a certain tipping point for gold supply-side payments, funders will have the ability to regulate this market. At the risk of future gazing, this could be done through the agglomeration of grant and dissemination costs. In other words, funders could state that the total amount awarded in a grant must cover both the research activities undertaken and the work's open access dissemination, with no distinction specified. This devolution of spending agency to grant recipients is a form of soft power, to appropriate Joseph Nye's concept, through which authors will be made sensitive to pricing of publishing as a service.[65] If faced with the choice of spending grant funds on publishing as opposed to staffing/equipment, cash-strapped researchers will place APCs under intense scrutiny. Through such a system of mandates in which researchers would be directly confronted with both the services offered and the expenditure of their own potential research funds on such services, this market might be spurred to competition.

Even with this being the case, there are also emerging models that seek to fund gold publishing infrastructures collaboratively, rather than competitively. The precedent for this, once more, comes from high-energy physics and the arXiv project (pronounced 'archive'). arXiv is a pre-print server that was founded by Paul Ginsparg in

1996 and that hosts non-peer-reviewed material.[66] The idea is that, in the disciplines covered, it is important that new discoveries are circulated as quickly as possible to allow others to verify findings as well as to establish the author's precedence and claim to originality, even while peer review is ongoing. To this end, arXiv allows researchers to put their manuscripts online for public access while the processes of review and publication in scientific journals are in progress. More relevant for the discussion at hand, however, is the fact that arXiv's revenue model is one under which Cornell University Library (CUL), the Simons Foundation, and a global collection of institutions support arXiv financially: 'Each member institution pledges a five-year funding commitment to support arXiv. Based on institutional usage ranking, the annual fees are set in four tiers from $1,500–$3,000. Cornell's [the host of arXiv] goal is to raise $300,000 per year through membership fees generated by approximately 126 institutions.'[67] A similar model has been implemented by another project, SCOAP[3], for high-energy physics, except this time for fully peer-reviewed, final publications.[68] Likewise, Rebecca Kennison and Lisa Norberg have proposed a model for the humanities under which there would be a central fund, created through an annual or multi-year payment from every institution of higher education, to which institutions and scholarly societies can apply through a competitive grant process.[69] With funding from the Andrew W. Mellon Foundation, my Open Library of Humanities project is also attempting to implement a similar model for journal publishing in the humanities.

These are models in which a moderate number of institutions come together to support a publishing platform. Because the ensuing research is freely and openly available to all, supporting institutions are not, themselves, 'buying' a commodity item. Instead they are banding together to bring to fruition projects that would not otherwise exist. Such an approach circumvents the economic problems engendered by the inherent micro-monopolies that are seen in scholarly communications. It could also make possible gold open access publishing without processing charges, which could work extremely well for the humanities discipline. However, it also comes with two distinct problems of its own: (1) the 'free-rider' problem in which even those who do not pay receive the benefits and (2) the difficulty for such initiatives of finding the optimum balance point between the level of contribution and number of institutions.

The first of these difficulties, the so-called 'free-rider' problem, relates to the economic understanding that rationally self-interested actors do not wish to pay for commodities from which others benefit for free. In other words, except in philanthropic modes or systems of taxation for public good, most people usually resist paying for goods for which only they pay, but from which non-purchasers also derive benefit.[70] This results, for gold open access publishing, in a kind of prisoner's dilemma. If all library entities behave in a purely self-interested way and disallow free riders, these collectively underwritten, non-APC models cannot emerge. Admittedly, the increasing enclosure of universities within market logics doubtless makes it harder for acquisition librarians to justify expenditure on projects where there are free riders to senior managers. That said, as Rebecca Bliege Bird and Eric Alden Smith point out, the 'generosity' of participation in such initiatives is not devoid of return to member institutions. Indeed, as they note, 'individually costly but collectively beneficial (or at least prestigious) behaviors such as public generosity or extravagant piety are a form of social competition: the most generous or self-sacrificial individuals gain higher prestige, and the recipients or observers gain material benefit at the expense of their own prestige'.[71] In this light, there is a potential direct return to institutions who behave generously, even in the face of free riders. This aside, through institutional cooperation it becomes possible to build scholarly communication systems that are not feasible within systems of pure market economics. arXiv recognises this problem and notes that 'arXiv's sustainability should be considered a shared investment in a culturally embedded resource that provides unambiguous value to a global network of science researchers. Any system of voluntary contribution is susceptible to free-riders, but arXiv is extremely cost-effective, so even modest contributions from heavy-user institutions will support continued open access for all while providing good value-for-money when compared with subscription services.'[72] If a similar business model was shown to be viable for the humanities, one that also covered the costs of coordinating peer review but that was still collectively underwritten, many of the fears about the exclusionary aspects of article and book processing charges for gold OA could potentially be reduced.

On the other of these two problems, that of finding the optimum balance point between level of contribution and number of institutions, arXiv has chosen to focus on the top 200 institutions worldwide because 'they account for about 75% of institutionally identifiable downloads'.[73] This has the substantial advantage of yielding a smaller number of (wealthier) institutions to target but, conversely, means that it is necessary to ask for a larger amount from each while also ensuring that the commodity perk that is exclusive (membership of the arXiv governance board) is primarily restricted to these already-prestigious (and wealthy) institutions.

*

How, then, can a transition to OA be affordable for the humanities? The only honest answer is that nobody can be certain that it is. This fact should always be accompanied, however, by the additional knowledge that at the moment it is possible to pay, globally, for all the research that is published. This means that, in theory, OA must be affordable, even in a switched, supply-side gold economy. The most likely short-term answer to this question, however, is that the currently available research shows that the green route poses no immediate danger to subscriptions for journals but allows open access. Books work differently and are covered below. In the longer term, for journals, two possibilities present themselves. The first is a market for APCs where researchers have developed price sensitivity, perhaps through funder encouragement. The second is a system of collective funding wherein many libraries collaborate to make possible an infrastructure to support publication that does not require a direct author-for-article/author-for-book payment. Such models can never ignore the costs of scholarly publication and should not underestimate the labour required. However, the current models cannot afford the opportunity costs of being left behind as open access gains increasing traction.

INTERNATIONAL CHALLENGES

At present, the economic challenges of the shifts to both gold and green open access are amplified by the fact that there is no unified global response, despite the international and collaborative nature of the original declarations. This creates a problem because academia and the publishing industries are clearly global in their natures. This is not to say, however, that there have been no efforts at coordination. The European Research Council's 'Working Group on Open Access' agreed, in April 2013, upon a clear set of principles for a transition to open access. These principles, adopted by the fifty-two member organisations from twenty-seven countries that constitute 'Science Europe' (which, despite its name, also includes humanities disciplines and funders such as the UK's AHRC), included recommendations that:

- both the green and gold routes should be supported
- institutional and subject repositories should be regarded as 'key strategic research infrastructure' and should comply with standards
- open access should occur no later than twelve months after publication for humanities subjects
- efforts should be internationally coordinated to ensure the efficient use of funds
- OA fees should be transparent and incorporate 'a clear picture of publishers' service costs'
- publishers should implement reductions in subscription payment as supply-side payments increase
- hybrid open access (in which OA content also appears in subscription journals) must be deemed a failure and any future transition models must prevent 'double dipping' and increase cost transparency
- there will be budgetary upheaval and redirection.[74]

Likewise, in May 2013 a weaker set of principles was endorsed by the Global Research Council (GRC), which is 'a virtual organization, comprised of the heads of science and engineering funding agencies [with "science" again including the humanities] from around the world, dedicated to promoting the sharing of data and best practices for high-quality collaboration among funding agencies worldwide'.[75] Among the key endorsements from this meeting were that:

- the negative perception of open access should be tackled through a positive PR campaign
- best practices for rewarding OA provision should be documented

- awareness-raising workshops on open access should be organised, especially in developing countries
- publishers should be encouraged to further develop open-access models
- funding agencies should work with libraries to begin diverting funds to the supply side through hybrid OA (in contrast to the damning ERC Working Group statements on hybrid)
- the affordability of open access should be monitored and assessed
- scholarly society journals should be helped to transition to OA
- green self-archiving should be supported through funder mandates and copyright regulations
- negotiations should be entered into with publishers to enable green deposit on behalf of authors
- interoperability and metadata standards of repositories should be developed and improved (so that unified search and cataloguing mechanisms can be developed)
- new assessment measures for quality and impact of research articles should be explored.[76]

At the time of writing, the GRC's 2014 meeting, hosted in Beijing, had been held and included a discussion of an 'Action Plan on Open Access for Publications'. Details of this meeting had not, however, been released beyond a statement that open access had been discussed.

The differing recommendations of just these two bodies is sadly symptomatic of a field in which the same motivations and problems are faced globally but meet with different responses. Speed, efficiency, return on investment, public gain and equal access are all widely sought benefits of open access. Likewise, the same controversies seem to have emerged in different global pockets as OA has come to the foreground, as demonstrated by the need for a positive press campaign: the quality or otherwise of open-access venues, copyright, sustainability, infrastructure and integration with national and career-reward metrics. Yet despite these shared objectives and challenges, the international field remains highly fragmented. As Michael Jubb of the Research Information Network noted at a recent (2014) international meeting on open access convened by Research Councils UK, there is a serious lack of consistent and authoritative information on the progress of implementation. Furthermore, as he also pointed out, there are now more than a dizzying 600 OA policies/mandates in force worldwide with huge variance in their scope and approach, from national through institutional and up to funder level. Those who would like to view a more complete list of such funder mandates should consult the online 'ROARMAP' (Registry of Open Access Repositories Mandatory Archiving Policies) resource maintained by Stevan Harnad.[77]

In terms of specific national developments, it is, of course, impossible for a volume such as this to give a comprehensive report on the current state of play. Remarks on this aspect will also, naturally, be among the parts of this volume to look the most dated in the shortest space of time. That said, to convey a sense of the diversity of progress worldwide I will venture into some summaries. While I have tried, here, to focus on developments in the humanities, I have also veered beyond this disciplinary purview where it looks likely that other fields have set national precedents for policy that will be followed by the humanities or where no explicit policies for the humanities currently exist. In terms of the national mandates discussed here, it is a sad fact that the humanities receive comparatively little research funding from governments. However, there is also a case to be made that publicly funded humanities research is likely to be of an extremely high quality because resources are scarce and competition is intense. This is significant if there are then mandates to make such work open access as it will counter perceptions of OA being intrinsically lower quality. As discussed below in Chapter 4, monographs are usually exempted from funder mandates at present, except in the case of the Wellcome Trust, so this section deals predominantly with journals. Where no source is given, this information came from the presentations given at the Research Councils UK (RCUK) International Meeting on Open Access in March 2014. Where no presenter is listed, the information was presented by Michael Jubb at that same event.

*

On 15 May 2014, the National Natural Science Foundation of **China** (NSFC) and the Chinese Academy of Sciences (CAS) announced that 'researchers they support should deposit their papers into online repositories and make them publicly accessible within 12 months of publication'.[78] Efforts to enable open access have been ongoing in this country since at least 2005 when Yongxiang Lu of the Chinese Academy of Sciences signed the Berlin Declaration, joined shortly thereafter by Yiyu Chen of the Committee of the National Natural Science Foundation of China.[79] Focus in the country largely rests upon the green route (and for the sciences) although there are also discussions on how to fund gold open access. All research funders allow the use of grant funds to support article processing charges. There are currently around 300–600 OA journals reportedly originating from the country although the number listed in the Directory of Open Access Journals is far lower (around fifty). These developments have led one recent article to proclaim boldly that 'OA is to become the future of academic library exchanges in China.'[80]

India, likewise, has no national mandate in place but there has been a recommended OA policy, drafted by the National Knowledge Commission, since 2007. Between 2006 and 2012 there was, however, a large expansion of open-access provision in India as a remedy to the reality that '[t]raditional avenues of publishing are closed to many authors in developing countries' coupled with the facts that 'poor access to international journals and the low visibility of papers are major problems facing Indian researchers'.[81] Although a later 2012 paper concluded that 'India has made important contributions towards the growth of open access publishing', it is also clear that 'Even though the overall picture of open access publishing in India looks promising, it makes an unhappy situation for subjects in social science, arts and humanities. The quantity and impact of journals in these subjects are not at par with subjects like medicine, sciences and technology.'[82]

South America, and in particular **Brazil**, has made huge advances in open access, most notably through their origination of the SciELO (Scientific Electronic Library Online) platform, which was created in 1997. Once more, as with Science Europe, despite its name, SciELO also contains humanities journals. The importance of this platform has been recognised by Thomson Reuters, who now include a 'SciELO Citation Index' to aid discovery of research in Latin America, Spain, Portugal, the Caribbean and South Africa.[83] This platform hosts approximately 1,100 journals, with 900 listed in the Directory of Open Access Journals coming to a total of half a million articles; a fairly staggering achievement. This has been reflected elsewhere on the American continent with the president of **Mexico** signing amendments to various national laws in May 2014 to create the National Repository of Open Access to Quality Scientific, Techno-logical and Innovative Information Resources of Social and Cultural Interest. This is a national-level green OA repository with mandated deposit for any publicly funded work, although the mandate has been criticised by advocates for its weak wording and potential loopholes.[84]

Open access in **Australia** also marches ahead. Both the Health and Medical Research Council and the Australian Research Council have OA mandates that require green deposit of articles with a maximum of a twelve-month embargo. All Australian universities now have institutional repositories. Researchers are also allowed to spend 2% of grants awarded by these organisations on article processing charges to facilitate gold. It is unclear how the current massive funding cuts to Australian higher education will affect these provisions. By contrast, there is no governmental policy on open access in **New Zealand** but there have been individual institutional mandates at Otago Polytechnic, Lincoln University and the University of Waikato.[85]

According to Ted Hewitt, the Executive Vice-President of **Cana-da**'s Social Sciences and Humanities Research Council (SSHRC), Canadian efforts in open access have focused heavily upon the green approach and a unified policy from the three federal research funding agencies, including the SSHRC, was expected in September 2014. Since 2006, the SSHRC has had an awareness-raising, optional policy that supported and encouraged transitions to open access. The current state of feedback on draft provisions indicates similar emergent anxieties as those experienced by countries further along the process (quality, career progression etc.).

Michel Marian, of the French Ministry of Higher Education and Research, and Serge Bauin, an open-access expert at the Centre National de la Recherche Scientifique observed that there is currently a mixed open-access ecosystem of both green and gold at work in **France**. However, the high degree of institutional budgetary auton-omy in this country has led to most efforts centring on individually controlled institutional repositories. It is also important to note that there are fewer large academic publishers, or at least that there is a perception that this is the case, in France than elsewhere, which also contributes to a greater decentralisation in French research dissemination. There has been concern in the country over how OA might affect French-language journals, as these are less likely to attract international support. That said, as covered below, France is home to the OpenEdition platform, which is a pioneer in trialling freemium models for gold OA.

Roberto di Lauro, the Scientific Attaché in the **Italian** Embassy, London, reported that, as of 7 October 2013, Italian law dictates that any material supported by public funds that appears in a journal with at least two issues published per year must be made open access through either the gold or the green route. For green OA an embargo of up to twenty-four months is allowed in humanities disciplines. A more recent call for research proposals at the national level halved the allowable embargo period and made compliance a condition of funding. Likewise, in **Denmark** there is a new commitment to achieving open access to 80% of articles produced in Danish research institutions by 2017 and 100% by 2022, primarily through the green route.[86]

OA in **Japan** is also well under way, with the infrastructure provided by the National Institute of Informatics. The green and gold routes are given equal weighting here although funds from national funding agencies are allowed to be spent on APCs. There are nearly 300 institutional repositories although a challenge remains in the digitisation of Japanese-language publications.

The Netherlands, home to the OAPEN project – a key early player in the OA books scene, as covered below – has been committed, since November 2013, to a three-year transition to gold OA, according to Jos Engelen of the Netherlands National Organisation for Scientific Research. The country is currently (May 2014) in an awareness-raising phase while developing mechanisms for reporting. If it is deemed that there has not been enough voluntary progress by 2016, the government intends to put in place legislation to mandate OA, although the details of such a move have not been discussed in detail.

In the **United States**, as reported by Neil Thakur of the National Institute of Health and the Department of Health and Human

Sciences, a recent 2013 directive required all data from publicly funded research to be archived and made available to the public. While the USA's system is much more devolved and decentralised than its counterparts in many other countries, federal funding agencies are now implementing their specific policies and procedures with a twelve-month embargo for greenly deposited content. The National Institute of Health has required a deposit in a subject repository called PubMed Central since 2008 and sanctions for non-compliance are now in place. Of more direct relevance, the National Endowment for the Humanities (NEH) directly funded the Digital Public Library of America (DPLA) to the tune of $1m in 2012, an open access project that aims to digitise and make available historical material from library collections that is out of copyright. Likewise, when digital humanities projects produce software outputs, the NEH strongly encourages (but does not mandate) that the results be open source.[87] This said, general awareness of open access, especially in the humanities, remains fairly low in the States and most OA mandates, where they do exist, are more likely to come from individual institutions rather than any state or funder requirement.

Finally, in the **United Kingdom**, there are green and gold mandates from HEFCE (the Higher Education Funding Council for England) and RCUK respectively. For any post-2014 Research Excellence Framework, it is a requirement that the 'accepted and final peer-reviewed text' of any journal article be uploaded to 'an institutional repository, a repository service shared between multiple institutions, or a subject repository such as arXiv' and that this be done 'as soon after the point of acceptance as possible, and no later than three months after this date'.[88] Monographs and edited collections are excluded from these requirements. Various exemptions are allowed, although these are mostly concerned with instances where deposit would be illegal (threats to national security etc.). There is one exception for when 'the publication concerned actively disallows open-access deposit in a repository, and was the most appropriate publication for the output'.[89] Since the overwhelming majority of publications for REF2014 would have been admissible for green deposit, however, it is not expected that this exemption will be frequently invoked. The maximum allowable embargo for humanities disciplines under the current provisions is twenty-four months (it is unclear whether this will be reduced after a transition period).[90] The UK's Research Councils (RCUK) support both green and gold open access (and mandate that the author choose one form for journal articles), providing a block grant to institutions to cover APC payments for the latter. During the transition period, an embargo on the green route of up to twenty-four months is permissible in humanities subjects, a move with which HEFCE deliberately aligned itself in order to avoid confusion.[91] RCUK requires that outputs be licensed under the Creative Commons Attribution License.[92]

This list could expand almost indefinitely in both depth and breadth as mandates change and new conditions come into force, but the above does give some idea, even if less than comprehensive, of the scale and range of change that has happened fairly recently. Certainly, if open access was thought to be purely a localised phenomenon this has been proved definitively untrue. That said, the diversity of mandates, policies and preferences poses an enormous challenge for policymakers, publishers and academics who find that they must exist within an international ecosystem, subject to competing pressures.

*

In this chapter I have broached some of the complexities of scholarly economics that underpin approaches to open access. From notions of prestige and symbolic capital through to questions about the commodity form of research, it is not a straightforward task to appraise the changes that will be engendered by a switch to supply-side payment systems or that green will have upon the current subscription mode. Furthermore, given the differences in international implementation and preferences for gold/green, the road ahead is not entirely clear. However, it is also apparent that the traditional economics of scholarly publishing are already extremely tangled and that while a switch to supply-side economics for gold open access could act as a stabiliser for academic publishing as a service industry, albeit without the high-risk/high-payoff potential that has previously existed, the regulation of scholarly economics is also tied to a regulation of gatekeeping in at least some forms. With this in mind, however, it is now worth turning attention away from these economic matters and back to the other side of the economics of open access: the lowering of permission barriers through open licensing and the opening of research to modification and redistribution.

CHAPTER 3

Open licensing

Among the arguments surrounding open access in the humanities that have caused controversy, few have been so fierce as those concerning open licensing.[1] Sceptics believe that liberal reuse rights will fuel an epidemic of plagiarism-like practices, will allow commercial re-enclosure of academic work and will fundamentally violate the moral rights of the academic author. Proponents, conversely, have cited the technological and social advances that could be made with the possibility of reusing material. In this chapter I explore these claims from both sides in order to ascertain the risks and the benefits of open licensing provisions but also to give some pragmatic information about the licenses under discussion.

AN INTRODUCTION AND CONTEXT TO FREE AND OPEN LICENSING

Picking up where Chapter 1 left off, 'open licensing' refers to conditions under which a copyright holder allows others to reuse material in ways that go beyond those specified within the fair use (or 'fair dealing') provisions of copyright law. Open and free licensing, like open access, has a history rooted in the free software movement. However, to truly get to grips with licensing, whether open or not, it is first important to understand how these phenomena sit in relation to copyright. Licensing does not override, and its goal is not to abolish, copyright. Licensing, instead, depends upon the legal provisions of copyright.

Copyright law, in the UK, was introduced under the Statute of Anne in 1709, was cemented by the Copyright Act of 1911 and is currently implemented under the Copyright, Designs and Patents

Act of 1988. In the United States, copyright was enshrined in the constitution in 1787 and designed 'To promote the Progress of Science and useful Arts, by securing for limited Times to Authors and Inventors the exclusive Right to their respective Writings and Discoveries'.[2] The international enforcement mechanism for copyright is the Berne Convention for the Protection of Literary and Artistic Works of 1886 in which signatories agreed to recognise the copyright of all signatory nationals as though they were home nationals. Copyright is automatically conferred on eligible works; simply by creating a work, the author invokes the legal protections. However, some things simply cannot be copyrighted: facts and ideas being the most notable categories. Instead, in these instances, what falls under copyright is the *expression of* the facts or ideas. Because expressions of the same idea can be similar, copyright also exists on a spectrum of enforcement and strength that must be weighed by a court when a challenge is made.

Copyright is generally held, in its contemporary usage, to separate economic rights from moral rights. Economic rights (the ability to reproduce the work, to make derivative works, to perform the work publicly, to display the work publicly and to transmit the work[3]) can be sold or transferred and treated as though they were any other form of property. Moral rights (such as the ability to be named as the author of the work, the right to be published anonymously and the right to the integrity of the work) cannot usually be sold or transferred but can be waived.[4] The time period for which copyright applies is, counter-intuitively, incredibly difficult to ascertain accurately. To grossly simplify, however, in the case of 'a personal author who produced a work on or after January 1, 1978, it is covered for the life of the author plus seventy years'.[5] As an amusing aside, critics of the current copyright regime note that there appears to be a direct coincidence of legislation to extend copyright terms at the moments when the still highly lucrative works of The Walt Disney Company are to become public domain.[6]

Under the contemporary system of academic publishing as of 2014, there are a variety of approaches taken by different publishers towards licensing and copyright: most publishers ask for a copyright assignment or transfer; some ask for an exclusive license to publish; occasionally, a non-exclusive license to publish may be appropriate;

and last, but not least for the context at hand, comes a request for a non-exclusive license to publish under a Creative Commons (or other open) license.

In a **copyright assignment** or **transfer** model, the author agrees to transfer (irrevocably give) his or her economic rights to the publisher. The publisher then may, at its discretion, permit the author to perform certain activities that go beyond fair use with the material (such as deposit in an institutional repository – green OA). This is implemented so that the publisher may protect the author against copyright violations, libel or plagiarism and to facilitate requests for reprints.[7] Of course, a publisher could offer either financial or in-kind legal advice to their authors without such a provision. There is, therefore, a case for balancing the rhetoric of author protection against the economic advantages for a publisher of a copyright transfer. It seems more probable that publishers prefer copyright transfer both because it gives them full and exclusive ownership of the material for the entire term, including distribution in new geographical areas or in new forms not covered explicitly under licenses to publish, and also because it centralises their ability to protect intellectual property. The argument in favour of this is that publishers often invest substantial quantities of labour time (at a price) into taking on work and that, within the current sales/subscription model, it may be easier to recover costs and/or make a profit with this form of ownership. Conversely, the author permanently signs away his or her economic rights to the work and has no comeback if he or she later wish to make such work open access and this was not initially agreed.

Under an **exclusive license to publish**, the author retains his or her economic rights, but signs away most of the practical benefits of so doing, usually for the entire term of the copyright. In this form of license, the publisher has the right to publish and make money from the work (and to act to legally protect those rights) and the author agrees never to give the specifically negotiated rights to anybody else. The reason that this mode has emerged is that it is marginally more beneficial to authors. If a specific type of publishing is not covered under an exclusive license to publish (for example, distribution in certain regions or formats), the author can renegotiate for new, better terms at a later date if the publisher (or another publisher) wished to then undertake these activities. This may financially disadvantage a publisher whose contracts are not sufficiently 'future proof' or it may simply mean that an author is free to publish the work in other formats elsewhere, depending upon the contract. It also allows publishers who know that they do not wish to operate in a certain sphere to give the author the opportunity to exploit this aspect elsewhere.

With a **non-exclusive license to publish**, the author keeps his or her copyright but gives the publisher the right to publish the material. However, the author retains the right to license others to do the same (or to make the piece public on his or her own initiative). This is seen by advocates as a good step for open access as the author will retain the right to deposit his or her work and to republish it wheresoever he or she chooses without requiring publisher dispensation. Of course, it also gives less favourable terms to publishers who need to ensure their economic return on the labour invested (see the remarks in Chapter 2 on the co-existence of green open access with sales/subscriptions, though, for reasons why this may still be possible). This mode does not, however, permit reuse of material beyond fair dealing, as detailed below.

Open licenses

Open licenses, which fulfil the lowering of permission barriers enshrined in the BBB definitions of OA, come in a variety of forms, but the most common for scholarly articles and books so far have been those designed by the Creative Commons Foundation, which have proved enforceable in courts of law worldwide.[8] The second most commonly used open text license is the GFDL (the GNU Free Documentation License), which was Wikipedia's choice until May 2009 (when it was then superseded by the Creative Commons Attribution-ShareAlike License).

Those who would like to know much more about Creative Commons licensing for humanities researchers (particularly on a practical basis) may wish to consult the *Jisc Collections Guide to Creative Commons Licensing for Humanities and Social Science Researchers* from which much of the information in this section is derived, which is itself made available under a Creative Commons Attribution license.[9] The other source for the information provided here is the Creative Commons site itself, also available under a CC Attribution license.[10]

The Creative Commons organisation provides seven mechanisms through which creators can allow others to use their work more permissively. The absolute, most liberal of these is the CC0 license, which 'enables scientists, educators, artists and other creators and owners of copyright- or database-protected content to waive those interests in their works and thereby place them as completely as possible in the public domain, so that others may freely build upon, enhance and reuse the works for any purposes without restriction under copyright or database law'.[11] Because it is unusual for scholars to wish to waive their right to demand attribution – and because, as I have already discussed, economies of prestige within the academy function as core drivers of academic output – I will primarily deal with the six other Creative Commons licenses that all carry an 'attribution' clause. That said, and as I will discuss below, academic citation norms and anti-plagiarism measures are so strong that even work under a CC0 license would probably not be subjected to misuse within the academy.

Beyond CC0, then, there are six, core, Creative Commons licenses, each with its own (at first) perplexing acronym: CC BY, CC BY-NC, CC BY-SA, CC BY-ND, CC BY-NC-SA and CC BY-NC-ND. The 'CC' clause in each case stands for 'Creative Commons', clearly enough. The wording 'BY' in each of these phrasings is not an acronym but literally means 'by'. Anybody using works licensed under these provisions with the 'BY' clause must give attribution, citing the original, and specifying *by* whom it was created. The modifiers then stand for 'Non-Commercial' (NC), 'ShareAlike' (SA) and 'NoDerivatives' (ND) respectively. As is clear from the above list, these modifiers can, in some circumstances, be compounded.

In order to explain what each of these licenses means for the licensor (the author, in this case), it is worth reproducing with minor modifications a table that can be found on page nine of the Jisc Collections guide (see Table 1).[12]

Note that the only two incompatible clauses are ND and SA; there is no way that a ShareAlike clause can apply if the NoDerivatives directive is also present as this would be nonsensical: there is *no* future *derivative* on which to compel sharing under the same license. Applying one of these licenses to a piece of work is as simple as writing a line of text

Table 1 *The Creative Commons Attribution Licenses*

License Designation	License Name	What does this mean for you as an author?
CC BY	Attribution	The most liberal of the Creative Commons licenses apart from CC0 Public Domain Dedication. This license allows others to distribute, remix, tweak, and build upon a work – even commercially – provided they credit the author for the original creation and clearly indicate that changes were made to the work.
CC BY-SA	Attribution ShareAlike	Similar to CC BY; however, others must license new creations under identical terms. Therefore, all new works based on such work will carry the same license, so any derivatives will also allow commercial use. This is the license used by Wikipedia.
CC BY-ND	Attribution NoDerivatives	This license allows for redistribution, commercial and non-commercial, provided it is passed along unchanged and in whole, with credit to the author.
CC BY-NC	Attribution Non-Commercial	Similar to CC BY; however, others must not remix, tweak, or build upon the original work for commercial purposes. Although new works must also acknowledge the author and be non-commercial, reusers do not have to license their derivative works on the same terms.
CC BY-NC-SA	Attribution Non-Commercial ShareAlike	This license lets others remix, tweak, and build upon the author's work non-commercially, provided they credit the author and license their new creations under the identical terms.
CC BY-NC-ND	Attribution Non-Commercial NoDerivatives	This is the most restrictive of the six licenses, only allowing others to download works and share them with others as long as they credit the author, but they cannot change them in any way or use them commercially.

specifying the conditions under which the work may be reused and distributed, as can be seen on the copyright page of this book. Placing work under a Creative Commons license is an irrevocable act; one cannot rescind the rights one has bestowed on others after the fact.

It is important to reiterate, as above, that these licenses do not replace or abolish copyright because, without copyright, an author could not make any claim over the work, including the right to attribution. Furthermore, when the copyright term expires, the license will no longer hold any binding force; the material will enter the public domain. Indeed, the Creative Commons licenses 'are, in fact, built on copyright and last for the same length of term as the copyright in the work'. The Creative Commons foundation believes that this gives a sense of freedom back to authors, noting that such licenses 'enable you, as an author, to specify the condi-tions of re-use that best suit your needs, while ensuring that you are credited for your work'.[13] As will be seen, others disagree with such an assessment and find the rhetoric of 'enabling' reuse, couched in terms of 'freedom', to be misleading, particularly when funding agencies require that researchers apply such licenses to their work.

As noted in Chapter 1, these licenses – and particularly the clauses that allow modification of work – derive from a history in computer science and open-source programming cultures. It is worth saying, however, that the contexts are slightly different, which may have a bearing upon the rationales for open licensing in the humanities as opposed to computer science. With a piece of computer software, there are usually two different aspects: the source code (which is text that can be read) and the compiled binary (which is the version that can be run). The process of authoring a program is (usually – there are exceptions) to write code (a series of instructions that tell the computer, sequentially, what to do) in a high-level language that resembles words and instructions familiar to speakers of the English language. These instructions are then fed to a 'compiler', which translates and optimises them into an object code (usually assembly or machine code), an extremely low-level format that is difficult for people to understand, but easy and quick for machines to execute. The important point to note, however, is that it is extremely hard, albeit not impossible, to change the behaviour of the program or to understand its workings without the original source code. It is also not easy automatically to change a program back from its compiled form to its source code.

This explains the importance of open source (or 'free software' as he prefers it to be termed) within Richard Stallman's philosophy of computer science.[14] In a world where we are surrounded by technology and somewhat at the mercy of software, he would argue, the obfuscation introduced by the compiler is a potentially powerful tool for control. This is because there is no easy way for others to audit, alter or fix the behaviour of important software (such as, for example, speed cameras that automatically fine people; bank machines that change our balances; credit scoring algorithms that determine whether one can obtain a mortgage to buy a house; life support machines; the list goes on).

In terms of academic research, however, and particularly that produced in the humanities disciplines, there is a different set of considerations as to why researchers might make derivative works, in which originals are altered or incorporated into another piece. Examples of derivative works in the humanities include any outputs featuring quotations or images from other sources, translations, scholarly editions and new presentations (such as digital humanities projects featuring XML encoding). In small quantities, some of these activities (such as limited quotation for the purposes of criticism and review) are permitted under law without any changes, the so-called 'fair use' or 'fair dealings' provisions. Other uses, such as inclusion of images, have far stricter criteria for fair use as the reproduction is often total, thereby obliterating the financial protections of copyright. Indeed, then, although open licensing may have emerged from the free culture movement in computer science, it is unclear as to how far the analogy to source code can be stretched in the applicability of open licensing to humanities work. For instance, the writing (or drawing, or performance, or whatever form the work deploys) within a piece is equivalent to its source code, for the software analogy. By altering these constituent parts and their arrangement, one can change the function and effective work of a piece of research, which may be undesirable or may hold value (and the perspective on this may be viewed differently in each case by different parties). Derivatives can be grand or minor in scale, drastically altering or only subtly recontextualising existing work. Within the academy, researchers already make use of the notion of derivative works when they cite the research of others, be this in the use of ellipses, changes of emphasis ('emphasis mine') or in the inclusion of images. The centrality of such inclusions also varies in scope/scale and spans a range of types of producer, from other academics to artists/performers and beyond. Nonetheless, these are derivatives in copyright terms that are allowed, at a small scale, within the bounds of fair use. Other cases that are desirable for the academy, such as inclusions of larger portions of material in course packs (which is then potentially a derivative work), as set out below, may not be considered fair use.

The case for open licensing in the humanities, then, is substantially different from its historical context in computer science. For the humanities, open licensing should be less about the rhetoric of liberation of data/code and the attachment of 'the language of personal freedom ... to information', as Paul Duguid points out, and more concerned with potential use cases.[15] In other words, this should not simply follow the business mantra that 'information wants to be free' but should instead be predicated on whether existing copyright provisions are adequate easily to allow activities desired by academic researchers. Advocates of open licensing claim that they are not.

ARGUMENTS IN FAVOUR OF OPEN LICENSING

Among the first questions that must be considered are whether and why open licensing might be required or desired. As I will suggest, below, there are multiple areas in which advocates construe benefits and this section presents arguments from that perspective. The foremost of these, however, are the assertions in recent years that the current system of copyright is actively preventing scholarly research from fulfilling its potential. For instance, a report by the Ad Hoc Committee on Fair Use and Academic Freedom in 2010 for the discipline of communication studies noted, of their survey research, that:

Nearly half the respondents express a lack of confidence about their copyright knowledge in relation to their research. Nearly a third avoided research subjects or questions and a full fifth abandoned research already under way because of copyright concerns. In addition, many ICA members have faced resistance from publishers, editors, and university administrators when seeking to include copyrighted works in their research. Scholars are sometimes forced to seek copyright holders' permission to discuss or criticize copyrighted works. Such permission seeking puts copyright holders in a position to exercise veto power over the publication of research, especially research that deals with contemporary or popular media.

These results demonstrate that scholars in communication frequently encounter confusion, fear, and frustration around the unlicensed use of copyrighted material. These problems, driven largely by misinformation and gatekeeper conservatism, inhibit researchers' ability both to conduct rigorous analyses and to develop creative methodologies for the digital age.[16]

As a simple preliminary finding, this gives just one example of a set of difficulties to which open licensing could pose an easier solution than changes to international copyright law.

Within different spheres of endeavour, open licensing is claimed to have varying degrees of potential. It seems fair to say, however, that there is not a single researcher who would not benefit in at least one fundamental way from even the more restrictive forms of open licensing (such as CC BY-ND). That is, without open licensing, even if one were to have monetarily *free access* to an article or book, this does not entail *permission to redistribute* that material beyond the basic provisions of fair use. Every year, universities pay to redistribute photocopies of critical material, produced by academics, to their students. This is because, for instance, despite the fact that this is use for the purposes of teaching in an educational establishment, in the UK 'Making copies by using a photocopier, fax, and so on, on behalf of an educational establishment for the purpose of non-commercial instruction generally requires a licence from the Copyright Licensing Agency.'[17] Organisations such as the UK's Copyright Licensing Agency and the US's Copyright Clearance Center act as mass collection agencies, requiring licensing agreements from universities in order to use, in many cases, material written by their own scholars and imposing limits on the amount that can be used for teaching in such cases. Furthermore, these agencies often require universities to re-purchase material that they already own, simply so that it can be reprographically distributed to students. The CLA's HE license states that, '[u]nless there are valid pedagogical reasons for using a superseded edition, all copies should be made from the current published edition' and economic hardship of one's library at having to buy the latest edition of a work that one already owns is not a valid pedagogical reason.[18] This seems to affect all those who teach in higher education and provides a good rationale for at least the more restrictive forms of open licensing that permit redistribution as a minimum of open access.

Certain other fields of endeavour within the humanities benefit differently under open licensing. Peter Suber lists some of these benefits as the abilities:

- to quote long excerpts
- to distribute full-text copies to students or colleagues
- to burn copies on CDs for bandwidth-poor parts of the world
- to distribute semantically tagged or otherwise enhanced (i.e. modified) versions
- to migrate texts to new formats or media to keep them readable as technologies change
- to create and archive copies for long-term preservation
- to include works in a database or mashup
- to make an audio recording of a text
- to translate a text into another language
- to copy a text for indexing, text mining, or other kinds of processing

all of which are impossible under most 'fair use/dealings' provisions.[19] While it should be clear from even a cursory glance at this list that every single one of these items might be applicable to the humanities disciplines, some are especially pertinent. Of especial note are: the possibility to quote longer excerpts and include academic images; the ability to translate texts; and the ability to text-mine works for digital humanities projects. The remainder of this section will be dedicated to exploring these exemplar use scenarios.

Use beyond 'fair dealing'

One way among many of conceiving of research work in the humanities is as an argument/refutation dialectic between scholars. Under such a formulation, research work is supposed to be an ongoing effort of communicating in public to negotiate on areas of contention in order to reach a shared truth or understanding. Given that this is the case, it can be surprising to see how little engagement there often is between scholars in print. This is jointly driven by incentives for originality and, on occasion, by a prohibitive copyright situation. On the first front: very few scholars get ahead by spending their time critiquing the arguments of others at length. Indeed, even more so in a culture where public 'impact' is becoming important, greater emphasis is placed on working from scratch than from pausing on the work of others.

That said, assuming that one did wish to mount a piece of substantial, engaged criticism of an academic's work, it is unlikely that the current system of copyright would be amenable. Indeed, to reproduce anything more than the bare minimum will place such use outside of 'fair', particularly if this represents a substantial portion of the original (even if required to make a point). Line-by-line critiques are, therefore, out of the question. Epigraphs from scholarly work could likewise be prohibited (this is contended but an increasing trend to prohibit epigraphs has been seen among some academic publishers in recent years, under counsel that this may not constitute fair use).

The images that academics produce are even more thorny. Anyone working in the discipline of art history will be able to attest to the enormous problems and costs in securing the rights to image reproduction. In fact, fair use provisions are applied differently and more stringently than images under some copyright jurisdictions. Because academics currently retain or transfer their copyright, the same goes for images produced by academics, even if these particular images/ illustrations/photographs were given away for free. Although it is clear that the ability to relicense images produced by academics provides another revenue stream for academic publishers, advocates question whether this is desirable given the difficulties of image inclusion. Furthermore, some authors have argued against liberal open licensing (and open access more generally) of their own works on the grounds that it will make it harder for them to include images that are under copyright. In fact, this problem only applies to the dissemination of work as gratis OA (work that is free to read) and is not a problem of libre OA (work that is also openly licensed). This is because it is possible, when openly licensing work, to exclude third-party images from the license provisions, thereby allowing the original copyright holder to continue to license their work.

A final use case can be seen in the broader dissemination and amplification of research work that could be possible through resources such as Wikipedia, if open licensing provisions were in place. Regardless of whether one favours the anarchic construction of this online encyclopaedia (and irrespective of the quality controls in some areas), it is a remarkable resource and the first port of call for many lay readers who wish to learn about a topic. While it is already possible to quote portions of research works within Wikipedia under fair use provisions, to extend this reuse to include larger portions of work, or even whole articles, would give a far more visible presence to humanities research in a popular, public space. While some will remain wary of Wikipedia, the potential to incorporate research work within similar ecosystems will be far easier if compatible open licensing provisions are adopted.

Translation

At present, English dominates scholarly discourse.[20] In a networked world, this is a huge challenge as, in the quest for practical solutions to overcome language barriers, the risk of erasing cultural specificity is omnipresent. To date, the mutually exclusive options to militate against this have been authorised translations or neglect. The question then becomes one of canonisation: which forces allow authorised translation, what are their motivations and who is allowed to translate? The answer, in most cases, will contain at least some degree of commercial interest for works that are within their copyright term.

This is where advocates claim that open licensing could help. To return to my previous argument from Weber, humanities communities should be at least partially concerned with plurality and the communication of difference. By giving permission, in advance, to anybody to translate a work, through open licensing, a greater degree of plurality could emerge, it is argued.

Such arguments have emerged implicitly and explicitly from the work of John Willinsky and Kathleen Fitzpatrick. In the former of these arguments, John Willinsky proposed that, in the online environment, acts of reading should be supplemented by technological 'helpers' that provide side-by-side context: contextual reading.[21] These helpers could, in Willinsky's view, give information on external references, allow quick lookups of words and many other features. It is not a huge leap to extend this to a mode whereby these helpers might also provide inter-lingual information and contexts. When thinking about translation, however, some have argued that it could be possible to extend this to the other extreme and to perform contextual *writing* on other documents. Arguments of this nature can be seen in Kathleen Fitzpatrick's deployment of Chris Kelty's notion of a 'recursive public' to illustrate how communities could become involved in 'working towards a common goal' that is 'focused on improving the communication systems that fosters its [that community's] work'.[22] In Kelty's terms, a recursive public is '*a public that is vitally concerned with the material and practical mainten-ance and modification of the technical, legal, practical, and conceptual means of its own existence as a public*'.[23] A recursive public would certainly be one that built a system whereby community translation efforts were both technologically and legally possible. Indeed, trans-lation that uni-directionally privileges English, it could be argued, is not truly respectful of the difference with which humanities communities can be said to be concerned and could be seen as an imposed controlled phenomenon, rather than a democratically recur-sive formation. Instead, if it is believed that there should be space in the university for critical thinking reflexively to consider academic practices (as a recursive public) and if it is thought that the preserva-tion of difference is to be valued, then, in one fashion, allowing bi-directional community translation of works through open licens-ing could begin to achieve this.

The counter-argument, of course, centres on the problem of bad translation. What is to be done in the instance of an incorrect translation? Often, the author himself or herself cannot evaluate whether the translation is correct or of quality and there is a fear of negative reputational association. Thus, while Sandy Thatcher points out that the CC licenses prohibit reuses that would 'distort, mutilate, modify or take other derogatory action in relation to the Work which would be prejudicial to the Original Author's honor or reputation', he also correctly notes that 'This provision might provide grounds for action against an intentionally bad translation, but not just a poor one innocently done.'[24] Such debates, however, already rage around professional translation of scholarly material. For just one single instance, Mark Philp contends that there are problems in the translations of some of Michel Foucault's best-known works, noting that Alan Sheridan's translation of 'rapports de force' as 'relations of power' leads to a circular definition of 'power', perhaps far from Foucault's intention.[25]

None of these arguments should serve simply to denigrate the skills of translators or even to point out the fairly obvious fact that academics sometimes dispute such translations in the services of their own arguments. It is rather to note that there is a vast corpus of material where no professional translation exists (or will exist) and that advocates argue that some translation could be better than no translation in such cases. If coupled with technological measures to ensure that bad translations could be vetted and/ or rated, the prospect of community translation might be exciting. There are, however, reputational challenges and fears that would have to be overcome before this could realistically become a mass proposition, not to mention the problems of incentivising such activities and of ensuring fair remuneration for professional translators.

Text/content mining and experimental re-presentation

Text and content mining are computer-aided techniques for sweeping a large corpus of material and looking for links and trends (or, in fact, simply for finding relevant information). The most well-known exposure of these techniques is Google's 'ngram viewer'.[26] An 'ngram' is a series of linguistic attributes ('n' refers to an arbitrary number and 'grams' is simply a shorthand for the grammatical portion of text/speech under discussion, which can be a phoneme, a word, a letter etc.). Google's viewer presents a search interface for trawling a large section of their scanned book corpus that makes it very easy to spot the emergence and correlation of various terms. As has also been made abundantly clear, though, through the proliferation of lawsuits against the service from copyright holders and their representatives, the legality of Google's practice is hotly disputed as claimed fair use.

In the biomedical sciences and other scientific disciplines, it is clear why text and content mining is important. As the volume of literature grows, it becomes necessary to trawl for existing research that may have a bearing on one's own work, but which lies within an entirely different sub-field. While the same is true for the humanities, it could be argued that nobody is actively harmed compared to a situation where, for instance, previous clinical data indicating a danger to life remained unearthed. That said, just because 'nobody will die if we can't adopt text mining' hardly seems a brilliant rationale, in the eyes of advocates, for leaving this route unexplored.

Text mining offers novel ways of exploring an academic corpus. For instance, should one wish to trace the historical genealogy of a specific concept, it becomes possible to see how ideas enter broader circulation. These techniques also offer the opportunity to search in ways beyond those implemented by publishers. While publishers have a good rationale for ensuring that people can find the material that they have published, it also makes sense to allow others to be able to create discoverability and readability experiments. Indeed, eLife's 'lens' software – which offers an innovative new presentation layer for already-published material – is one such example. The lens viewer is a system to re-present the same information in a published article within a new interface that focuses on aligning multimedia and reference elements alongside text so as not to distract from the reading experience in an exceptionally aesthetically pleasing fashion. In order to allow those who are thinking about such issues to have the chance to *try* new experimental technological presentations and data collection, open licensing is necessary, despite some jurisdictions loosening the prohibitions on such activities within fair use provisions. The computational techniques provided by text mining will not be of use to all humanities academics but they will be of use to some, especially if the broad field of digital humanities continues to grow at its present rate.[27]

These aspects constitute some of the reasons why advocates believe that it would be beneficial to apply open licenses to academic work in the humanities. It is not a comprehensive list but it does give a flavour. However, sceptics argue that there are risks that come with open licensing – and particularly the more liberal forms of the Creative Commons licenses – and it is to these arguments that I now turn.

THE CHALLENGES OF INTEGRATING OPEN LICENSING
INTO THE ACADEMY

In terms of controversies pertaining to open access and the humanities, Creative Commons licensing has aroused fervent opposition. As outlined in Chapter 1, and beyond the economic arguments in Chapter 2, the main oppositions to CC licensing take two forms: concerns over scholarly integrity and broader worries about undesirable activities that could be enabled by such lowering of permission barriers.

In this section, I want to spend a little more time airing these claims and evaluating the dangers that could arise from the implementation of CC licenses. It is worth noting, upfront, however, that personal preference for a specific license may not, in the end, be a choice that rests with most authors. Many funding councils have mandated Creative Commons licenses for work that they fund. The EU's Horizon 2020, the UK's RCUK and the Wellcome Trust, as notable humanities funders, already have mandates for forms of open licensing.[28] Given the Australian Research Council's move towards open-access mandates, one could speculate that a licensing condition will only be a matter of time for this funder also. Authors who dissent from Creative Commons licenses are then faced with the (non-)choice of deciding whether they will accept funding from a particular source (under its rules) or spurn the funding in favour of principle. Given institutional pressure to attract funding, it seems unlikely that many will stick to their guns. That said, a recent survey by Taylor & Francis also indicated that authors remain extremely wary of CC BY, an aspect reiterated by Wiley, although advocates continue to criticise the methodology of these surveys.[29]

Concerns over scholarly integrity

The first worry regarding Creative Commons licenses concerns the integrity of academic research material and the author's moral rights. While some see the ability to rework material as a benefit, others think this a problem. Without a No-Derivatives clause, each license is *designed* to allow maximum reuse, including modifications to the language used. While this might seem strange, understanding some of the logic around the creation of the licenses can help to provide a rationale. Lawrence Lessig, as the founder of Creative Commons, describes these provisions as circumventing what he sees as the unnatural provisions of copyright: 'The extreme of regulation that copyright law has become makes it difficult, and sometimes impossible, for a wide range of creativity that any free society – if it thought about it for just a second – would allow to exist, legally ... I then want to spotlight the damage we're not thinking enough about – the harm to a generation from rendering criminal what comes naturally to them.'[30]

This is an interesting stance because Lessig clearly predicates his belief in free culture on the fact that creativity requires the reuse of preceding works. He also explicitly here signals that this desire to create and to build upon the work of others is, in his worldview, the *natural state* of humankind. Richard Stallman often uses exactly the same logic: 'people have been told that natural rights for authors is the accepted and unquestioned tradition of our society ... As a matter of history, the opposite is true. The idea of natural rights of authors was proposed and decisively rejected when the US Constitution was drawn up. That's why the Constitution only permits a system of copyright and does not require one; that's why it says that copyright must be temporary.'[31] At least part of the controversy over open licensing can probably be attributed to different ideas of natural and moral rights with regard to copyright.

It is also within such contexts that claims for protection of scholarly integrity should be considered in the humanities. Clearly, it remains important that protections against libel or utterly false attribution remain and all of the Creative Commons licenses continue to provide these. Rather, however, these provisions are thought of in terms of allowing others to build upon and modify scholarly works to create new versions. The analogy that Lessig uses for this is another from technology: he suggests there is a paradigm of 'read only' (RO) culture and a coming wave of 'read/write' (RW) that is to do with democratic participation in production.[32] While critics often argue that people should work creatively from scratch, advocates would counter that most humanities work is already based upon the scholarship of others and 'derivative' readings of culture/history.[33] Furthermore, that 'critical editions' of certain texts are already created does show, to some extent, that derivative practices already exist in the humanities. With this background context out of the way, however, it is worth turning to some of the specific concerns that fall under this heading.

Among these is the claim that open licensing promotes plagiarism.[34] This has been put forward in a number of forms. The first is an outright accusation of facilitating plagiarism and the second is a version of the argument that notes that the derivatives clause encourages activities that 'look like' plagiarism. To explore such claims, an accurate definition of 'plagiarism' is needed. Plagiarism is a specific form of copyright infringement with a legal meaning that informs, but that is separate from, the intra-academic contexts. Plagiarism usually refers 'to the subcategory of copyright infringement which involves false designations of authorship and other unattributed uses of copyrighted material. This is usually distinct from the other common subcategory of copyright infringement called "piracy," which involves the production and sale of unauthorized literal copies of a work.'[35] In other words, plagiarism involves making a claim to authorship of a work created by someone else.

Plagiarism is enforceable both in law and, also, within academic institutional contexts, where the penalties can be severe. The intra-institutional context is slightly different from the purely legal realm. Because the academy often uses fair dealing, or fair use, provisions to allow the reproduction of small portions of works upon which it performs analysis, there is a strict requirement to delineate quoted words from the author's words, which would not apply in other contexts where no degree of copying would have been permissible. There is also a requirement to represent accurately the original source (and its author) in both specific quotations and broader semantic terms.

The Creative Commons Attribution licenses grant specific additional rights in the legal realm but leave the academic institutional context unchanged. Just because additional reuse is possible under the law does not mean that academic citation practices will necessarily change. Whether legally allowing additional activities might eventually change the norms of the academic institutional context remains impossible to predict, however. These licenses allow anybody (except in the case of the Non-Commercial clause, which restricts any non-personal reuse) to copy any quantity of the text that they would like, even beyond those allowed under fair use. They are also allowed to change the contents as they see fit. These licenses do not, however, allow this unconditionally.

Any user of a Creative Commons work must, 'expressly', retain an 'identification of the creator(s) of the Licensed Material and any others designated to receive attribution, in any reasonable manner requested by the Licensor (including by pseudonym if designated)'. In other words, a reuser *must* identify the original creator under legal penalty *in the manner chosen by the author* (within reason). This is designed to protect the moral right to be named and seems to avoid the risk of outright plagiarism. After all, by crediting the original author, one disclaims authorship. As an end reuser, it is also imperative under the terms of the license, if you have changed the work, that you 'indicate if You modified the Licensed Material and retain an indication of any previous modifications'. This means that it is crucial that an end-user indicates whether the work has been changed, a provision that is designed to protect the moral right to integrity of the original. It does not, however, mean, as Peter Mandler has rightly taken pains to reiterate on many occasions, that the author must legally show *what* changes have been made. That said, Mandler concurrently acknowledges that academics have their 'own norms of how best to incorporate one work within another', which he claims 'derivative use [under a CC BY license] denies'.[36] Mandler's concern seems to be that the CC BY license will interfere with academic norms because it allows (or perhaps even endorses) activities that the academy would not permit within its intra-institutional rules. What remains unclear within such an argument, at least to me, is why academic practice would change, simply because it is legally permissible to use the work differently; these two contexts can be different yet co-exist. After all, works whose copyright has expired (therefore holding none of these protections and which the law explicitly permits anyone to use in any fashion) are still subject to these intra-academic norms. Conversely, others have sometimes built valuable, digital, scholarly projects around such works; enterprises that would be practically impossible without permission to modify the original. For just one example of this, one could consider the Nietzsche Source project, which aims to create a freely accessible, citable, reliable XML-encoded version of Nietzsche's works.[37] As another instance, one might also consider the liberal rewriting of academic material into a Wikipedia article, always with citation of course. A more extensive list of such projects can be found on the website of the Text Encoding Initiative.[38]

It is also important to note that nothing in the CC BY licenses 'constitutes or may be construed as permission to assert or imply that You [as a reuser] are, or that Your use of the Licensed Material is, connected with, or sponsored, endorsed, or granted official status by, the Licensor'. In other words, a reuser cannot imply that the original author (the licensor) condones the subsequent reuse of the work. Finally, as a reuser, 'if requested by the Licensor, You must remove any of the information required [to attribute the work] to the extent reasonably practicable'.[39] This means that the licensor (the original author) may request that their attribution be removed and thus they be disaffiliated from the work. The licensor (the original author) cannot, however, request that the work be taken down.

For the academy, this is interesting. Broadly speaking, the requirements of the CC BY licenses are: (1) attribution (without implying endorsement); (2) indication of modification; (3) the right to removal of attribution. This sounds similar to the definition of the needs of a researcher. Researchers need to be able to reproduce material and they need to attribute it. They also need, through the intra-institutional context, to specify any changes, including any ellipses, changes of emphasis etc. On this last point, the legal aspects of the Creative Commons license are not wholly in alignment with the social needs of the academy since the CC BY licenses do not require the modifier to say *how* they have changed the material. The licenses also do not allow for the material to be removed if the academy objects (although the alternative to this situation is one in which an author could censor critique through legal copyright mechanisms). It is unclear, however, whether this matters if the social mechanisms of the academy could protect against such behaviour. It is also uncertain what the likelihood and impact of such actions might be when counterpoised with potential benefits.

Concerns over undesirable reuse

The second broad category of concern over CC licensing pertains to undesirable reuse. This generally takes two sub-categories of its own: politically undesirable reuse and commercially undesirable reuse, although in the case of the latter, particularly, this is a case of: 'undesirable for whom?' Let us begin with politically undesirable reuse.

In an article at the extreme fringe of such claims, but one that can be applied more moderately, Robert Dingwall makes the accusation that 'open access is good news for neo-Nazis'.[40] In a fine instance of Godwin's law – a humorous axiom of the internet that 'as an online discussion grows longer, the probability of a comparison involving Nazis or Hitler approaches one'[41] – Dingwall hypothesises a paper about a (fictional) group of neo-Nazi racists:

This might well result in a journal paper which demonstrates that the group's members are not demons but ordinary men and women responding to economic and social challenges with strategies that seem reasonable to them, even if based on partial information or analysis by others' standards . . . For the author, the paper presents evidence that it is unhelpful to dismiss these people as bigots: the political system needs to recognize and address their grievances, without adopting their racist solutions. With a CC-BY [*sic*] licence, however, nothing stops the group taking hold of the paper, editing it down and using it as a recruitment tool: 'Famous professor says we are just ordinary people responding in a reasonable way to the problems of our community . . .'[42]

This argument does not seem particularly solid. For one, such a group could likely attempt a claim under 'criticism and review' fair dealing provisions anyway, as do news outlets (it would be libel for which they could be taken to court, not for their actual use of the material). While Dingwall's claims are perhaps too extreme to be credible, one might consider undesirable use by more mainstream parties, whether fringe or even moderate, and the problems that this could have for the neutrality of research work.

The second concern over undesirable reuse surrounds commercial appropriation. Building on the remarks in Chapter 2, this requires a little more time to unpack as it is, itself, split across two different axes: a wholesale rejection of any kind of utilitarian appropriation of humanities work, or an antipathy towards specific commercial entities using university research. To deal with the first of these objections, it is worth noting, as Helen Small points out, that 'the spectre of trial by proven utility [which is necessary for any commercial appropriation] has accompanied universities in one version or another since they came into existence'.[43] Indeed, Small also ably points out that while the reductive language of utilitarian thinking ought to be resisted, the humanities contribute to society through: a 'distinctive relation to the idea of knowledge as being inextricable from human subjectivity'; in a provision 'of the skills for interpreting and reinterpreting ... culture to meet the needs and interests of the present'; in their 'vital contribution to individual happiness and the happiness of large groups'; in the role of a clinician ensuring 'the health of the democracy'; but most importantly that 'none of these arguments is sufficient without a supporting claim that the value of the objects and cultural practices the humanities study and the kinds of scholarship they cultivate have value "for their own sake" – that they are good in themselves'.[44] In this light, it is certainly true that attempts to defend the humanities need not take a purely anti-utilitarian turn, even when that utility is within industry, so long as this does not remain the driving force for the investigation.

With this in mind, it is important to acknowledge that Creative Commons licenses do facilitate commercial reuse of academic work if the Non-Commercial clause is not present. Those who wish to counter this aspect of Creative Commons licensing have asked whether appending the NC clause to mandated licenses might pose a solution. This list of anti-NC advocates includes a set of twenty learned societies who form the Arts and Humanities User Group, whose license recommendation was CC BY-NC-ND.[45] Based on recent court decisions, however, I would suggest that this may not be the most helpful approach. As Erik Möller points out, the definitions of 'commercial' are unclear.[46] This confusion has been made worse by a recent German ruling that NC licenses must refer *only to private uses*, thereby disallowing universities, charities and other organisations from redistributing and using such material.[47] Given that many universities charge student fees and make money off research patents, they are very much commercial in their own rights, even if this is not how many of those within the walls of the academy would wish it. By appending the NC clause, universities potentially lock their own communities out of the benefits of open licensing in a baby-with-the-bathwater situation. Furthermore, if derivatives are prohibited, so too are the benefits of extensive quotation, academic image inclusion, rewriting for popular consumption, community translation and longer excerpts for course pack distribution, as well as text mining for the digital humanities in jurisdictions where there are no legal exemptions.

Given these controversies, it is unsurprising that it has been suggested that Creative Commons licenses are unsuitable for academic research and that a new set of licenses is needed instead.[48] However, writing licenses from scratch is a difficult business as they require court precedents to be trustworthy and also have jurisdictional specificity that needs expert legal counsel worldwide. Furthermore, new licenses may be incompatible with existing CC licenses used elsewhere, which could, for just one example, make the inclusion of material within Wikipedia impossible. It is also clear that a proliferation of licenses comes with problems. For example, when the International Association of Scientific, Technical & Medical Publishers recently drafted its own set of licenses, Andrés Guadamuz noted that, aside from being non-compliant with BBB definitions of open access, these new licenses served to 'taint the open access licensing environment by generating more licence complexity and more confusion [for] the academic authors'.[49] A potentially better solution for those who would like the humanities to be less utilitarian, but who also recognise both that open licensing comes with some benefits and that potential industry collaborations need not always be resisted, could be to impose a ShareAlike (SA) clause on material. This would mean that industry would be under the same obligation to give back to the community as the original academic. Indeed, any new derivatives that were made by industry as a result of using academic research licensed under CC BY-SA would also have to carry that license, meaning that the academy could benefit in turn from any transformation of the work, if valuable.

This brings me, finally, to consider the role that CC licensing could play in the broader structural changes pertaining to the marketisation of higher education, a concern that has been mentioned several times already. Some figures, most notably John Holmwood, have argued that Creative Commons licensing of academic research will fuel this process by allowing bodies that do no teaching, but which hold degree awarding powers, to alter the material for their own ends (compiling it into a sort of online anthology or textbook) and to thereby undercut the research university on cost, leading to its extinction. This represents a serious danger to academic autonomy and the financial cross-subsidisation of research from teaching. The standardisation and mass production of academic degrees, set by an external entity, is just another factor that would take the university ever further from its ideal as a community of self-organising scholars.[50] Although Holmwood does not specify exactly how he envisages that such providers could not already use such material under the guise of 'educational' fair use, or by simply buying the material – which they could afford anyway – his argument is that there have been progressively more aggressive policy moves towards commercialisation of the university, particularly in the UK (with which is hard to disagree). Indeed, he notes that 'universities are also enjoined to increase value for money for students through efficiency savings. Here the model is one of the "unbundling" of different activities, to identify those which can be taken to market by "outsourcing" and made subject to the proper rigours of the profit-motive.' However, in a parallel to education, Holmwood then goes on to note that 'Open Access under CC BY is one of the measures designed to speed up commercialization, by making scientific innovations more immediately accessible, especially to small and medium-sized enterprises.'[51] An analogous argument could certainly be made between the cultural industries and the humanities.

I do not dispute that this seems to tally with governmental agendas. For those who support open licensing but wish to counter such approaches, however, there are a variety of responses. Holmwood clearly supports the addition of the NC clause to licenses (his own book is CC BY-NC[52]), while I believe that ShareAlike would be a better solution to the same problem: ensuring that if others benefit from the public work of academia, it remains a public good.

In this section, I have appraised some of the most common objections to the CC BY licenses: plagiarism and undesirable reuse. I remain unconvinced that plagiarism is a strong argument, but this is not a view universally held. The latter arguments about undesirable reuses, both political and damaging to the university as it currently stands, conversely, certainly have traction in some specific areas.

*

Open licensing is contentious and, in some senses, it is possible to have open access without open licensing ('gratis' versus 'libre'). However, advocates point out that many other benefits are available under open licensing, including: dissemination for teaching, extensive quotation, text/content mining and community translation. Advocates also claim that the copyright system as it currently stands often does not fulfil the needs of academics, acting as a barrier to research, rather than a protection. Conversely, others feel that the dangers of relaxing these provisions are too great. A variety of suggestions, from new licenses through to NC-ND clauses, have been suggested as compromises. However, the Non-Commercial (NC) clause of the Creative Commons licensing scheme might be less useful than it sounds as this will exclude the university from redistribution and use. The No-Derivatives (ND) clause allows redistribution but prohibits more radical experimentation. Writing new licenses is a difficult task that complicates the licensing environment and should not be undertaken lightly.

The final point that we might wish to consider before moving on is the place of economics within the contexts of open licensing. While it should be clear that the open licensing agenda intersects with my earlier remarks on the commodity form of research work and sites of use-value that are distant from the academy, a more immediate concern comes from a particular stakeholder group: publishers. There is very little reliable evidence to know, one way or another, whether open licensing damages the sales prospects of scholarly material in print form. As I shall show when I now move to monographs, this could pose problems for models in which print subsidy forms part of those particular economic sustainability arrangements.

CHAPTER 4

Monographs

By now, it is trite and clichéd to note that the scholarly mono-graph is in crisis. Indeed, several papers given at a conference in 1997, now seventeen years ago, questioned whether the rhetoric of crisis was better framed as 'chronic illness' as the state seems perpetual.[1] It is also fair to say, as Robert McPherson notes, that there are disciplinary differences in the nature and/or severity of the crisis.[2] Nonetheless, because humanities departments exist within budgetary constraints set throughout the institution and not in isolation, the economics of monograph purchasing are intrinsically bound to the forces determining journal finances and are, therefore, rarely stable; the rhetoric of crisis is here to stay.[3] This crisis, though, is not singular; it is in fact the same phenomenon that we saw with journal publishing wherein the term 'crisis' denotes two paradoxical supply-side and demand-side crises. Nobody ever complains of having too little to read, as Richard Fisher, the managing director of Cambridge University Press's academic division, has put it at many conferences. Yet, most humanities academics feel the need to publish books for their jobs and, more importantly, simply to disseminate their findings. This chiastic formulation was challenged by an MLA committee in 2002, which asked: 'On a practical level, how can ever-increasing demands for publication as a qualification for tenure and promotion be sustained when scholars find it harder and harder to publish their books?'[4] It is, of course, a rite of passage for new academics to publish their Ph.D. theses as reworked monographs, a fact that often hampers the imposition of OA mandates on doctoral work.[5] However, this 'need' to publish in a quasi-trade market has also led to claims of the erosion of esoteric research in favour of populist agendas and an impact of finance upon the type of scholarship that is conducted.[6]

In this chapter, I turn my attention to open access and monographs. I begin by asking whether there is a fundamental difference between monographs and other forms of scholarship. I then undertake a survey of different projects that seek to bring an open-access ecosystem to scholarly monographs. Finally, I look at the economic models that could support open-access monographs. Before proceeding, however, there is one aspect of terminology that must be clarified. In this chapter, I use the term 'monograph' to refer to scholarly books on a single, specialised subject with coherent thematic unity, authored by one or more persons, but that are not edited collections of disparate essays. In this way, the term 'monograph' is distinct from 'book', with the latter term encompassing monographs, edited collections, scholarly editions and other forms. This is a conscious decision intended to limit scope for the purposes of meaningful discussion: an enabling constraint. It is also helpful because the types of labour involved in the academic production of different types of 'book' are so diverse as to make discussion within the practical bounds of a chapter almost infeasible. This chapter will, therefore, primarily concern itself with monographs, although in some instances the argument may also apply to other forms of books, particularly so in the final section when I will venture into discussion of scholarly editions, as these are often bound up with the business models of learned societies. I would also like to note that, where possible, I have tried to avoid becoming too embroiled in a historical study of the emergence of the scholarly book. Such a task would constitute at least another work in its own right and sits beyond the scope of this text. Finally, anyone wishing to know more on this topic would do well to consult Ellen Collins' excellent literature review for the OAPEN-UK project.[7]

WHY ARE MONOGRAPHS DIFFERENT?

It is often remarked that monographs are different from other, shorter types of academic publication. For instance, as covered in more detail below, the Higher Education Funding Council for England (HEFCE) has a strong OA mandate for its next national research assessment evaluation but has deliberately chosen to exempt 'monographs and other long-form publications' from the open-access requirement.[8] However, regardless of the number of times such a truism is reiterated, without a definitional framework for *why* the monograph should be thought of differently, it is impossible to consider its role within an open-access world. Beyond the challenges, then, of how to read long-form material in a digital format (let alone open access), which comes with well-documented problems, it is first necessary to ask *what* the monograph is for; *how* it is produced; and *why* it should be seen as different from other forms.[9] The first part of this chapter is dedicated to such an unravelling as the answers to these questions must inform any perspective on open access.

The purpose of the monograph

To ask what the monograph is (used) for is to invite the preliminary question: by whom? Indeed, in a 2010 report on 'user needs' regarding digital monographs for the OAPEN project, Janneke Adema and Paul Rutten identified at least four groups that each have a stake in the monograph: scholars, publishers, libraries and funding agencies.[10] Furthermore, even within the scholar subset there is a large degree of disciplinary variance in the use, and authorship, of monographs.[11] To consider another group, briefly – to demonstrate the problems in thinking about a single 'use' of the monograph – for libraries the current use is to be purchased, to be catalogued, to take up shelf space and to slowly degrade over hundreds of years, even with acid-free paper. However, these functions are changing. Although no current digital solution exists that can replicate the functionality of the material codex, making it unlikely that the print monograph will disappear in the near future, a mixed environment is emerging in which researchers use print for end-to-end reading and digital for search and other functions.[12]

Given this heterogeneous set of uses, it may instead be better to ask what scholars want and need from the monograph. Although Adema and Rutten identify four groups of stakeholders, and although it is true that the object called a 'monograph' depends upon publishers and funders, it is clear that without scholars there would be no need for that long-form object to exist. Scholars, or academics, are writers, citers, submitters, readers, editors, reviewers and quality-control accreditors.[13] That scholars are often the only primary target audience as a readership for these objects is lamentable but also renders their involvement all the more central. Collins notes that most studies of the monograph to date have 'focus[ed] upon researchers'.[14] I contend that there is good cause for this.

The fundamental idea of the monograph is that it provides the necessary greater space to work through, and in which to present enough evidence for, an argument than is possible in a journal article. The standard has evolved to the 80,000 word mark in many disciplines because it is a well-known fact that academics must be told when to stop speaking. However, various experiments with the form's length have been undertaken in the last thirty years. For instance, Ken Wissoker notes that Duke University Press published a range of short-form books in the mid-nineties at the behest of book shops, who felt that 'somebody who wasn't an academic might read something that was 125 pages while they wouldn't read the 300 page version'. Wissoker then extends this line of thinking to note that 'Presses have been interested in having shorter forms – and having a variety of forms – for a long time. And with the digital, if you take out the production part, you should be able to accommodate a whole range of lengths, including much longer things than would fit into a book.'[15]

It is in this historicised light that Palgrave Macmillan has also recently launched its 'Pivot' programme, featuring original research at approximately the 30,000 word mark (but not described as a monograph). This programme, according to Hazel Newton, 'seeks to challenge the assumption that research could only be published at these [80,000 word] lengths' and is made possible by developments in technology that eliminate the previous constraints of 'the practicalities and costs of printing, binding and paper'.[16] This is, in many ways, fascinating, because it demonstrates how the commercial histories and constraints of technology may continue to bear upon the way in which ideas are communicated between scholars, even in the age of the internet. We are, after all, historically conditioned subjects. Taking this to an extreme and depending upon how one thinks about the interaction between writing and thinking, there is also the possibility that such space constraints – engendered by historical limitations of technology – could also impinge upon the very possibility of thought. To return to the topic at hand, however, it is clear that digital technologies, XML-first workflows[17] and print-on-demand are already transforming the scope, potential and even *definition* of a monograph. What the monograph is 'for' (in the sense of 'what scholars need') is communicating ideas at greater length, but even that scope is under attack, for where do we place the cut-off point for 'long-form' if mid-form titles are also counted as 'monographs'?

When speaking of value and use, it is also worth finally noting that the current monograph/book supply chain bestows greater value on items that are bought at a price and that are material, both of which are the opposite of pure open access (although print for a price can co-exist with OA). Indeed, at least one commercial study has correlated the print form with readers' 'emotional connection' to books, and particularly those with 'classic' status.[18] There is, furthermore, an understanding that pricing should be correlated with perceived value.[19] While a zero-price exponentially increases demand for a product and damages competitors' offerings disproportionately in most fields of commodity purchase, book readers are used to finding best-sellers in book shops and may be suspicious of the supposed lack of investment by a publisher if there is no option to purchase.[20] In other words, value ascription to books is often shaped within social spaces and by commercial entities (book shops and publishers) in such a way that readers are accustomed to paying. Part of this payment is to ensure that a reputable intermediary will filter out the 'nonsense' through which the reader would otherwise have to trawl if anyone could place their book in a book shop and if everything was free. While this is being challenged in the trade world through new self-publishing paradigms, in the realm of monographs there remains a problem with trade crossover titles. If academics desire to be as widely read as possible, then, at present, the ultimate goal is to reach the general public with one's book (ideally with a tie-in television series etc.). However, present mechanisms of discovery for the general public do not include searching for high-quality academic titles online, to be read free of charge. Indeed, it seems likely that this would cast suspicion on a volume: 'why is it free?' As will be seen below, it is possible to have open-access models in which print partner volumes can be sold, which is probably the best answer to this problem. However, it is notable that this paradox exists and that, hypothetically, it is conceivable that a shift to pure open-access monographs could reduce the reach of some academic work because the public would neither find the book, nor value it outside of those socio-economic trappings.

How monographs are produced

Involvement in monograph production represents an academic's exposure to both the most commercially crass and also the most procedurally sophisticated and nuanced portions of any academic publication process. As John Thompson puts it:

> On the one hand, publishing organizations in these fields [the academic book market] are concerned with questions of quality and scholarship – indeed, for most university presses these questions are paramount. But publishing organizations are also driven by commercial concerns.[21]

The economics of this commercial system are paramount because, as Jennifer Crewe has put it, 'the crisis in scholarly publishing is essentially a numbers problem'.[22] In other words, as budgets contract but costs remain the same or rise, the economic viability of the monograph is continually threatened. Although, in the current age of 'impact', academics are encouraged (or forced) to think about their audience and the potential changes engendered by their work, there is at the same time a belief that scholarship should not be determined through markets masquerading as democracy, as seen in earlier discussions of utilitarianism and higher education. However, authors are also all used by now to completing the 'marketing' section of a book proposal, specifying its audience, assessing its commercial viability (or otherwise) and thereby its potential appeal to a press. This is not to say that all books are published by academic presses for profit. Far from it; many presses, and especially university presses, formally exist to circulate academic excellence and deploy massive cross-subsidy between their commercial success stories and their esoteric-yet-valuable monographs. Some presses are even sub-sidised by their host institution to achieve these goals (while others resubsidise their host institutions). Despite this, however, something still rankles about the fact that the gatekeeper – whose blessing can, after all, determine whether an academic is hired or promoted and may condition how highly their work is valued by others – might here be deciding on the basis of commercial viability, however defined. Even within market logic, this is flawed. Who, for instance, can predict the future emergence of figures culturally neglected within their time? As with many forms of peer review, the scholarly monograph world is inclined towards a conservative model that privileges normative scholarship: work that will sell at the time of publication.

This, however, is merely the most negative sharp end of the book publication gatekeeping system. In the current setup, the form of editorial curation that takes place before peer review in the case of monographs, conducted by those with extensive experience in publishing, albeit not necessarily specialists in the field, also has a discoverability function. This is because a well-curated list at a press is supposed to exhibit coherence and quality. It is supposed to be a space wherein a reader will find a selection of the latest and greatest material on the particular subject at hand. This function, which is inextricable from the commercial aspect, is key to many presses' successful online book bundles (the University Publishing Online system, for example, or Oxford University Press's 'Oxford Scholarship Online'). As will be noted below in Chapter 5, this function could be changing. Although it in no way requires it, open access does offer a moment in which to re-evaluate other publication practices, such as peer review. While I will leave a full discussion of these aspects until later, it is worth noting, at this point, that the value of discovery through a coherent list may be diminished through digital mechanisms. For instance, as full-text search and online ranking mechanisms mature, the community might be able to rate good material internally while burying the bad. This is not to say anything of the value of curation by quality, however, which should mostly be handled by the academic peer-review process anyway. Monograph selection nonetheless continues to differ from its journal counterparts in one final way. It is expected, with monographs, that a good non-academic editor or copyeditor will work with an author to improve the work. This view can be incredibly useful as those locked within a disciplinary discussion often cannot give the same perspective as a voice with expertise in publishing and argument, but less immanently placed with respect to the subject.

In the realm of technical production, there are differences between monographs and journals, but these are predominantly now the result of legacy systems. There is no reason why books should not feature the same XML-first workflow that is widely used in journal production. After all, the technology behaves in the same way when dealing with 8,000 words or 80,000 words. There are, however, as I have implied, some differences. Most notably, monographs are distributed through aggregation channels with comparatively long lead times and this explains the ways in which the same marketing copy arrives at all the various different outlets (Amazon, Barnes and Noble, Waterstones etc. all get their data from the same sources). Likewise, this digital-first[23] format now gives an easy route to print; print on demand (POD). This advance in technology has enabled the total unification of technological processes for print and digital.

If, then, production differences between monographs and journals are primarily of scale, rather than of kind, there are nonetheless difficulties that come with such a scaling, predominantly in the legal realm. Within a monograph there is a far greater scope for copyright infringement as more space is granted and a greater number of sources are deployed. While open licensing of scholarly works could help in this regard (as seen earlier in Chapter 3), obtaining permission to reproduce images and texts that are under copyright can be an incredibly expensive process. This cost is massively increased within a gratis open-access environment since, basing their calculations off a legacy model of 'print runs', an openly accessible, digital reproduction is often treated as though it were an *infinite run*. The logic behind this is that if something is distributed gratis on the internet, the ability to exchange it at a financial price point is lost, which again ties in well with this work's previous analysis of the tension between the open-access work and the commodity form. As will be seen below in my discussion of business models, new ways of thinking about this are needed if open access for monographs is to succeed.

Why should the monograph be seen differently?

In the contemporary technological landscape, several factors that differentiate the monograph from journals are destroyed. The core technological and labour differences that remain are larger scales of typesetting, copyediting and proofreading. That said, differences of distribution channel remain, at least for now. Instead, it is clear that the differentiating factors for the monograph are social: they involve publisher expertise and list gatekeeping. Many hard-line advocates of OA would disavow that even these functions are necessary and that they will be eroded over time. For now, however, regardless of such speculation, there are significantly more barriers, both social and technological, to entry into book publication than into journals.

These barriers to entry are simultaneously a reflection of the differences in scale noted above and also a result of a lack of transition strategies for new start-up publishers. In the journal sector there has already been a small but growing degree of publisher disintermediation (in which academics adopt a do-it-yourself approach to publishing, removing the intermediary) through the development and use of freely available tools, such as the Public Knowledge Project's Open Journal Systems: the software that hosted almost 5,700 active journals at the end of 2013. Until very recently, no such alternative has been available for monographs, although this is now changing with the launch of Open Monograph Press. Because platform development – an effort replicated over and over by many presses who seek a unique online presence – requires a large degree of initial organisational capital investment, there is a greater monetary barrier to entry.[24] At the same time, however, scholars are less willing to commit their monographs into unproven hands. Writing a monograph is a substantial commitment of a magnitude many times greater than that of producing a journal article. For this reason, scholars expect a commensurate return on their investment, largely in the form of reputational capital. This will not be provided by new presses until they have a significant number of high-quality titles under their brand, regardless of how experienced the team members may be. It will, however, be harder for new presses to attract high-quality submissions because they do not yet hold prestige; this is a chicken and egg situation. In both cases, these are, again, merely differences in scale. The people who perform the labour of publishing, however, move about between jobs and set up new companies, as in any other field. That the same individuals, with the same skill-sets, could have different reputational appeal to scholars based upon brand illustrates, once more, the idiosyncrasies of prestige as it currently stands.

The differences between books and journals, in these respects, are often over-stated. There is a nonetheless pressing need to ensure that the transition to an open-access model preserves those aspects of the monograph that are of use to scholars. On this front, even if hard-liners believe the differences between books and journals to be over-stated (because they are 'merely' differences of scale), they should nonetheless see the commensurately larger responsibility to ensure that the work of scholars during a transition period does not become collateral damage. Monographs may merely take longer, or they may never come to open-access fruition. This is not to say, though, that experiments are not under way and it is to an examination of current projects that I will now turn.

OPEN-ACCESS MONOGRAPH PROJECTS

There are, broadly speaking, two types of open-access monograph project currently in existence. The first of these consists of social scientific research projects investigating economic and academico-structural changes engendered by open-access monographs. The second grouping is a band of publishers and business model inter-mediaries, who are either already publishing open-access books, or facilitating such action. In this portion of the chapter I will detail the first group of these projects and the contribution that they make to the field. The second group will be explored under the section 'Economic models for monographs' below. As a preliminary and crude observation: the field is changing incredibly quickly and some of these projects have had the ground shift beneath them even as they proceed. As with all social science, this is the risk; social environments are incredibly complex phenomena and academic publishing is no exception. Finally, for this section's introduction, it is important to note that, while I have tried to include as many as possible, the list of projects below is not comprehensive. Instead, it is hoped that named initiatives are seen as representative of specific types of project (and no slight is intended upon those not listed).

Studies of the OA monograph

The leading studies of the open-access monograph, at present, are: the OAPEN-NL project; Jisc Collections' OAPEN-UK initiative; and the HEFCE Open Access Monographs investigation. The first of these (OAPEN-NL) concluded in 2013. The OAPEN-UK study is ongoing and will end in 2015. The HEFCE panel is currently also ongoing but due to end in 2014 (some time near to the submission of this book's manuscript). All three studies feature involvement from publishers, libraries and researchers but each has slightly different aims and objectives. This section will give a brief summary of each and, when possible, the findings. It is worth noting, before proceeding and in the interests of fair disclosure, that the nature of early OA studies is that they are often run by those with an interest in seeing open access come to fruition. Furthermore, while there are some strong headline findings from various projects, these must remain provisional and some publishers are sceptical of their real-world applicability (or at least are not willing to be the first to take the two-footed jump into the unknown).

OAPEN-NL

The OAPEN-NL project – headed by Eelco Ferwerda, Ronald Snijder and Janneke Adema – was based on a broader OAPEN (Open Access Publishing in European Networks) project, originally established in 2008, with a shared aim between the investigations to explore the business model implications for OA books. From the project's description:

OAPEN-NL was a project to gain experience with Open Access publication of monographs in the Netherlands. Between June 2011 and November 2012, 50 Open Access monographs in various subject areas were published in [gold] Open Access by 9 participating publishers. For every Open Access title, the publishers provided a similar title that was published in the conventional way … Data were collected about usage, sales and costs, to study the effect of Open Access on monographs. OAPEN-NL consisted of a quantitative and a qualitative research component, measuring the effects of Open Access publishing and the perceptions and expectations of publishers and authors.[25]

This concept of 'similar titles' is difficult to pull off. As many publishers will attest, no two books are alike in their sales profile or content and there is no such thing as a 'typical' monograph. Faced with such difficulties, for the OAPEN-NL project, similarity was defined in terms of publication date, number of pages, price and subject area. The OAPEN-NL project was finished in 2013 with data returned from Koninklijke van Gorcum, IOS Press B.V., Springer Science & Business Media, Techne Press, Wageningen Academic Publishers, Koninklijke Brill NV, KITLV Press and Amsterdam University Press.[26] This resulted in a sample size of fifty books with a total expenditure of €239,615.85 by the project at a maximum of €5,000 per book paid to publishers.[27]

The project's headline findings from its quantitative data used a statistical technique called Analysis of Variance between groups (ANOVA) that is designed to ensure minimal risk that the result was derived by chance. From this analysis, the OAPEN-NL project concluded that 'no significant effect of Open Access on monograph sales could be found' but that there was significant increase in digital usage (the number of times a book was viewed on Google Books) when it was OA. There was no observed citation benefit to a book being open access, a result that contradicts several studies in the journal sphere.[28] Finally, the project also examined the costs of publishing and concluded that an OA edition is approximately 50% cheaper to produce than the total cost of a conventional, print monograph, although I have heard non-participating publishers exhibit scepticism towards this finding in particular (and there is the temptation to believe, once more, that the intangible digital object should always cost less, regardless of the labour invested).[29]

For OA advocates, there are two positive outcomes in these findings and one unexpected negative result. However, a sequential and sceptical look at these findings reveals that each can be interpreted differently. The first result of the project, that open access does not act to the detriment of other sales, can be viewed sceptically if one considers the fact that the open-access route is not so well embedded within researcher-specific discovery channels as traditional books. This could mean that those who might have been dissuaded from purchasing the book were it open access ended up buying the monograph purely because they were unaware that they could get it for free. Although the study notes that discoverability of monographs was generally increased (the second finding) through one particular route (Google Books), it is not clear whether this is the discoverability route of those who are academic monograph purchasers. Furthermore, during and since the period of the OAPEN-NL study, open access has exploded in international recognition, even in the monograph sphere, through funder mandates such as Wellcome. It is entirely possible that acquisition librarians – one of the core audiences for academic monographs – are now more on the lookout for OA editions. Finally, however, the lack of a citation boost is unexpected (and certainly contradicted the expectations of the book authors surveyed in the study, 94% of whom expected to see a rise in citations).[30] In the same spirit of contradiction, however, it is entirely possible to explain this result through the long publishing cycles in the humanities against the relatively short run-time of the OAPEN-NL study. The citation findings were due to be reviewed in August 2014.

Clearly, these early results showed promise for open-access monographs, but were not fully cemented; an extremely interesting and valuable starting point, even if not conclusive. Indeed, what seemed necessary was an extension of this monitoring experiment as, in some cases, it was simply too early to tell. To that end, enter OAPEN-UK.

OAPEN-UK

The OAPEN-UK experiment is, in many senses, a continuation of the OAPEN-NL project, except that it introduces the concept of 'matched pairs', in which profiled books are designed to be compared with one another. In contrast to the OAPEN-NL project, OAPEN-UK contains ninety titles, forty-five of which constitute the experimental gold open access group, while the other forty-five remain as a traditional, purchased control group.[31] The publishers involved in OAPEN-UK are Routledge, University of Wales Press, Liverpool University Press, Palgrave Macmillan, Berg Publishers and Oxford University Press. The disciplinary range of the monographs included spans international criminal law, classics, literature and history, through to marketing, among many others. As the OAPEN-UK project is still running, no definitive results from the quantitative portion of the experiment/control study are yet available. That said, the project has already released some extremely valuable findings from various case studies and focus groups as part of a structured qualitative research programme.[32]

The first round of OAPEN-UK focus groups was held between November 2011 and February 2012 and consisted of institutional representatives, publishers, researchers, funders, learned societies and eBook aggregators. The core issues raised in these fora, among many others, were: quality and prestige; dissemination; versioning, preservation and archiving; and costs.[33] While the matter of 'costs' will be dealt with shortly in the section below on economic models for monographs, among the most prominent remarks to emerge in this portion of OAPEN-UK's investigation was that:

Most commentators identified a perception that OA content is, per se, lower quality than books published in more traditional ways, although not all agreed that this is necessarily the case. The prestige of print publication was recognised as very important to researchers, and there were concerns that they would be slow to adopt OA, as both authors and readers, although the researchers themselves did not mention this as a potential problem.[34]

While this view on OA as lower quality ties in well with my earlier remarks on perceived value and pricing, it is also clearly false. Open access is supposed to refer to peer-reviewed research and there is no reason why it should be lower quality. As awareness of OA grows and as traditional publishers expand their efforts, this view will probably become less common.

Another area in which there was some consternation surrounded the official version of record. In a green OA environment for monographs, were copies to be distributed among repositories, for instance, there was a fear that a proliferation of different versions would cause trust in the monograph to decline.[35] This was also linked to the supposed challenges for perpetual access to OA content. While this is an important area and shouldn't be taken for granted and to reiterate a point made in the introduction to this book, Kathleen Fitzpatrick also does much to challenge such repeated mantras through two chiastic statements: 'The first is simply to note that [hard-copy/print] books are often far more ephemeral than we often assume. Bindings give way and pages are lost ... Second, and by contrast, bits and the texts created with them can be far more durable than we think.'[36] Fitzpatrick explicitly notes that she does not by this 'mean that we can be cavalier about their preservation',[37] which is crucial for continued access, but that it is a red herring to believe that it is impossible or that such mechanisms do not exist. This is not to say that such systems are not complex, as Donald J. Waters notes, but rather to point out that the digital revolution has been long anticipated and efforts are already fairly advanced.[38] For instance, the CLOCKSS, LOCKSS and Portico systems are all digital preservation systems that are capable of preserving open-access books as they currently stand by distributing copies of the same book to hundreds of locations worldwide. Of course, if one really wished to push this, one could arrive at the logical conclusion that we depend on electricity for any kind of digital preservation and imagine a situation where such a resource is no longer available. In that eventuality, however, the systems of environmental control that preserve our print works would also fail.

The second piece of interesting material published to-date by the OAPEN-UK project is their 'humanities and social science research-ers survey' results. Running from March to May 2012, this survey solicited 690 usable results from a self-selecting respondent group (meaning that the results may be skewed towards those with precon-ceived ideas on the subject). Interestingly, the largest group of respondents was Ph.D. candidates, perhaps showing that an upcom-ing generation of scholars have been more aware of these issues for longer than those already in academic employment (or simply that the reward incentives of Amazon vouchers were more keenly sought by this group!).

Of the respondents, 53.8% classed themselves as 'aware' of OA, against 38.7% who said they were 'familiar' and 7.2% who had 'never heard' of open access. Interestingly, given that a large number of publishers are commercial and shareholder-driven entities, only 20% of researcher respondents felt that it was acceptable for publishers to make a profit and to do with this what they wished, as opposed to supporting the discipline and/or future publication.[39]

Finally, and perhaps most usefully at present, the OAPEN-UK project conducted two case studies of learned societies (the Royal Historical Society [RHS] and the Regional Studies Association [RSA]), as groups who have, in some instances, objected to the new business models proposed for gold open access. While OAPEN-UK is a project examining monographs, this particular part of their qualitative research situated its work on learned societies within the broader journal landscape, hence there may be some slippage in the below section between the formats. In the case of the eminent RHS, business models were clearly a concern, despite 'all interviewees ... stating their firm support for the principle of open access'. However, interestingly, at the point of this case study, 'the financial issues were not the main concern for most interviewees' when considering OA. Instead, it was 'the effect on volunteer networks, and the academic freedom of Society members' that were deemed the most problematic. As the latter issue of academic freedom has already been covered above, I will not reiterate those arguments here. The former argument is more difficult to place, however. One interviewee 'suggested that removing profits from publishing would also remove the "fun"', by which it was meant that part of the reward to society volunteers (upon whom much depends for their labour) was in 'seeing their effort and passion turned into book sales, especially when the book performs unexpectedly well', an aspect that was intensified when the profits went back into supporting the discipline. Conversely, though, 'another interviewee suggested that explicitly putting a price on the work done to publish a book, through an APC or similar, would anger academics who give their time for free to undertake peer review'.[40] This is a curious statement because, while it has been estimated that the unpaid non-cash costs of peer review undertaken worldwide by academics is £1.9 billion per year, many book publishers do pay reviewers for their time, given the proportionately larger degree of labour involved.[41]

The OAPEN-UK case study of the Regional Studies Association took a slightly different tack, with the primary concerns being 'the effect upon scholarship for their members, and the effect upon the Association's business models'. The former of these points was linked both to 'ensuring trusted brands [and especially the Society's brand] are not undermined' and to an emphasis on maintaining high standards of peer review. There was also concern in this area over 'the new ways that work could be used and cited, and the loss of control over their own work that academics might experience', presumably referring to conditions of open licensing covered above in Chapter 3. As a positive counterbalance, however, Society members suggested 'quicker publication speeds and more open discussions around articles, benefits for policymakers and practitioners, and the ability to disseminate different types of content' as among the benefits of OA.

Secondly, on the financial front, it was noted that 'income from publications makes up a significant proportion of the Association's budget, and it is subsequently used to support conferences, dissemination, research projects, overseas networks, early career researchers and all the Association's other activities'.[42] It is unclear what a shift to gold open access would do to the Society's finances. Interestingly, however, the RSA's journals (*Regional Studies, Spatial Economic Analysis, Territory, Politics, Governance* and *Regional Studies, Regional Science*) are published by Routledge, an imprint of Taylor & Francis, an organisation that is in turn owned by the Informa group, the extremely healthy profits of which were discussed earlier in Chapter 1. In fact, the RSA's journals seem to have always been enmeshed with commercial publishers, unlike some societies which originally produced their publications in-house. The first issue of *Regional Studies*, for instance, was published in 1967 by Pergamon Press, now owned by the largest international commercial publisher and hate-figure for uncompromising advocates within the Open Access movement: Elsevier. This is not to deprecate the claims that there may be financial challenges for associations and societies in any transition to open access. It is, rather, to note that calls to protect society revenue models are often inextricable from calls to protect publisher profits; the two are interwoven. This rhetoric of economy and sustainability, it must also not be forgotten, will always make one group's sustainability possible only at the expense of another: usually the library. Hard-line OA advocates would call, therefore, for the learned societies to forgo their revenue in the service of knowledge dissemination. Hard-line Society figures would argue that the services supported by publishing revenue are more important. Perhaps the moderate ground that we need is to find the point of sustainable balance?

HEFCE open-access monographs investigation

HEFCE (the Higher Education Funding Council for England) is a quango (quasi-autonomous non-governmental organisation) in the United Kingdom that translates the government's higher education budget allocation into usable funds. Some of this goes in a teaching grant for STEM (Science, Technology, Engineering and Mathematics) subjects (this funding has been withdrawn for the humanities subjects), while other portions of the budget are devolved to the major UK research councils. Aside from specific project funding, the other major way in which HEFCE funds research is called quality-related (QR) funding. This is awarded to institutions on the basis of an assessment exercise known as the 'Research Excellence Framework', which was preceded by a series of 'Research Assessment Exercises', which in turn have their root in the 1986 'research selectivity exercise'.[43] These exercises now take place approximately every five years and are, it is fair to say, widely hated by UK academics who often consider them as bureaucratic exercises in quantification.

Of interest to the subject at hand, however, is that, in April 2014, HEFCE announced that eligibility to submit to a post-2014 Research Excellence Framework (presumed to be 'REF2020') would depend upon an open-access component: a mandate. Specifically, authors must deposit the accepted version of their articles at the time of acceptance.[44] However, as already mentioned in passing, it is notable that monographs ('and other long-form publications'), edited collections, non-text outputs and data are all excluded from the mandate.[45]

From the rhetoric deployed by HEFCE and the Research Councils, some academics have surmised that these bodies would like to mandate monographs for a future exercise; after all, why should one form be deemed different from others in their eyes when both are supported by QR funding?[46] However, in recognition of the additional barriers (and researcher sensitivities) surrounding open-access monographs, HEFCE has instead opted for now to mount an investigation into the subject, the first national-level funding council investigation of its type. The investigation is being led by Professor Geoffrey Crossick, an ex-Vice Chancellor of the University of London and a Distinguished Professor of History. Crossick's findings were expected to be released in the late summer/autumn of 2014.

These, then, comprise the majority of the social scientific studies of open-access monographs. However, there are also a number of presses who have simply decided to try publishing monographs in an OA format. In the next section, I want to draw attention to several projects with innovative aspects that show signs of emergent and viable economics for OA monographs. It is, of course, impossible to gain full coverage of all the exciting new projects working on OA books but this will give a flavour of the experiments that are under way.

ECONOMIC MODELS FOR MONOGRAPHS

As of mid 2014, a small number of presses, such as Amsterdam University Press, allow green open access deposit for monographs, usually with an embargo of 18–24 months. The central model emerging for gold open access monograph publishing, conversely, is one of book processing charges (BPCs). The current rates requested by established presses under such a system are high and pose real, possibly insurmountable, challenges for unfunded research: $2,450/chapter from de Gruyter; €640/chapter from InTech; £5,900 from Manchester University Press for books of up to 80,000 words; £11,000 from Palgrave; and approximately €15,000 from Springer, to name but a few.[47] Each of these presses does, of course, offer a different service: although not exclusively limited to the more expensive presses, the higher end tend to allow more liberal reuse rights by default (CC BY) while others have more restrictive criteria and may not allow ePub downloads (a format for mobile reading devices). One of the central drivers of the introduction of this model has been the strong open-access mandate of the Wellcome Trust, which, in contrast to HEFCE, includes 'scholarly monographs and book chapters authored or coauthored by Trust grantholders that arise as part of their grant-funded research'.[48] The first Wellcome-funded OA book was released in late 2013.[49]

Despite the emergence of the BPC as the model of choice for many publishers, several other economic models are appearing (some of which are experimental), including: print subsidy, freemium and consortia. These models remain immature and unproven but are showing signs of working at the present time within specific contexts.

This final section will sequentially detail some of these projects in order to think beyond a purely BPC-driven market. As with OA journals, it is also worth noting that some open-access book efforts are scholar-led and subsist entirely on volunteerism, a model that certainly will not scale to cover the entire field but does seem to work within niche contexts.

Print subsidy

Among the most common forms of alternative revenue streams for open-access monographs has been print subsidy. In this model, the open, online version is available free of charge but the revenues from the sales of print – or specific alternative digital versions – are retained by the publisher. Such a model relies on the continuing desire for print or for formats that can be read exclusively by digital reading devices. In other words, this rests on what Gary Hall has termed a 'paper-centrism', a phenomenon wherein the hard-edged format of paper is transferred to a digital medium, seen most clearly in the persistence of the paginated PDF.[50] In this model the confidence in sales as a revenue stream is based upon a belief in continuing desire for the features of print that are currently hard to replicate in an online environment. There is no guarantee that this will continue to be the case but, for now, it looks an appealing model; the codex is an enduring form. This model can also, of course, be used alongside other forms, such as a BPC.

Although there are many projects that utilise this model – such as the University of Adelaide Press and Monash University Publishing, both based in Australia – the case study I have opted to focus upon for this model is Open Book Publishers (OBP), a new small press based in Cambridge, UK and headed by Alessandra Tosi, a fellow of Clare Hall, and run by Rupert Gatti, a fellow of Trinity College. OBP has a strict emphasis on strong peer review with the mantra that, if a book doesn't meet the highest of academic standards, it will not be published. Using a streamlined workflow, they hope to be able to outperform traditional publishers, publishing material of an equal quality faster and cheaper. As of mid 2014, OBP have published forty-three open-access books. The press has several routes to funding, the first of which (although only constituting 25% of their

current income, according to Gatti) is to ask authors to request a
BPC payment from their institutions. Lack of funding does not
preclude publication, however, because there is an additional revenue
stream from the demand side. Titles are available through high-
quality print-on-demand. It is unclear, at present, whether this
model will prove sustainable but, as mandates come into force,
OBP will emerge as a strong market contender when other presses
are charging thousands of pounds per book, although it is unclear at
what scale they might eventually operate.

Institutional subsidy

OBP's loose affiliation with various Cambridge colleges also raises
another potential funding source for open-access monographs: institutional subsidy. Under this type of model, universities or other
types of institution pay to support the publishing operation because
it is in their economic and strategic interests to do so. This move was
given additional credibility in mid 2014 when the Association of
American Universities and the Association of Research Libraries
issued a joint proposal for an institutionally funded first-book
subvention, noting 'the inability of a market model to adequately
support research monograph publication based primarily on scholarly merit'.[51] One of the more prominent examples of this type of
project is the Open Humanities Press (OHP) initiative, established
by Gary Hall, alongside Sigi Jöttkandt. This project has strategic
partnerships with the University of Michigan Library's Scholarly
Publishing Office, UC-Irvine, UCLA Library and the Public Knowledge Project, the former of whom is 'subsidizing the production and
distribution costs and providing its services in kind, in keeping with
its mission to provide an array of sustainable publishing solutions to
the scholarly community'.[52] OHP also intends to cover costs through
the sale of print-on-demand copies and ePub versions.

In a similar vein, some institutions have directly affiliated OA
book components. Purdue University has a subsection of its libraries
entitled 'Purdue e-Pubs', the name of which is unaffiliated to the
ePub file format. This service offers open access to a selection of
books published by Purdue University Press in the PDF format.[53]
A similar scenario, wherein a university library cooperates with an

associated press, has also been put into operation at Pittsburgh on a two-year embargo model.[54]

These types of project may implement alternative sources of funding such as a print subsidy scheme, for example. However, this model is not the same as a *grant*. It is, rather, a long-term financial arrangement with a continual flow of cash from institution to press. There have been several projects funded by start-up grant, such as the MediaCommons initiative – a scholar-run setup started by Kathleen Fitzpatrick and Avi Santo – that began with a grant from the US National Endowment of Humanities, but these are not the same as permanent institutional subsidy arrangements.[55]

Freemium

The next most obvious way of finding revenue for open-access publications is to create a version of the monograph that has functionality and features above and beyond those provided for free by the open-access edition. A French platform named OpenEdition, with a component called 'OpenEdition books', adopts this approach in which the HTML versions (those read online in a web browser) are available freely and openly to read while the PDF version (a paginated typeset edition that corresponds to a print counterpart) is accessible only to those who pay.[56] Other features available for a charge through OpenEdition include enhanced technical support for the digital items, more metadata (including machine-readable formats for libraries), statistics on usage and a governance stake for subscribing libraries. Likewise, the open-access Athabasca University Press in Canada sells ePub format versions of its free books.[57]

This approach does, of course, have the downside that the open-access version must inherently be the poor relation of its purchased counterparts. Conversely, it does offer a breath of fresh air in an otherwise painful transition to supply-side funding mechanisms. There are also some other assumptions upon which this model is predicated. As formulated by Moshe Y. Vardi and Richard Baraniuk at Rice University in 2012, the model requires a cheaper system to make up for lost sales, one in which 'most authors would prefer to forgo income in order to maximize dissemination', with the goal being purely to cover the expenses of publishing, rather than including 'large profits'.[58] Many publishers would deny, however, that the 'large profits' to which Vardi and Baraniuk refer actually exist in the sphere of research monographs. All of which is to say that it remains unclear as to whether additional services with premium features ('value added' in management terminology) will cover the costs inherent in monograph production.

Collective funding

The final model that I want to discuss here is one of collective, or collaborative, funding. The most substantial cost for monograph production in a digital or print-on-demand environment is getting to the first copy; the costs of subsequent reproductions in the digital domain are comparatively slim and warehousing/inventory management concerns are substantially lessened.[59] Back in 2010 – an age ago in digital publishing terms – Hugh Look and Frances Pinter proposed a model for collectively underwriting the risks and costs based on 'aggregating demand in the form of a consortium and paying publishers for getting to first copy stage'. Look and Pinter continue:

> if, say 1,000 libraries paid into a fund that 'bought' the non-commercial open access rights to a book that carried, for the sake of the arithmetic, a 'getting to first copy' cost of $10,000, then each library would contribute $10.00. The average monograph today costs approximately $80.00. This would not only get libraries eight times as many titles online, it would be truly contributing to making knowledge accessible globally. If, say 5,000 libraries subscribed to the scheme (although we feel this is unlikely) the cost would be $2.00 a title, representing a 97.5% reduction on the current print or eBook price.[60]

While Look and Pinter acknowledged the difficulties of establishing new models in the midst of extant markets, this proposition came to fruition in 2014 under the auspices of Pinter's 'Knowledge Unlatched' (KU).[61]

Knowledge Unlatched's pilot collection consisted of twenty-eight new books from thirteen renowned scholarly publishers (Amsterdam University Press, Bloomsbury Academic, Brill, Cambridge University Press, de Gruyter, Duke University Press, Edinburgh University Press, Liverpool University Press, Manchester University Press,

Purdue University Press, Rutgers University Press, Temple University Press and the University of Michigan Press). The basic premise of the pilot was as Look and Pinter described, albeit at a smaller scale. While Pinter had earlier proposed 1,000 libraries, for the KU Pilot a more achievable 200 were sought, with almost 300 libraries eventually participating. This included 137 from North America, 77 from the United Kingdom, 27 from Oceania and 55 from elsewhere.[62] The amount requested from each library was capped at US $1,680, which was an average of $60 per book with 200 libraries participating. As the eventual goal of 200 libraries was superseded by almost 50%,[63] this was eventually closer to $40 per book, which is substantially cheaper than the cost of most academic books when bought outright, let alone for those that can now be distributed ad infinitum for free.[64]

Interestingly, although this model for making material open access depends upon the internet for its success, it has been traced far further back by Sandy Thatcher. Indeed, Thatcher notes the affinity with the description furnished by Adrian Johns of seventeenth-century practice: 'another option, of increasing importance after 1660, was to publish by subscription ... It involved persuading a number of prosperous individuals to invest enough money in the proposed publication that the project would be sufficiently capitalized to proceed to completion.'[65] Other projects to implement a model of this kind include the Gluejar initiative, which is designed to enable 'individuals and institutions to join together to liberate specific ebooks'[66] and my own Open Library of Humanities project, which works slightly differently as the predominant funding is for journals, but working to cross-subsidise monographs.

Concluding thoughts on monograph economics

While book processing charges are the predominant form of current implementation for open-access monographs, they are not to be considered the be-all and end-all. A diverse range of experiments are under way to establish alternative bases upon which gold open access monograph publication could be possible. It is clear that not all of these will succeed and that they should be considered experimental. It is also fair to say, though, that publishers' revenue models will have to change if any forms of national mandate for monographs come into play. While savvy publishers are already thinking ahead to such a scenario and beginning to experiment, others are only on the very cusp of understanding the implications of infinite, free, digital dissemination for their practice. Humanities academics, likewise, are playing catch-up against the science-driven journal market from which mandates have been derived. While, then, more time is needed to develop models that will circumnavigate the dreaded steep publication charges, it is worth ending with one final observation. The panic over the potential limitation of monograph publication in the switch to a supply-side economy (in which it is feared that one may not be able to publish because of the high cost borne by the institution publishing) is to some extent only an unravelling of the simultaneous crises of supply and demand in the scholarly publication market.

While green open access can now be secured for the vast majority of journal publications with no changes to the current system, even this level of access in the monograph world remains a harder goal. This is because the economic structures for monograph production are tightly bound into editorial and gatekeeping functions, yielding a high cost to reach first copy. This, in turn, leads to greater publisher anxiety over the long-term sustainability of a green model alongside a pay-to-purchase system. There are, however, many projects emerging that either study the ways in which monographs can be made open access or attempt to implement one of the proposed models. Furthermore, there are a variety of experimental ways in which gold open access book production can be funded that do not rely solely on recourse to publication charges.

CHAPTER 5

Innovations

As I have already noted, there is nothing in the concept of open access that means anything must be done differently except to lower price and permission barriers to research. Indeed, Peter Suber is at pains to specify that open access is not about circumventing peer review;[1] an especially important observation given some of the misconceptions identified by the OAPEN-UK project. In this light, it might be fair to ask why it is necessary to discuss innovation, changes to editorship or modifications to peer review at all. After all, such discussions surely muddy the waters of open access. I would suggest, however, that there are three reasons why peer review and other forms of experimental innovation must not remain the elephant in the room when we talk about open access. Firstly, it is necessary to keep talking about peer review, in particular, because of the recurring misplaced belief that open access must *inherently* refer to lower standards of quality control (it means no such thing). Secondly, these shifts in publication practice allow us the space to rethink peer review and other practices and to ask whether there are analogous changes, facilitated either socially or technologically, that could be worth exploring at this time of transition. In fact, just as one of the arguments for open access is that it is culturally elitist and untenable to presume that a broader audience can neither understand nor appreciate scholarship, there are, I would argue, parallels in peer review and editorial practice that could reflect this same principle inside the academy. Thirdly, peer review is a key element for discussion because the economics of scholarly publication are intertwined with systems of value.

In this chapter, I want to flag up several ways in which the current system of academic publishing *could* be reformed in a new digital era.

Nothing written here is to be taken as necessary for open access. Instead, these musings are designed as thought experiments to determine the risks and benefits of potential modifications. It is also true that much thinking has already taken place on such issues over the last twenty years.[2] That does not mean, however, that I do not wish us to continue to think about this. As I hope has been made clear throughout this volume, I consider thinking about academic publishing as a form of reflexive critique. It is the histories of academic publishing that shape current practice and determine the possibilities for academic discourse and, therefore, communication. Thinking, in the contemporary tradition of this mode, must involve, as Michel Foucault reframed it, 'a historico-practical test of the limits we may go beyond'.[3] While this is twisting Foucault a little for current purposes, it is in a similar vein of thinking about the historically contingent practices that structure our writing that I wish to proceed.

PEER REVIEW

Peer review is often thought of as inviolable and can be held in extremely high regard. After all, what could be better than a community of self-regulating experts deciding on the merit of a piece of work, in some cases without knowing the author's identity? It sounds like the ultimate form of meritocracy. All is not, however, quite so rosy in actual implementation. Indeed, as far back as 2003, it was proposed by Carlos Alonso, Cathy N. Davidson, John Unsworth and Lynne Withey that the problems of scholarly communication cannot merely be confined to access and economics. As they note, 'the "crisis" of the scholarly monograph, then, is not merely a crisis in the economics of scholarly publishing, but also in the processes of peer review and academic self-governance, prompting reflection on practices of scholarly evaluation that we have simply taken for granted'.[4] In this first section, I want to outline provocatively the potential flaws in the extant systems of peer review before moving on to suggest new alternatives in an open-access, digital world. Some of the criticisms here will only apply in the most negative of cases; often, existing forms of review work fairly well. Nevertheless, if we value quality control mechanisms, it is important to consider the potential failings of our models, even if we eventually reject proposed alternatives. In other words: there is always merit in playing devil's advocate, at least temporarily.

The first point to note is that the gatekeeper model – that is, the system of deciding on permissibility before publication through both publisher policies and peer-review practice – works on a series of unspoken ideological assumptions that are never wholly objective and apolitical, but are rather, at the extreme end, based on a series of exclusions and marginalisations. While much review certainly is aimed at improving work and there are often substantial efforts to bring work up to standard through iterative commentary, at high-end journals and publishers there must be a percentage of rejections based on notions of importance in order to match page budgets and preserve prestige. This is because a gatekeeper model sometimes pre-defines its audience and disregards a series of important questions. For example, how can one wholly know the value of the material that is pre-excluded given that we exist within ideologies that are not always explicitly clear from our immanent positions? How can we know what *will* be of value in the future? What do we make of the exclusions and other spaces that, under the gatekeeper model, we cannot even know at present? In other words, the model of review, as it currently stands, can only be bound by temporal norms: the conditions of the present. This makes it very good at selecting work that will be highly valued in the current instance, but contributes towards a significant weakness in our system of pre-excluding material that might be of worth at a later date.

Secondly, in one (admittedly somewhat negative) reading of peer review, it is possible to see the filter-first method as a development entwined as much with economics as with quality. Historically, one of the key functions of the gatekeeper has been to reduce the quantity of permissible material; clearly, for economic reasons, not everything that is submitted can be published. This was not only an effort to avert what is now called 'information overload' and what are perceived as low standards, but also because each issue of a print journal or each book had a specified page budget. In the world of print and physical commodities, there is a need to restrict the quantity of output because there is a material cost for each page that is printed and distributed. This is, clearly, no longer directly the case (although every output has correlative labour that must be compensated and so has an economic scarcity) but persists through a culture that, as I have already noted, Gary Hall calls our 'paper-centrism'.[5] Under this traditional model of review and economics, the price of a subscription to a journal must cover not only the cost of the material that is printed and owned but the cost of the editorial labour that was invested in administrating the pieces that are rejected. As it is with icebergs, so it can be with editorial labour; it is easy to forget that, in a filter-first mode, the majority lies hidden below the surface.

Thirdly, single- or double-blind forms of peer review assume an honourable motivation for reviewers and provide few ways of holding readers publicly accountable for their decisions. Hypothetically and provocatively: is it right that a mere two academics, in most instances, although sometimes only one, have the private, unaccountable, final word on an article's or book's acceptability, particularly when there has been intense debate over the statistical significance of the number of reviewers, even in scientific disciplines?[6] For Early Career Researchers (ECRs) this private decision can be the difference between a lifetime of employment in academia and a lengthy period of retraining. Furthermore, reviewers and journals are often only evaluating a piece with one specific audience group in mind; if judging on the 'importance' of work, it is crucial to ask 'for whom?' Different journals and presses, of course, have different target audience constituents, but even these sub-fields may be fractured and subject to competing notions of 'importance' within a discipline. In other words, how can one accurately pre-judge, within one's own temporal, geographical and disciplinary immanence, what may be of worth to scholars free of these constraints? While it could be argued that the specificity of journal and publisher remits renders such considerations irrelevant, this lack of accountability and, as will be explored below, logic in the admissibility of papers is a problem that is exacerbated by the traditional double-blind system.

Fourthly, the term 'double-blind', as well as carrying ableist insinuations about the partially sighted in its language, can actually be a misnomer. Theoretically, the author should be unaware of the identity of his or her reviewers and vice versa, a mode used in most journal reviewing. The benefits of this are easy to articulate: it is designed to encourage an impartial assessment of the work, rather than the author. Furthermore, reviewers are supposed to be protected from professional repercussions in cases where, for instance, the author is a prominent figure in his or her field. Often, however, this is utopian, in the sense of 'naïve'. In many small fields where work may have been presented in early versions at conferences, where authors are known for adopting a specific stance, or simply through flawed metadata erasure and/or slips of self-citation, the identity of the author can be ascertained. While it is less often that slips occur the other way around, it is sometimes possible to guess the most likely reviewer of one's work simply by dint of his or her expertise and by the idiom of his or her returned report.

Furthermore, anonymity can be problematic. The lack of accountability of readers, as above, can lead to harsh, penalising reviews, rather than to feedback that, while rigorous, intends to work in community to elevate a work to a publishable standard. Additionally, there is also something strange about the perseverance of anonymity after publication. As noted earlier with respect to the role of citation, universities and academia function on genealogies of validation; that is, on hierarchies of prestige that trace the flow of academic 'capital' and authority through publications.[7] As explored in earlier chapters, journals and presses are primarily only as valuable as the genealogies that validate their work as high quality, through submission quantity/quality and rejection rate, underpinned by the labour of peer review. However, in the current way of working, what remains is a situation where, instead of the process of review being visible in order to validate the work, the quality of the review process must be inferred from the perceived post-publication quality of the research.

To extend this argument: there are only two ways, both flawed, in which the quality of the review can be ascertained under current practice. The first of these is through trust in nominal journal or publisher brand; the problems of prestige to which much of Chapter 2 was dedicated. The second way in which journal or publisher quality is crudely measured and the one that surely most affects scholars' perceptions lies in the duplication of labour when reading an article or book; a type of second review in which academics bring their own evaluative skills to bear on already published work. During this constant re-evaluation, the blame for poor quality is often put down either to the author or to the journal/press brand. This is interesting; what seems to have failed is actually the peer review, gatekeeping function, but this is not, in a mode of journal or publisher brand, the way in which it is perceived. While in some ways this is a fair appraisal, there could be modes through which the journal could signal the degree of delegation and trust that has been relied upon and to which I will now turn my attention.

PROPOSED EXPERIMENTS IN PEER REVIEW

The most obvious way in which these problems might begin to be addressed at the moment of transition to open access is to rethink anonymity in the review process, as has already happened in many scientific disciplines. However, it is worth saying upfront that each of the various combinations of the review anonymity matrix comes with its own problems and it may be the case that none is, in the end, as satisfactory as some forms of blind review, except, perhaps, for at least being more honest about the potential flaws. The first of these potential changes would be to remove the author's anonymity while maintaining the anonymity of the reviewers, which, although common practice in book reviewing, seems to add very little. In this scenario, reviewers could judge solely on the past reputation of the author, rather than the merit of the piece alone while remaining unaccountable for their actions. The only debatable benefit here might be that the reviewer can assess the competence of the author to write on the topic at hand, although this seems dangerous; surely the sole criterion for being able to write on a subject should be through the production of valuable work, not a track record in the area?

Conversely, one could take the opposite stance and remove reviewer anonymity (at various stages in the process, but primarily after the review and regardless of outcome) while retaining the author's veil. This mode brings absolute accountability upon reviewers while protecting the author from pre-judgements. It also gives a clear genealogy of validation and militates against corruption to some degree as any conflicts of interest would be immediately clear. The disadvantages of this approach are also obvious, though. Any system that brings unbalanced extreme accountability will result in a conservative situation of strict, normative appraisals, thereby potentially ruling out a whole body of useful work that may be barred by fearful reviewers. While some may see such strictness as an advantage – a tightening of review standards – given the historical parallel to page budgets and evolutions in social and technological filtering processes (see below), the argument that this is solely about quality may be less solid than might be thought. Finally, although the revelation of reviewer identity in some ways helps spot corruption (as any affiliation to the author would be obvious), the extreme burden to 'make the right call' could encourage reviewers to seek the author's identity. This tactic exposes reviewers and makes a thankless task perhaps even more risky.

What, then, about completely removing all anonymity from the process? There are some advantages in this case (as outlined above) but there still remains no counter-balance to the problems that could arise as a result of exposing reviewers. Conversely, reviewers would surely also be prone to appraise the author's identity in this case.

Evidently, in each of the cases where anonymity is removed, during the review process itself, there are problems that seem, to some degree, worse than the flaws in a double-blind setup. However, this solely applies when discussing a gatekeeper model in which a paper only sees the light of day so that the journal may be associated with the most exclusive papers in order to protect its brand. Other, more radical, experiments in the sciences have worked to change this. For instance, the review criteria of *PLOS ONE* – now an enormous journal that has published over 100,000 articles since its launch in 2006[8] – reads as follows:

Too often a journal's decision to publish a paper is dominated by what the Editor/s think is interesting and will gain greater readership – both of which are subjective judgments and lead to decisions which are frustrating and delay the publication of your work. PLOS ONE will rigorously peer-review your submissions and publish all papers that are judged to be technically sound. Judgments about the importance of any particular paper are then made after publication by the readership (who are the most qualified to determine what is of interest to them).[9]

This model implements a fix for what Clay Shirky has called 'filter failure'. In an influential 2008 keynote at the New York 'Web 2.0' expo, Shirky identified a new form of post-Gutenberg economics in which he proposed the overturn of the filter-first model (i.e. advanced selective peer review). This is because the cost of putting something on the internet, in raw form, can be extremely low. Once the material is online, Shirky intimates, it might then be possible to create social and technological filter mechanisms that glorify the good and bury the bad.[10]

At first, this standard of publishing all papers that are 'technically sound' appears to have no analogue for many disciplines in the humanities. This may prove to be correct. As a hypothesis, though, a technically sound paper in the humanities could: evince an argument; make reference to the appropriate range of extant scholarly literature; be written in good, standard prose of an appropriate register that demonstrates a coherence of form and content; show a good awareness of the field within which it was situated; pre-empt criticisms of its own methodology or argument; and be logically consistent. These are, indeed, the exact checks that one would expect an editor to make before sending a piece out for review. While this is just a cursory stab at a definition and not meant to be finalised, implementable criteria, many of the problems of the review system as it stands could certainly be addressed through the formation of explicit consensus as to what constitutes an acceptable barrier to entry in the humanities.

Secondly, though, the inversion that *PLOS ONE* effects could leave it open, as was the very first scientific journal, the *Philosophical Transactions of the Royal Society*, to John Hill's 1751 critique: the inclusion of 'trivial and downright foolish articles'.[11] In other words, by inverting the review methodology, *PLOS ONE* could expose itself to admitting rubbish. The difference from the contemporary situation, however, lies in the economic models and technological filters at our disposal. In 2014, sophisticated full-text and social search mechanisms exist that can bury unpopular material on the furthest pages of results but without removing such items from the economy altogether. This is not, therefore, a removal of selection, but rather a different way of filtering. There is still selection of material but, at a later date, it also becomes possible to see those manuscripts that were not initially favoured. The advantage of this, as with the arguments for open access more generally predicated upon an anti-elitism, is that we do not presume to know what will be important for all time. Instead, we replace such a system twofold with the ability to ensure that what is relevant now is found and valued while also allowing those papers in niche fields or in areas that have yet to gain any prominence to be found, if and only if the seeker desires. In this mode of post-publication review, everything would be assessed, but it would be done after the fact and the exclusion of material would not be a permanent pre-silencing, but rather a process of continuous community consensus. There are a couple of assumptions that underpin this mode. Such a system would rely upon the correct translation of the community will by software and also upon the continued participation of academics; voting systems for article/book prominence must be hardened against gaming and academics would need to be engaged enough to signal value. Of course, there is no guarantee that the peer-review criterion of 'technical soundness', however translated, would be free of abuse in itself, but this could be a step in the direction of militating against some of the perceived failings of blind review. Hurdles, nonetheless, remain, especially because there are also no current incentive systems within the academy that adequately value peer review, especially in the sense of an open, post-publication mode.

To close this section, however, it is worth once more referring to Kathleen Fitzpatrick, the most lucid thinker of these problems for the humanities to date. In her seminal book on the subject, *Planned Obsolescence*, Fitzpatrick systematically interrogates humanities' peer-review practices in the age of the digital and concludes that what is required is a mode that is less certain of the merits of 'the stability that we've long assumed in the print universe' and one that is more adaptive to generative possibilities.[12] What Fitzpatrick addresses, in essence, is the problem of the fundamentally anti-collaborative nature of humanities research in most cases. At present, review is not usually a community endeavour but rather an activity that expects to see a final artefact in which no traces of the construction remain visible, in much the same way as I have traced some of the problems of anonymity here. Experiments such as McKenzie Wark's collaboration with the Institute for the Future of the Book on his 2007 *Gamer Theory* suggest, however, that while an online collaborative model currently solicits sub-optimal levels of participation, there can be merit in the process.[13] Indeed, a draft of Fitzpatrick's own book was first published through the CommentPress system, open for comment and revision, before being released by New York University Press. Likewise, Palgrave Macmillan ran their own form of open peer-review experiment (although, for reasons of caution, they selected titles that had already been through a traditional process first).[14] From what is visible on the archive of that project, it seems there was, likewise, a low degree of takeup as it is very difficult to incentivise something without specifically targeted readers and deadlines.

Most importantly, though, I want to use my final words here to reiterate, but modify, my opening gambit. Fitzpatrick astutely notes that, in this case (and others), 'the system that needs the most careful engineering is less technical than it is social'.[15] Bearing this in mind, it is crucial never to succumb at any point to a techno-fetishism but always to consider whether technology facilitates desirable social changes.[16] The academy has built, over many years, systems for appraising the individual rather than acknowledging the way in which knowledge is collaboratively produced and, for the first time in many years, there may be an opening through which to address this. Open access does not require any changes to peer-review practices any more than the codex meant that readers had to abandon their palaeographic antecedents. There might, however, be practical ways in which a moment of technological change could enable us to see, with apologies for inverting Winston Churchill's well-known aphorism, that perhaps our review practices are not so wholly democratic, not so entirely objective, fair or community-based; that they may only be the best that have been tried, apart from all the others.

Overlay journals: editing as social curation

A further region in which new experiments are emerging in an online, open-access ecosystem is in the editorship space. This can be seen in the rise of a specific type of formation known as an 'overlay journal'. The term 'overlay journal', originally coined by the creator of arXiv Paul Ginsparg in 1996,[17] can be specified as:

An open-access journal that takes submissions from the preprints deposited at an archive (perhaps at the author's initiative), and subjects them to peer review. If approved (perhaps after revision), the postprints are also deposited in an archive with some indication that they have been approved. One such indication would be a new citation that included the name of the journal. Another could be a link from the journal's online table of contents. A third could be new metadata associated with the file. An overlay journal might be associated with just one archive or with many. Because an overlay journal doesn't have its own apparatus for disseminating accepted papers, but uses the pre-existing system of interoperable archives, it is a minimalist journal that only performs peer review.[18]

To unpack this a little, the basic idea of an overlay journal is that papers are deposited on preprint servers (i.e. the work is made publicly available in a repository prior to peer review) before an editor decides to arrange for peer review of a new manuscript. The manuscript is then reviewed in the traditional way, including the upload of a new postprint version (also to the repository) incorporating revisions if required. Finally, a version is uploaded that indicates that the paper was reviewed and accepted by an overlay journal and the journal itself adds the paper to the table of contents.

Overlay journals, though, have shifted in their definition and function. With the advent of the megajournal – a single, multi-disciplinary journal containing thousands of articles, sometimes operating on a post-review framework, exemplified by *PLOS ONE* – the concept of an 'overlay' has a different role. Instead of adding peer review outright, as the material is drawn from a megajournal with some form of quality control built-in, in this situation an overlay journal could bring the curational role of the editor to the fore in a fashion similar to an edited collection.

This concept of an overlay journal, which derives (as does much of the OA movement) from theoretical physics, is highly significant in specific scientific disciplines. Indeed, in physics, where the subject can change very rapidly, it is important for the field that information is available as quickly as possible and it is important for the scientists that their author precedence be recorded. Now, it could be argued that, in many humanities disciplines, these needs do not exist or are less significant. I would like to close this section with some observations to the contrary, noting that precedence, turnaround and, most importantly, the explicit positioning of the editor as the centre of prestige here, could have very real and positive effects for the humanities and that overlay journals are one such mechanism through which this could be rethought. Once more, I will note up-front that OA does not require any of these innovations; it merely provides a historical juncture where it may be possible to implement them should we so desire.

Speed of turnaround and establishing precedence

As noted above, peer review – in whatever form – remains an important part of the scholarly publishing apparatus. However, as anybody who has attempted to publish an article or book within a deadline for any kind of assessment framework knows, it can also be a lengthy process. Delays in peer review, except in the case of ineptitude, are hardly ever the fault of the publisher. Rather, it is that overworked academics take a long time to respond to requests, then go over the deadlines and require multiple follow-up emails to ensure timely review. In extreme cases this can take years in some disciplines. However, once this process is complete, some publishers then attempt to synchronise their hard-copy journals with their online efforts, thereby re-introducing the artificial page budgets that I pointed out earlier and causing further delays. In journals this can result in a total publication delay of years from submission and often even longer in edited collections.

While some have argued that this delay is acceptable in humanities fields, there are problems with such stances. First of all, one of the most common rebuffs to a need for speed is that 'nobody dies if work in the humanities isn't published in a timely fashion', supposedly in contrast to certain medical disciplines. I would contend, despite having touched upon such a claim myself earlier, that this may not always be the case. Is it not possible to conceive of humanities works that focus on immigration and hate crime – as just one example – in historical and/or cultural terms and that could change policy, thereby saving lives? If the answer is that the humanities can never have this kind of impact, then something is going very wrong given the ethical purchase that is often claimed for humanities work. To argue, conversely, that all humanities work must have this kind of impact is also nonsensical. Secondly, in many sub-fields, such as my own area of contemporary fiction, it is deeply frustrating to have to wait two or more years for work to emerge when there is a dearth of critical material. Certainly, much of the material surfaces at conferences, but these are frequently closed enclaves and it seems bizarre that, with the advent of the internet, our means of communicating is restricted to either flying across the globe – thereby contributing further to the crisis of global warming – or waiting two years, with a further delay of at least two years before any future work will be citing the first piece.

There is also a further reason why it could be desirable to speed up the process of scholarly communication – for we might consider it thus, rather than being termed exclusively 'publication' – and that is establishing precedence. While it may be nice to envisage a scenario where ideas were free and there was no need to attribute authorship because researchers worked in harmony rather than competition, this is the road not taken. Indeed, academia becomes ever more competitive and the imperative for novelty – no matter how contentious that word may prove – is given increasing credence. While there have been many excellent arguments for the 'slow humanities' and the value therein, even the scholar who worked slowly but published quickly would be at an advantage over those who abhor speed in both camps. In short, regardless of how long it takes to produce an article or volume of research, for which there may be extremely good reasons, there seems little rationale for slower publication after that point. A 'slow humanities' may lead to more rigorous work, greater care, higher levels of feedback and better research. How slow publication, after peer review, might also contribute to any of those aspects is less clear.

This, then, is my argument in favour of preprints, with overlay journals (or even overlay book publishers) as a potential mechanism on top of this: speed of turnaround can have important social and intra-disciplinary ramifications. Making work available for the purposes of communication, rather than purely for certification, could help to foster a better international research community. Likewise, establishing precedence will serve scholars better within a competitive framework. Although it may be desirable to eliminate such a competitive environment, it is worth noting that opposition to faster publication turnaround through preprints does not seem to serve that goal either.

Restoring the editor function

To move now to the second point raised by the concept of overlay journals, it has been my contention throughout this book that prestige, while a pragmatic and useful filtering mechanism for both assessment and readership purposes, comes with many potentially damaging side effects, both social and economic, when applied at the journal/publisher level. The idea of an overlay journal, in which pre-reviewed material is curated by trusted and respected editors into issues that they feel will be of value for their readers, puts editors at the centre of the system and displaces the purely service function of a publisher.

There are, of course, problems with such a setup. For instance, how is such material to be cited without diluting the version of record? As the provisions currently stand, unless material is strictly delineated from original publications in an issue, it might also fall foul of the recommendations of the Committee on Publication Ethics (COPE) on duplicate publication and/or self-plagiarism. One potential solution is to specify precisely on the cover sheet the original venue of publication while placing the 'curated' item in its own separate zone within an issue.

The other advantage of this type of curational setup worth mentioning is that it provides us with a further metric. Pieces that are re-curated by high-profile and respected editors are likely to be valuable themselves. This then gives a mark of prestige to an article based not upon the original publication venue or brand but rather upon the academic 'brand' of the curating editor. This is already the case, at least partially, with respect to special issues and to edited collections. In this way, the value of different publishers will become perspicacious free of a historical legacy of prestige. It may well be, in this new world, that old publishers really do know best. Indeed, the specific reach provided by presses with a history of targeted dissemination and trusted brand is fairly clear, even as critiques are mounted of those systems and companies. However, without a shift away from brand at the publisher level being conflated with academic quality, rather than with the quality of the production and other aspects with which publishers are concerned, it is impossible to evaluate the field fairly. It is, therefore, worth closing this volume with a remark that seems far from the concept of overlay journals that prompted this discussion but that is, actually, the logical conclusion engendered by such thinking.

It makes no sense for open-access advocates to be 'anti-publishers'. Publishers perform necessary labour that must be compensated and any new system of dissemination, such as open access, will require an entity to perform this labour, even if that labour takes a different form at different levels of compensation. One may be opposed to specific practices of extant publishers, or particular hypothetical publishing enterprises, but it is not possible to desire the functions of filtering, framing and amplification without there being a publisher, even if this publisher is also the author. Nor, I would suggest, should one be opposed to competition between publishers, which can foster benefits for researchers. What seems problematic, instead, are historical genealogies that make it difficult to modify the current system of publication, which was born in an era before the internet. It is also clear, however, from the investigations mounted throughout this book that the economics of scholarly communications are extremely complex and that there are some genuine risks for publishers who dip their toes into these waters, so caution is to be advised and the rhetoric of 'disruption' avoided. However, as the music industry has perhaps best shown us, the internet is not going away and to find new models sooner appears to be a more sensible approach.[19] As the opportunity cost of not venturing into these territories mounts, it becomes incumbent on researchers, librarians, publishers and funders not only to enter into dialogue about suitable transition strategies but also to ensure that our thinking is not bounded by what merely exists. Without a broader horizon of possibility for what our practice might look like, even in the face of pragmatic difficulties, we will not have lived up to McGann's call, the epigraph to this book, to mount a practical self-criticism.

Notes

1 Although the concept of 'open access' has existed since the 1980s: Open Access Directory, 'Early OA Journals' http://oad.simmons.edu/oadwiki/ Early_OA_journals [accessed 21 April 2014]. Note also that, in this volume, I refer to the lowering of price and permission barriers with the lower case 'open access' (abbreviated as 'OA') and to the movement dedicated to making this a reality with the title case 'Open Access movement'.

2 Malina Thiede, 'On Open Access Evangelism', *Serials Librarian*, 67 (2014), 21–6 (p. 23) http://dx.doi.org/10.1080/0361526X.2014.915608; Kathleen Fitzpatrick, 'On Open Access Publishing', *Society for Critical Exchange*, 2010 http://societyforcriticalexchange.org/blog/blog3.php/ 2010/01/15/on-open-access-publishing [accessed 3 May 2014].

3 Peter Suber, *Open Access*, Essential Knowledge Series (Cambridge, MA: MIT Press, 2012), p. 8 http://bit.ly/oa-book. The term 'barrier', of course, comes laden with a specific value judgement and perspective. The barrier is facing the reader and/or reuser in each of these cases. Other perspectives might contest this term and instead see a 'barrier' to their business model within open access itself, as I will cover shortly.

4 Peter Suber, 'Creating an Intellectual Commons through Open Access', in *Understanding Knowledge as a Commons: From Theory to Practice*, ed. Charlotte Hess and Elinor Ostrom (Cambridge, MA: MIT Press, 2007), pp. 171–208 http://dash.harvard.edu/handle/1/4552055.

5 Stevan Harnad, 'Overture: A Subversive Proposal', in *Scholarly Journals at the Crossroads: A Subversive Proposal for Electronic Publishing*, ed. Shumelda Okerson and James J. O'Donnell (Washington, DC: Association of Research Libraries, 1994), pp. 11–12 (p. 11) http://hdl.handle.net/2027/ mdp.39015034923758 [accessed 8 May 2014].

6 George Veletsianos and Royce Kimmons, 'Assumptions and Challenges of Open Scholarship', *International Review of Research in Open and Distance Learning*, 13 (2012), 166–89 (p. 167).

7 The specific forms of open access will be covered shortly.

8 Throughout this work I use the invariant US spelling of 'license'.

9 Neil Selwyn, 'Editorial: In Praise of Pessimism – the Need for Negativity in Educational Technology', *British Journal of Educational Technology*, 42 (2011), 713–18 (p. 167) http://dx.doi.org/10.1111/j.1467–8535.2011.01215.x.

10 Nigel Vincent and Chris Wickham, 'Debating Open Access: Introduction', in *Debating Open Access*, ed. Nigel Vincent and Chris Wickham (London: British Academy, 2013), pp. 4–12 (p. 6).

11 Cameron Neylon, '@d_mainwaring . . . I've Also Been Described as "Neo Liberal" (alongside Uber Capitalist) and "Marxist" in the Past Year Which Is Fun . . .', *@CameronNeylon*, 2013 https://twitter.com/CameronNeylon/status/410035300388597760 [accessed 18 January 2014].

12 Veletsianos and Kimmons, 'Assumptions and Challenges of Open Scholarship', p. 172.

13 Although it is interesting to note that the movement's origins were couched in terms of 'subversion'. Harnad, 'Overture: A Subversive Proposal'.

14 See the submission of Nature group House of Commons Science and Technology Committee, 'Supplementary Evidence from Nature Publishing Group', *UK Parliament*, 2004 www.publications.parliament.uk/pa/cm200304/cmselect/cmsctech/399/399we163.htm [accessed 7 January 2013].

15 Sara L. Rizor and Robert P. Holley, 'Open Access Goals Revisited: How Green and Gold Open Access Are Meeting (or Not) Their Original Goals', *Journal of Scholarly Publishing*, 45 (2014), 321–35 (p. 329) http://dx.doi.org/10.3138/jsp.45.4.01.

16 As with any manner of digital resource (for scholarship must now be thought of in such a way), it is never simply that there is one single way of funding its production, dissemination and continued existence. Although, as will be seen, dominant models are emerging, a relatively recent Ithaka report noted that 'There is no formulaic answer or single approach to achieving sustainability.' Kevin Guthrie, Rebecca Griffiths and Nancy Maron, *Sustainability and Revenue Models for Online Academic Resources* (New York: Ithaka, 2008) www.jisc.ac.uk/media/documents/events/2010/04/ithakasustainabilityreport.pdf [accessed 4 May 2014]; Suber, *Open Access*, p. 53.

17 Directory of Open Access Journals, 'Journals by Publication Charges' www.doaj.org/doaj?func=byPublicationFee&uiLanguage=en [accessed 20 January 2014].

18 Jisc, 'Publisher Copyright Policies & Self-Archiving', *SHERPA/RoMEO* www.sherpa.ac.uk/romeo/ [accessed 20 January 2014].

19 For a good summary of the economic challenges presented by issues of digital preservation, see Blue Ribbon Task Force on Sustainable Digital

Preservation and Access, *Sustaining the Digital Investment: Issues and Challenges of Economically Sustainable Digital Preservation*, December 2008 http://brtf.sdsc.edu/biblio/BRTF_Interim_Report.pdf [accessed 2 May 2014].

20 Kathleen Fitzpatrick, *Planned Obsolescence: Publishing, Technology, and the Future of the Academy* (New York University Press, 2011), p. 122.

21 The evidence for the claims that green open access does not result in subscription cancellations is discussed below in Chapter 2.

22 Peter Suber, 'Helping Scholars and Helping Libraries', *SPARC Open Access Newsletter*, 2005 http://dash.harvard.edu/handle/1/4552051 [accessed 1 May 2014].

23 For introductory material, see Robert Darnton, 'What Is the History of Books?', *Daedalus*, 1982, 65–83; Robert Darnton, *The Business of Enlightenment: A Publishing History of the Encyclopédie, 1775–1800* (Cambridge, MA: Harvard University Press, 1987); *The Book History Reader*, ed. David Finkelstein and Alistair McCleery, 2nd edn (Abingdon: Routledge, 2006); Michael Bhaskar, *The Content Machine: Towards a Theory of Publishing from the Printing Press to the Digital Network* (New York: Anthem Press, 2013).

24 John Willinsky, 'The Unacknowledged Convergence of Open Source, Open Access, and Open Science', *First Monday*, 10 (2005) http://firstmonday.org/ojs/index.php/fm/article/view/1265 [accessed 9 July 2014].

25 University of Illinois Library at Urbana-Champaign, 'The Cost of Journals', *University of Illinois Library at Urbana-Champaign*, 2009 www.library.illinois.edu/scholcomm/journalcosts.html [accessed 25 November 2013]; Björn Brembs, 'A Fistful of Dollars: Why Corporate Publishers Have No Place in Scholarly Communication', *bjoern. brembs.blog*, 2012 http://bjoern.brembs.net/2013/08/a-fistful-of-dollars-why-corporate-publishers-have-no-place-in-scholarly-communication/ [accessed 27 November 2013]; Martin Paul Eve, 'Tear It Down, Build It Up: The Research Output Team, or the Library-as-Publisher', *Insights: The UKSG Journal*, 25 (2012), 158–62 http://dx.doi.org/10.1629/2048-7754.25.2.158.

26 Association of Research Libraries, 'ARL Statistics 2009–2011', 2014 www.arl.org/storage/documents/expenditure-trends.pdf [accessed 1 July 2014].

27 Stephen Bosch and Kittie Henderson, 'Periodicals Price Survey 2013', *Library Journal*, 2013 http://lj.libraryjournal.com/2013/04/publishing/the-winds-of-change-periodicals-price-survey-2013/ [accessed 6 May 2013].

28 Ian Sample, 'Harvard University Says It Can't Afford Journal Publishers' Prices', *The Guardian*, 2012 www.theguardian.com/science/2012/apr/24/harvard-university-journal-publishers-prices [accessed 31 May 2014].

29 See, for contrasting views on the relative degree of dysfunction, Martin Paul Eve, 'Utopia Fading: Taxonomies, Freedom and Dissent in Open Access Publishing', *Journal of Victorian Culture*, 18 (2013), 536–42 (p. 538) http://dx.doi.org/10.1080/13555502.2013.865979; Peter Mandler, 'Open Access for the Humanities: Not for Funders, Scientists or Publishers', *Journal of Victorian Culture*, 18 (2013), 551–7 (p. 557) http://dx.doi.org/10.1080/13555502.2013.865981.

30 For more on markets and the problems of competition in scholarly publishing, see Peter Suber, 'Open Access, Markets, and Missions', *SPARC Open Access Newsletter*, 2010 http://dash.harvard.edu/handle/1/4322590 [accessed 21 April 2014].

31 Suber, *Open Access*, p. 39.

32 Theodore C. Bergstrom and Carl T. Bergstrom, 'Can "Author Pays" Journals Compete with "Reader Pays"?', *Nature: Web Focus*, 2004 www.nature.com/nature/focus/accessdebate/22.html [accessed 1 May 2014].

33 For more on the expansion of higher education, see Thomas Docherty, *For the University: Democracy and the Future of the Institution* (London: Bloomsbury Academic, 2011), p. 136.

34 This phenomenon is exemplified in the UK's Research Excellence Framework (REF) and its predecessors, the Research Assessment Exercises; Australia's Excellence in Research for Australia; and the brutal and infamous tenure-track appointment system in the States. Key Perspectives Ltd, *A Comparative Review of Research Assessment Regimes in Five Countries and the Role of Libraries in the Research Assessment Process: A Pilot Study Commissioned by OCLC Research* (Dublin, OH: OCLC, 2009) www.oclc.org/content/dam/research/publications/library/2009/2009-09.pdf?urlm=162926 [accessed 19 January 2014].

35 This was most recently flagged in a report by the MLA that noted that academics should 'challenge expectations for book publication as the primary criterion for conferral of tenure'. MLA Task Force on Doctoral Study in Modern Language and Literature, *Report of the MLA Task Force on Doctoral Study in Modern Language and Literature* (Modern Language Association of America, 2014), p. 15 www.mla.org/pdf/taskforcedocstudy2014.pdf [accessed 16 July 2014].

36 For more on the rhetoric of utility, see *Humanities in the Twenty-First Century beyond Utility and Markets.*, ed. Eleonora Belfiore and Anna Upchurch (London: Palgrave Macmillan, 2013).

37 See Suber, *Open Access*, p. 46.

38 The exception is when attackers deliberately overwhelm a server by over-taxing its resources in order to block others, a 'denial of service' (DoS) attack.

39 Veletsianos and Kimmons, 'Assumptions and Challenges of Open Scholarship', p. 173.

40 As is the license on this book.

41 *Fox Film Corp. v. Doyal* (Supreme Court of the United States, 1932), my emphasis.

42 Stallman also believes that the term 'intellectual property' is nonsensical and refuses to use it.

43 Richard Stallman, 'Misinterpreting Copyright: A Series of Errors', in *Free Software, Free Society: Selected Essays of Richard Stallman* (Boston, MA: Free Software Foundation, 2010), pp. 111–20 (p. 113).

44 See Suber, *Open Access*, pp. 9–15.

45 There are also a small proportion of academic authors who do make substantial money out of their book sales. These are by no means the majority, though.

46 Bhaskar, *The Content Machine*, pp. 103–36.

47 Suber, *Open Access*, p. 7.

48 See Suber, *Open Access*, pp. 86–90 for a note on why the term 'mandate' is problematic, though.

49 Peter Suber and others, 'Bethesda Statement on Open Access Publishing', 2003 http://dash.harvard.edu/handle/1/4725199 [accessed 4 May 2014].

50 Helen Small, *The Value of the Humanities* (Oxford University Press, 2013), p. 30.

51 Jerome McGann, *A New Republic of Letters* (Cambridge, MA: Harvard University Press, 2014), p. 4.

52 Just as John Thompson differentiates fields of publishing on the basis of Bourdieu's work, I think this kind of definition works here to separate the sciences from the humanities. They are different 'structured space[s] of social positions' each with their own 'resources and power with [their] own forms of competition and reward', with some overlaps. John B. Thompson, *Books in the Digital Age: The Transformation of Academic and Higher Education Publishing in Britain and the United States* (Cambridge: Polity Press, 2005), p. 6.

53 Hannah Arendt, *The Human Condition* (University of Chicago Press, 1998), p. 155; see also Elizabeth Markovits, *The Politics of Sincerity: Plato, Frank Speech, and Democratic Judgment* (University Park, PA: Penn State Press, 2008), p. 57, which first reminded me of this part of Arendt's thought.

54 See, of course, C. P. Snow, *The Two Cultures*, Canto edn (Cambridge University Press, 1993).

55 Commonly paraphrased and listed in several quotation books as: 'academic politics is the most vicious and bitter form of politics, because the stakes are so low'.

56 '[T]he production of research output fulfils two distinct but equally important functions – dissemination and certification.' Thompson, *Books in the Digital Age*, p. 82.

57 It is notable that much humanities work criticises the individualist nature of neoliberal late capital, particularly in literary and sociological fields, while also clinging to single-authored works as the benchmark of quality. Indeed, despite Foucault's well-known observations on the 'death of the author', Lisa Ede and Andrea Lunsford have picked up on the degree to which there are 'disjunctures or contradictions between theory and practice in the academy', noting that 'Literary scholars such as Jonathan Arac, James Sosnoski, Evan Watkins, Maria-Regina Kecht, and Paul Bove have pointed out the extent to which contemporary academic practices in English studies constitute, as Sosnoski puts it in the title of his 1995 study, "modern skeletons in postmodern closets".' Indeed, as they go on, 'In his *In the Wake of Theory*, Bove explores the relation of theory and practice in English studies, noting that too often scholars have assumed "that 'theory-work' somehow would or could stand outside the given realities of our time and place" (5). Similarly, in *Work Time* Watkins calls attention to the importance of acknowledging that "actual practices of resistance depend on specific working conditions" and to the danger of "the dream of transubstantiation" – the dream that work done in one location (the writing of an article or a book, for instance) will effect political change in another location (28–29).' Lisa Ede and Andrea A. Lunsford, 'Collaboration and Concepts of Authorship', *PMLA*, 116 (2001), 354–69 (p. 356).

58 Anthony Grafton, *The Footnote: A Curious History* (Cambridge, MA: Harvard University Press, 1999), p. 233.

59 Steve Hitchcock, 'The Effect of Open Access and Downloads ("hits") on Citation Impact: A Bibliography of Studies', 2013 http://opcit. eprints.org/oacitation-biblio.html [accessed 21 April 2014]; Alma Swan, 'The Open Access Citation Advantage: Studies and Results to Date', 2010 http://eprints.soton.ac.uk/268516/ [accessed 24 March 2014]. While advocates would claim that this 'citation benefit' is evidence of broader use of material, the counter-argument of sceptics is that such a focus could prioritise accessibility over relevance or appropriateness.

60 This is an extremely common misconception about OA. See Thiede, 'On Open Access Evangelism'.

61 Robin Osborne, 'Why Open Access Makes No Sense', in *Debating Open Access* (London: British Academy, 2013), pp. 96–105 (p. 104).

62 Osborne, 'Why Open Access Makes No Sense', p. 97.

63 Osborne, 'Why Open Access Makes No Sense', p. 104.

64 Osborne, 'Why Open Access Makes No Sense', pp. 104–5.

65 I am well aware, following Thomas Docherty, that the term 'taxpayer' is a hideously loaded phrase that summons to mind a miserly caricature who believes only in self-gain; one that probably doesn't actually exist.

Indeed, there is clear benefit to society in simply having educated people who have access to research. I nonetheless use the term because of its prevalence in political discourse.

66 For more on the strong and weak forms of the 'taxpayer' argument see Peter Suber, 'The Taxpayer Argument for Open Access', *SPARC Open Access Newsletter*, 2003 http://dash.harvard.edu/handle/1/4725013 [accessed 1 May 2014].

67 ROAPE Editors, 'Yes to Egalitarian "Open Access", No to "Pay to Publish": A *ROAPE* Position Statement on Open Access', *Review of African Political Economy*, 40 (2013), 177–8 (p. 177) http://dx.doi.org/ 10.1080/03056244.2013.797757.

68 Editors of History Journals, 'Written Evidence', *UK Parliament*, 2013 www.publications.parliament.uk/pa/cm201213/cmselect/cmbis/writev/ openaccess/m44.htm [accessed 24 January 2014].

69 Peter Mandler, 'Open Access: A Perspective from the Humanities', *Insights: The UKSG Journal*, 27 (2014), 166–70 (p. 168) http://dx.doi. org/10.1629/2048–7754.89.

70 Mandler, 'Open Access for the Humanities', p. 556.

71 See Andrew McGettigan, *The Great University Gamble: Money, Markets and the Future of Higher Education* (London: Pluto Press, 2013), pp. 79–95.

72 For more on this, see McGettigan, *The Great University Gamble*.

73 John Holmwood, 'Markets versus Dialogue: The Debate over Open Access Ignores Competing Philosophies of Openness', *Impact of Social Sciences*, 2013 http://blogs.lse.ac.uk/impactofsocialsciences/2013/10/21/ markets-versus-dialogue/ [accessed 24 January 2014].

74 I use the term 'left-spectrum' here for those OA advocates who wish to eradicate the profit motive from scholarly communications.

75 Bob Grant, 'Elsevier Abandons Anti-Open Access Bill', *The Scientist*, 2012 www.the-scientist.com/?articles.view/articleNo/31798/title/ Elsevier-Abandons-Anti-Open-Access-Bill/ [accessed 21 January 2014].

76 Alicia Wise, 'Evidence to House of Commons Select Committee Inquiry', in *Inquiry into Open Access: Fifth Report of Session 2013–2014*, by House of Commons Business, Innovation and Skills Committee (London: House of Commons, 2013), pp. Ev1–Ev11 (p. Ev3).

77 Robert L. Bradley, 'Oil Company Earnings: Reality over Rhetoric', *Forbes*, 2011 www.forbes.com/2011/05/10/oil-company-earnings.html [accessed 21 January 2014].

78 'The Cost of Knowledge' http://thecostofknowledge.com/ [accessed 21 January 2014].

79 Heather Morrison, 'Taylor & Francis Open Access Survey: Critique', *The Imaginary Journal of Poetic Economics*, 2013 http://poeticeconomics.

blogspot.co.uk/2013/03/taylor-francis-open-access-survey.html [accessed 21 January 2014]; Taylor & Francis, 'Open Access Survey', 2013 www.tandfonline.com/page/openaccess/opensurvey [accessed 21 January 2014].

80 Informa, *Annual Report*, 2012, p. 1 www.informa.com/Documents/ Investor%20Relations/Corporate%20Governance/Informa%20Annual %20Report%202012-web.pdf [accessed 22 January 2014].

81 Informa, *Annual Report*, p. 9.

82 Informa, *Annual Report*, p. 1.

83 While Peter Mandler claims that the situation in the humanities is one wherein journals are less frequently owned by large commercial entities, I am unaware of any actual surveys that measure this and the prevalence of mega-presses seems to contradict such a view. Mandler, 'Open Access: A Perspective from the Humanities'.

84 For more on mergers in the book world, see Thompson, *Books in the Digital Age*, pp. 54–64.

85 Bloomsbury Group, *Annual Report*, 2012, p. 7 www.bloomsbury-ir.co. uk/annual_reports/2012/pdf/2012ar.pdf [accessed 22 January 2014].

86 Jane Park, 'An Interview with Frances Pinter of Bloomsbury Academic', 2008 http://creativecommons.org/weblog/entry/10100 [accessed 22 January 2014].

87 Friedman's doctrine that shareholder profit is the only social factor for which businesses should be held responsible is widely disseminated and equally widely criticised. See Milton Friedman, 'The Social Responsibility of Business Is to Increase Its Profits', *The New York Times Magazine*, 13 September 1970, pp. 32–3, 122–4.

88 Thompson, *Books in the Digital Age*, p. 45.

89 Thompson, *Books in the Digital Age*, p. 167.

90 PLOS, 'Written Evidence to House of Commons Select Committee Inquiry', in *Inquiry into Open Access: Fifth Report of Session 2013–2014*, by House of Commons Business, Innovation and Skills Committee (London: House of Commons, 2013), pp. Ev80–Ev87 (p. 83).

91 For more on symbolic capital in book publishing, see Thompson, *Books in the Digital Age*, pp. 32–4.

92 Bergstrom and Bergstrom, 'Can "author pays" journals compete with "reader pays"?'

93 Linguistic Society of America, 'Journal Sponsorship', *Semantics and Pragmatics*, 2014 http://semprag.org/about/journalSponsorship [accessed 22 January 2014].

94 Caroline Sutton, Peter Suber and Amanda Page, 'Societies and Open Access Research', *Harvard Open Access Project*, 2014 bit.ly/hoap-soar [accessed 26 June 2014].

95 Amherst College Press, 'Frequently Asked Questions', 2014 www.amherst.edu/library/press/faq [accessed 22 January 2014].

96 Adeline Koh, 'Is Open Access a Moral or a Business Issue? A Conversation with The Pennsylvania State University Press', *Chronicle of Higher Education*, 2012 http://chronicle.com/blogs/profhacker/is-open-access-a-moral-or-a-business-issue-a-conversation-with-the-pennsylvania-state-university-press/41267 [accessed 22 January 2014].

97 Eelco Ferwerda, Ronald Snijder and Janneke Adema, 'OAPEN-NL: A Project Exploring Open Access Monograph Publishing in the Netherlands Final Report', 2013, p. 17 www.oapen.nl/images/attachments/article/58/OAPEN-NL-final-report.pdf [accessed 24 March 2014].

98 Rod Cookson, 'Learned Societies More Confident about Future – and a "new Pragmatism" on Open Access', ALPSP: at the heart of scholarly publishing, 2014 http://blog.alpsp.org/2014/08/learned-societies-more-confident-about.html [accessed 12 August 2014].

99 Learned societies are organisations that promote academic disciplines and professions, often awarding grants and subsidising various activities through their membership base.

100 Agnès Henri, 'EDP Open Survey Reveals Learned Society Attitudes towards Open Access', 2014 www.edp-open.org/index.php?option=com_content&view=article&id=273&lang=en_GB.utf8%2C+en_GB.UT [accessed 28 May 2014].

101 Mary Waltham, *Learned Society Open Access Business Models* (Jisc, June 2005) www.jisc.ac.uk/whatwedo/topics/opentechnologies/openaccess/reports/learnedsociety.aspx [accessed 22 January 2014].

102 Paul Jump, 'Open Access Will Cause Problems for Learned Societies' Journals, Accepts Finch', *Times Higher Education*, 15 January 2013 www.timeshighereducation.co.uk/open-access-will-cause-problems-for-learned-societies-journals-accepts-finch/422395.article [accessed 22 January 2014].

103 'Steering Group' http://oapen-uk.jiscebooks.org/overview/steering-group/ [accessed 22 January 2014].

104 Martyn Wade, 'Thriving or Surviving? National Libraries in the Future' (presented at the RLUK Conference, Edinburgh, 2010) www.rluk.ac.uk/files/Martyn%20Wade%20-%202010%20Conf.pdf; Frances Pinter and Christopher Kenneally, 'Publishing Pioneer Seeks Knowledge Unlatched', 2013 http://beyondthebookcast.com/transcripts/publishing-pioneer-seeks-knowledge-unlatched/; Nancy Kranich, 'From Collecting to Connecting: Engaging the Academic Community' (presented at The Library in the Digital Age: Communities, Collections, Opportunities, Temple University, 2013).

105 See also John Bohannon's 'sting' and the retorts from its critics: John Bohannon, 'Who's Afraid of Peer Review?', *Science*, 342 (2013), 60–5 http://dx.doi.org/10.1126/science.342.6154.60; Martin Paul Eve, 'Flawed Sting Operation Singles out Open Access Journals', *The Conversation*, 2013 http://theconversation.com/flawed-sting-operation-singles-out-open-access-journals-18846 [accessed 23 January 2014]; Amy Buckland and others, 'On the Mark? Responses to a Sting', *Journal of Librarianship and Scholarly Communication*, 2 (2013) http://dx.doi.org/10.7710/2162–3309.1116.

106 Jeffrey Beall, 'The Open-Access Movement Is Not Really about Open Access', *tripleC: Communication, Capitalism & Critique. Open Access Journal for a Global Sustainable Information Society*, 11 (2013), 589–97 (p. 589); Joseph Esposito, 'Parting Company with Jeffrey Beall', *The Scholarly Kitchen*, 2013 http://scholarlykitchen.sspnet.org/2013/12/16/parting-company-with-jeffrey-beall/ [accessed 23 January 2014].

107 Wayne Bivens-Tatum, 'Reactionary Rhetoric against Open Access Publishing', *tripleC: Communication, Capitalism & Critique. Open Access Journal for a Global Sustainable Information Society*, 12 (2014), 441–6 (pp. 442–3).

2 DIGITAL ECONOMICS

1 Richard Smith, 'The Irrationality of the REF', *BMJ*, 2013 http://blogs.bmj.com/bmj/2013/05/07/richard-smith-the-irrationality-of-the-ref/ [accessed 11 February 2014]; Lindsay Waters, 'Rescue Tenure from the Tyranny of the Monograph', *Chronicle of Higher Education*, 20 April 2001 https://chronicle.com/article/Rescue-Tenure-From-the-Tyranny/9623 [accessed 18 May 2014].

2 Michael Jensen, 'Authority 3.0: Friend or Foe to Scholars?', *Journal of Scholarly Publishing*, 39 (2007), 297–307 http://dx.doi.org/10.1353/scp.2007.0027.

3 Pierre Bourdieu, *Outline of a Theory of Practice* (Cambridge University Press, 1977), p. 180.

4 Bourdieu, *Outline of a Theory of Practice,* p. 195.

5 Longina Jakubowska, *Patrons of History: Nobility, Capital and Political Transitions in Poland,* Google Books (Aldershot: Ashgate, 2012), no page.

6 Peter Suber, 'Thinking about Prestige, Quality, and Open Access', 2008 http://dash.harvard.edu/handle/1/4322577 [accessed 21 April 2014].

7 Peter Suber, 'Open Access and Quality', *SPARC Open Access Newsletter*, 2006 http://dash.harvard.edu/handle/1/4552042 [accessed 1 May 2014].

8 The most recent of which is Higher Education Funding Council for England, 'Independent Review of the Role of Metrics in Research Assessment', 2014 www.hefce.ac.uk/whatwedo/rsrch/howfundr/metrics/ [accessed 21 June 2014].

9 It is, of course, possible to put technological counter-measures in place to combat this type of technological cheating. However, this then becomes a game of catch-up, much like search engine optimisation practices, wherein those who are behaving badly ('black hats') are simply trying to stay one step ahead of the counter-measures.

10 See Fitzpatrick, *Planned Obsolescence*, pp. 27–30.

11 See Bhaskar, *The Content Machine*, pp. 131–4 for more on amplification in publishing.

12 See Osborne, 'Why Open Access Makes No Sense'.

13 Samuel Weber, *Institution and Interpretation*, Cultural Memory in the Present, expanded edn (Stanford, CA: Stanford University Press, 2001), p. 27.

14 Weber, *Institution and Interpretation*, pp. 32–3.

15 Weber, *Institution and Interpretation*, pp. 132–52.

16 Bill Readings, *The University in Ruins* (Cambridge, MA: Harvard University Press, 1996), pp. 2–3.

17 I am wary of the term 'neoliberalism' as an overly broad and empty term, but I here define it as in part entailing an at least nominal insistence on transparency, accountability and openness, in order to support the belief that all aspects of society are best handled on a for-profit basis through competition, for which a fixation on quantification and measurement will produce the ultimate rational market actor.

18 Docherty, *For the University*, p. 134.

19 Readings, *The University in Ruins*, p. x, emphasis mine; Keith Hoeller, 'The Academic Labor System of Faculty Apartheid', in *Equality for Contingent Faculty: Overcoming the Two-Tier System*, ed. Keith Hoeller (Nashville: Vanderbilt University Press, 2014), pp. 116–55 (p. 117).

20 UCU, 'Over Half of Universities and Colleges Use Lecturers on Zero-Hour Contracts', 2013 www.ucu.org.uk/6749 [accessed 6 September 2013].

21 Thompson, *Books in the Digital Age*, p. 113. Furthermore, covering the cost of fairly subsidising academic labour for the production of a book would cause the price of books to skyrocket, thereby further impeding access.

22 Suber, *Open Access*, p. 10.

23 'Submit to SAGE Open today to lock in the $99 APC before the price goes up!'

24 Stuart Lawson, 'APC Pricing', 2014 http://dx.doi.org/10.6084/m9.figshare.1056280 [accessed 13 June 2014]; see also David J. Solomon and Bo-Christer Björk, 'A Study of Open Access Journals Using Article Processing Charges', *Journal of the American Society for Information Science and Technology*, 63 (2012), 1485–95 http://dx.doi.org/10.1002/asi.22673 for an older study.

25 Palgrave Macmillan, 'Frequently Asked Questions', *Palgrave Open*, 2013 www.palgrave.com/open/faq.asp#section2 [accessed 21 December 2013].

26 For just one example, see Meera Sabaratnam and Paul Kirby, 'Open Access: HEFCE, REF2020 and the Threat to Academic Freedom', *The Disorder of Things*, 2012 http://thedisorderofthings.com/2012/12/04/open-access-hefce-ref2020-and-the-threat-to-academic-freedom/ [accessed 27 November 2013].

27 Mandler, 'Open Access: A Perspective from the Humanities'; Sabaratnam and Kirby, 'Open Access: HEFCE, REF2020 and the Threat to Academic Freedom'; Suber, *Open Access*, p. 79.

28 American Association of University Professors, 'Statement of Principles on Academic Freedom and Tenure', 1940 www.aaup.org/report/1940-statement-principles-academic-freedom-and-tenure [accessed 13 February 2014].

29 Benjamin Ginsberg, *The Fall of the Faculty: The Rise of the All-Administrative University and Why It Matters* (Oxford University Press, 2013), pp. 131–2.

30 'Education Reform Act 1988', para. 202 www.legislation.gov.uk/ukpga/1988/40/part/IV/crossheading/academic-tenure [accessed 9 July 2014].

31 As a disclaimer: I am a Co-Director of the Open Library of Humanities.

32 Beall, 'The Open-Access Movement is Not Really about Open Access'. See above, p. 57.

33 Joss Winn, 'Helplessness', *Joss Winn*, 2013 http://josswinn.org/2013/07/helplessness/ [accessed 29 January 2014].

34 Winn, 'Helplessness'.

35 I am a little wary of the glib way in which the word 'capitalism' is sometimes used in debates such as this, an aspect that I owe to a conversation with Joe Brooker. Indeed, beyond a return to nomadic bartering communities, I am unsure whether the term carries a huge degree of imaginative traction and, instead, feel that enterprises that exist within capital tend simply towards more or less egalitarian premises. That said, because research work in the humanities is so often theorised as an activity somehow separate from economic activity, it is nonetheless useful to deploy this thinking.

36 Amy E. Wendling, *Karl Marx on Technology and Alienation* (Basingstoke: Palgrave Macmillan, 2009), p. 52.

37 Richard Hall, 'On the Context and Use-Value of Academic Labour', *Richard Hall's Space*, 2014 www.richard-hall.org/2014/02/02/on-the-context-and-use-value-of-academic-labour/ [accessed 4 February 2014].

38 Nigel Tubbs, 'The Importance of Being Useless', *Times Higher Education*, 11 October 2012 www.timeshighereducation.co.uk/features/the-importance-of-being-useless/421413.article [accessed 4 February 2014]; Michael Bérubé, 'The Futility of the Humanities', in *Humanities in the Twenty-First Century: Beyond Utility and Markets*, ed. Eleonora

Belfiore and Anna Upchurch (Basingstoke: Palgrave Macmillan, 2013), pp. 66–76.

39 As Benjamin Ginsberg points out, there are ways in which all forms of research income grants are desired for universities as sites of direct value extraction from research work, even in the humanities. Ginsberg, *The Fall of the Faculty*, pp. 180–97.

40 This is also why Robin Osborne is mistaken: the liberation of research material is not impossible because teaching is bought, but rather it is ideal because teaching is a profit-making activity that can extract surplus value from research.

41 Raymond Hogler and Michael A. Gross, 'Journal Rankings and Academic Research: Two Discourses about the Quality of Faculty Work', *Management Communication Quarterly*, 23 (2009), 107–26 (p. 111) http://dx.doi.org/10.1177/0893318909335419.

42 Hogler and Gross, 'Journal Rankings and Academic Research', pp. 119–21.

43 For more see Thompson, *Books in the Digital Age*, p. 21.

44 Joss Winn, 'Is an Open Access Journal Article a Commodity?', *Joss Winn*, 2014 http://josswinn.org/2014/02/is-an-open-access-journal-article-a-commodity/ [accessed 15 February 2014].

45 For the explanation of the BBB definition, see above, p. 21.

46 Suber, *Open Access*, pp. 20–7.

47 Suber, *Open Access*, pp. 149–61.

48 Chris Beckett and Simon Inger, *Self-Archiving and Journal Subscriptions: Co-Existence or Competition?* (Publishing Research Consortium, 2006) http://eprints.ecs.soton.ac.uk/13179 [accessed 9 July 2014]; Stevan Harnad, 'Self-Archiving and Journal Subscriptions: Critique of PRC Study' http://users.ecs.soton.ac.uk/harnad/Hypermail/Amsci/5792.html [accessed 9 July 2014].

49 Association of Learned and Professional Society Publishers, 'ALPSP Survey of Librarians on Factors in Journal Cancellation', 2006.

50 Suber, *Open Access*, p. 158.

51 Jingfeng Xia and others, 'A Review of Open Access Self-Archiving Mandate Policies', *Portal: Libraries and the Academy*, 12 (2012), 85–102 (p. 98).

52 House of Commons Business, Innovation and Skills Committee, 'Open Access: Fifth Report of Session 2013–14', *UK Parliament*, 2013, p. 18 www.publications.parliament.uk/pa/cm201314/cmselect/cmbis/99/99.pdf [accessed 9 July 2014].

53 House of Commons Business, Innovation and Skills Committee, 'Open Access: Fifth Report of Session 2013–14', p. 18.

54 Rebecca Darley, Daniel Reynolds and Chris Wickham, *Open Access Journals in Humanities and Social Science* (London: British Academy, 2014).

55 House of Commons Business, Innovation and Skills Committee, 'Open Access: Fifth Report of Session 2013–14', p. 18.

56 Taylor & Francis, 'Information for Funders & Institutions', 2014 www.tandfonline.com/page/openaccess/funders [accessed 11 May 2014].

57 I am aware of institutions with budgets of £4,000 per year, which leads to approximately three articles on the levels outlined above.

58 Stevan Harnad, 'Pre Green-OA Fool's Gold vs. Post Green-OA Fair Gold', *Open Access Archivangelism*, 2013 http://openaccess.eprints.org/index.php?/archives/1007-Pre-Green-OA-Fools-Gold-vs.-Post-Green-OA-Fair-Gold.html [accessed 17 May 2014].

59 Consider as an illustrative example of this the evidence of Nature to the House of Commons select committee in 2004, justifying a £30,000 APC purely on the basis of their current practice: 'The £30,000 figure was arrived at simply by dividing the annual income of Nature (£30 million) by the number of research papers published (1,000).' House of Commons Science and Technology Committee, 'Supplementary Evidence from Nature Publishing Group'.

60 Alice Meadows and David Sweeney, 'Meet David Sweeney of HEFCE – the Higher Education Funding Council of the UK', *Wiley Exchanges*, 2014 http://exchanges.wiley.com/blog/2014/05/06/meet-david-sweeney-of-hefce-the-higher-education-funding-council-of-the-uk/ [accessed 17 May 2014].

61 Once more, consider Nature group's pricing: a print-only (and, therefore, single concurrent-user) institutional subscription to *Nature* in North America comes to $4,958.00. Nature, 'Pricing', 2014 www.nature.com/nmat/pricing/index.html#site_licence [accessed 17 May 2014]. It is also worth noting the extremely high costs paid by some institutions to Elsevier with huge variance even within the top tier of UK universities. Imperial College, for example, currently spends £1,340,213 annually. Tim Gowers, 'Elsevier Journals – Some Facts', *Gowers's Weblog*, 2014 http://gowers.wordpress.com/2014/04/24/elsevier-journals-some-facts/ [accessed 17 May 2014].

62 For a parallel in the sphere of online music distribution, see Aleksandr Dolgin, *The Economics of Symbolic Exchange* (Berlin: Springer, 2009), pp. 32–40.

63 Thompson, *Books in the Digital Age*, p. 24.

64 Note well that there are no current mandates that insist exclusively on gold open access. The Wellcome Trust's mandate, however, was fulfilled through the gold route in 85% of the compliant cases in 2012 according to Nature. Richard Poynder, 'Open Access Mandates: Ensuring Compliance', *Open and Shut?*, 2012 http://poynder.blogspot.co.uk/2012/05/open-access-mandates-ensuring.html [accessed 17 May 2014].

65 Joseph S. Nye, *Bound to Lead: The Changing Nature of American Power* (New York: Basic Books, 1991). The benefit of this approach for centre-right, market-orientated governments is that they do not have to set caps on APCs but can rather let the market 'guide itself'.

66 P. Ginsparg, 'Winners and Losers in the Global Research Village' (presented at the Electronic Publishing in Science, UNESCO HQ, Paris, 1996) www.cs.cornell.edu/~ginsparg/physics/blurb/pg96unesco. html [accessed 10 April 2014].

67 arXiv, 'FAQ', 2013 http://arxiv.org/help/support/faq [accessed 22 December 2013].

68 SCOAP³, 'Frequently Asked Questions and Answers', *SPARC*, 2014 www.sparc.arl.org/resources/papers-guides/scoap3-faq [accessed 20 May 2014].

69 Rebecca Kennison and Lisa Norberg, *A Scalable and Sustainable Approach to Open Access Publishing and Archiving for Humanities and Social Sciences* (K|N Consultants, 11 April 2014), p. 3 http://knconsultants.org/wp-content/uploads/2014/01/OA_Proposal_White_Paper_Final.pdf [accessed 5 May 2014].

70 In my view, such logic is societally disastrous if applied unilaterally as it negates the potential for any kind of communally underwritten social security.

71 Rebecca Bliege Bird and Eric Alden Smith, 'Signaling Theory, Strategic Interaction, and Symbolic Capital 1', *Current Anthropology*, 46 (2005), 221–48 (p. 221).

72 arXiv, 'FAQ'.

73 arXiv, 'FAQ'.

74 Science Europe, 'Principles for the Transition to Open Access to Research Publications', 2013 www.scienceeurope.org/uploads/PublicDocumentsAndSpeeches/SE_OA_Pos_Statement.pdf [accessed 17 May 2014].

75 Global Research Council, 'About Us', 2014 www.globalresearchcouncil. org/about-us [accessed 17 May 2014].

76 Global Research Council, 'Action Plan towards Open Access to Publications', 2013 www.dfg.de/download/pdf/dfg_magazin/internationales/130528_grc_annual_meeting/grc_action_plan_open_access.pdf [accessed 17 May 2014].

77 Stevan Harnad, 'ROARMAP' http://roarmap.eprints.org/ [accessed 25 July 2014].

78 Richard Van Noorden, 'Chinese Agencies Announce Open-Access Policies', *Nature*, 2014 http://dx.doi.org/10.1038/nature.2014.15255.

79 Dehua Hu, Aijing Luo and Haixia Liu, 'Open Access in China and Its Effect on Academic Libraries', *Journal of Academic Librarianship*, 39 (2013), 110–12 (p. 110) http://dx.doi.org/10.1016/j.acalib.2012.11.009.

80 Hu, Luo and Liu, 'Open Access in China and Its Effect on Academic Libraries', p. III.

81 Leila Fernandez, 'Open Access Initiatives in India – an Evaluation', *Partnership: The Canadian Journal of Library and Information Practice and Research*, 1 (2006) https://journal.lib.uoguelph.ca/index.php/perj/article/view/110 [accessed 19 May 2014].

82 Bhaskar Mukherjee and Bidyut Kumar Mal, 'India's Efforts in Open Access Publishing', *Library Philosophy and Practice*, 2012 http://unllib.unl.edu/LPP/mukherjee-mal.htm [accessed 19 May 2014].

83 Thomson Reuters, 'SciELO Citation Index', 2014 http://thomsonreuters.com/scielo-citation-index/ [accessed 19 May 2014].

84 Enrique Peña Nieto, 'Open Access in the Knowledge Society', 2014 http://en.presidencia.gob.mx/open-access-in-the-knowledge-society/ [accessed 25 May 2014]; Luis Reyes-Galindo, 'Mexican Policy-Making on OA: A Bitter-Tweet State of Affairs', *Sociology of science and Open Access* http://blogs.cardiff.ac.uk/luisreyes/121/ [accessed 3 June 2014].

85 Creative Commons Aotearoa New Zealand, 'Open Access to Research', 2014 http://creativecommons.org.nz/research/ [accessed 5 August 2014].

86 Henrik Bendix, 'Regeringen: Alle Danske Forskningsartikler Skal Være Frit Tilgængelige', *Ingeniøren*, 2014 http://ing.dk/artikel/regeringen-alle-danske-forskningsartikler-skal-vaere-frit-tilgaengelige-169271 [accessed 26 June 2014]; Danish Ministry of Higher Education and Science, 'Denmark 's National Strategy for Open Access', 2014 http://ufm.dk/en/research-and-innovation/cooperation-between-research-and-innovation/open-science/open-access-to-research-publications/engelsk-version-national-strategy-for-open-access.pdf [accessed 24 July 2014].

87 Lisa Spiro, '"This Is Why We Fight": Defining the Values of the Digital Humanities', in *Debates in the Digital Humanities*, ed. Matthew K. Gold (Minneapolis: University of Minnesota Press, 2012), pp. 16–35 (p. 24).

88 Higher Education Funding Council for England, 'Policy for Open Access in the Post-2014 Research Excellence Framework', 2014, paras. 17–19 www.hefce.ac.uk/media/hefce/content/pubs/2014/201407/HEFCE2014_07.pdf.

89 Higher Education Funding Council for England, 'Policy for Open Access in the Post-2014 Research Excellence Framework', para. 36.

90 Higher Education Funding Council for England, 'Policy for Open Access in the Post-2014 Research Excellence Framework', para. 30.

91 Research Councils UK, 'RCUK Policy on Open Access and Supporting Guidance', 2013, p. 6 www.rcuk.ac.uk/RCUK-prod/assets/documents/documents/RCUKOpenAccessPolicy.pdf [accessed 10 July 2014].

92 Research Councils UK, 'RCUK Policy on Open Access and Supporting Guidance', p. 2.

3 OPEN LICENSING

1 A reminder that I here use the invariant US spelling of 'license' throughout.

2 United States of America, 'U.S. Constitution: Article 1 Section 8', *The U.S. Constitution Online*, 2010 www.usconstitution.net/xconst_A1Sec8. html?ModPagespeed=noscript [accessed 21 February 2014].

3 Charles W. Bailey Jr, 'Strong Copyright + DRM + Weak Net Neutrality = Digital Dystopia?', *Information Technology and Libraries*, 25 (2013), 116–27, 139 (p. 117) http://dx.doi.org/10.6017/ital.v25i3.3344.

4 Intellectual Property Office of the United Kingdom, 'Copyright: Essential Reading', 2011, p. 2 https://ipo.gov.uk/c-essential.pdf [accessed 21 February 2014].

5 Bailey Jr, 'Strong Copyright + DRM + Weak Net Neutrality = Digital Dystopia?', p. 117.

6 See Lee Edwards and others, '"Isn't It Just a Way to Protect Walt Disney's Rights?": Media User Perspectives on Copyright', *New Media & Society*, 2013, http://dx.doi.org/10.1177/1461444813511402.

7 See, for instance, Palgrave Macmillan Journals, 'Copyright FAQs', 2014 www.palgrave-journals.com/pal/authors/copyright_faqs.html [accessed 22 February 2014].

8 Creative Commons, 'Case Law', 2013 http://wiki.creativecommons.org/ Case_Law [accessed 6 March 2014].

9 Ellen Collins, Caren Milloy and Graham Stone, *Guide to Creative Commons for Humanities and Social Science Monograph Authors*, ed. James Baker, Martin Paul Eve and Ernesto Priego (London: Jisc Collections, 2013) http://eprints.hud.ac.uk/17828 [accessed 23 February 2014].

10 Creative Commons, 'About the Licenses', 2014 https://creativecommons.org/licenses/ [accessed 23 February 2014].

11 Creative Commons, 'About the Licenses'.

12 Collins, Milloy and Stone, *Guide to Creative Commons*. Licensed under a CC BY license. I have removed legal and license code links and removed some portions of description text, including reference to CC0.

13 Collins, Milloy and Stone, *Guide to Creative Commons*, p. 10.

14 Richard Stallman, 'Why Open Source Misses the Point of Free Software', in *Free Software, Free Society: Selected Essays of Richard Stallman* (Boston, MA: Free Software Foundation, 2010), pp. 83–8.

15 Paul Duguid, 'Material Matters: The Past and Futorology of the Book', in *The Future of the Book*, ed. Geoffrey Nunberg (Berkeley: University of California Press, 1996), pp. 63–101 (p. 74).

16 The Ad Hoc Committee on Fair Use and Academic Freedom, *Clipping Our Own Wings: Copyright and Creativity in Communication Research* (The Media and Communication Policy Task Force, 7 May 2010) www. cmsimpact.org/fair-use/related-materials/documents/clipping-our-own-

wings-copyright-and-creativity-communication-r [accessed 1 May 2014].

17 Intellectual Property Office of the United Kingdom, 'Permitted Uses of Copyright Works: Teaching in Educational Establishments', 2006 https://ipo.gov.uk/types/copy/c-other/c-exception/c-exception-teaching. htm [accessed 4 March 2014].

18 It is extremely difficult to work out exactly how much the CLA license costs each institution in the UK, but the yearly charge that would allow a researcher to photocopy one chapter of a recent book for distribution to students is £A/B × C × 38.50 (where 'A' is the Licensee's income from UK industry, commerce and public corporations; 'B' is the total income of the Licensee; and 'C' is the full-time equivalent number of academic staff). Copyright Licensing Agency, 'Comprehensive HE Licence 1 August 2010', 2010 www.cla.co.uk/data/pdfs/he/uuk_basic_he_licence_specimen.pdf [accessed 23 April 2014]. The variance in cost between institutions is large and depends heavily upon the corporate revenue ratio. An estimated figure of £10,000 per year, however, is not unrealistic. Taking, for instance, the figures for Durham University in 2012/2013: A in this case is 57,334,000 (3,783,000 ('UK industries') + 35,789,000 (residences and catering), 6,487,000 ('other services rendered'), 11,275,000 ('other income')). B is 283,379,000. C is approximately 1,250 from UK HESA statistics. This yields a cost of £9,737 per year (57,334,000/283,379,000 × 1,250 × 38.50). Durham University, 'Annual Accounts 2013', 2014, pp. 24, 29, 30 www.dur.ac.uk/resources/treasurer/financial_statements/Accounts13.pdf [accessed 4 July 2014]. Although a drop in the ocean for an individual institution's budget, open licensing would circumvent the restrictions on quantity imposed here and also avoid the costs because anybody would have permission to redistribute the work.

19 Suber, *Open Access*, pp. 73–4.

20 See, for instance, Theresa Lillis, 'Economies of Signs in Writing for Academic Publication: The Case of English Medium "National" Journals', *Journal of Advanced Composition*, 32 (2012), 695–722.

21 John Willinsky, *The Access Principle: The Case for Open Access to Research and Scholarship*, Digital Libraries and Electronic Publishing (Cambridge, MA: MIT Press, 2006), pp. 155–71.

22 Fitzpatrick, *Planned Obsolescence*, p. 82.

23 Christopher M. Kelty, *Two Bits: The Cultural Significance of Free Software* (Durham, NC: Duke University Press, 2008), p. 3. Emphasis in original.

24 Klaus Graf and Sanford Thatcher, 'Point & Counterpoint: Is CC BY the Best Open Access License?', *Journal of Librarianship and Scholarly Communication*, 1 (2012), 2 http://dx.doi.org/http/10.7710/2162-3309.1043.

25 Mark Philp, 'Foucault on Power: A Problem in Radical Translation?', *Political Theory*, 11 (1983), 29–52 (p. 33).

26 Google, 'Ngram Viewer', 2013 https://books.google.com/ngrams/ [accessed 5 March 2014].

27 I am, of course, aware of the problems of defining digital humanities as a 'field' and use it only broadly as a shorthand within which to refer to the growth of various computational corpus analysis techniques.

28 Jisc, 'Research Funders' Open Access Policies', *SHERPA/JULIET*, 2014 www.sherpa.ac.uk/juliet/index.php [accessed 26 February 2014].

29 Taylor & Francis, 'Open Access Survey', 2014 www.tandfonline.com/page/openaccess/opensurvey/2014 [accessed 21 January 2014]; Verity Warne, 'To CC-BY or Not to CC-BY? A Vignette on Author Choice', *Exchanges*, 2014 http://exchanges.wiley.com/blog/2014/04/14/to-cc-by-or-not-to-cc-by-a-vignette-on-author-choice/ [accessed 23 April 2014]; Morrison, 'Taylor & Francis Open Access Survey: Critique'; Heinrich Mallison, 'Taylor & Francis Misrepresents DFG Guidelines on Open Access – an Innocent Error?', *dinosaurpalaeo*, 2014 https://dinosaurpalaeo.wordpress.com/2014/04/20/taylor-franics-misrepresents-dfg-guidelines-on-open-access-an-innocent-error/ [accessed 20 April 2014].

30 Lawrence Lessig, *Remix: Making Art and Commerce Thrive in the Hybrid Economy* (New York: Penguin Press, 2008), p. 18.

31 Richard Stallman, 'Why Software Should Not Have Owners', in *Free Software, Free Society: Selected Essays of Richard Stallman* (Boston, MA: Free Software Foundation, 2010), pp. 37–41 (p. 39).

32 Lessig, *Remix*, pp. 34–5.

33 '[W]rite your own work'. Mandler, 'Open Access: A Perspective from the Humanities', p. 169.

34 Editors of History Journals, 'Written Evidence'; Mandler, 'Open Access for the Humanities'.

35 Aaron Keyt, 'An Improved Framework for Music Plagiarism Litigation', *California Law Review*, 76 (1988), 421–64 (p. 422).

36 Mandler, 'Open Access: A Perspective from the Humanities', p. 169.

37 Nietzsche Source, 'Digital Critical Edition of Nietzsche's Works and Letters', 2009 www.nietzschesource.org/documentation/en/eKGWB.html [accessed 18 July 2014].

38 Text Encoding Initiative, 'Projects Using the TEI', 2014 www.tei-c.org/Activities/Projects/ [accessed 5 August 2014].

39 Creative Commons, 'Attribution 4.0 International Legal Code', 2014 http://creativecommons.org/licenses/by/4.0/legalcode [accessed 28 February 2014].

40 Robert Dingwall, 'Why Open Access Is Good News for Neo-Nazis', *Social Science Space*, 2012 www.socialsciencespace.com/2012/10/why-open-access-is-good-news-for-neo-nazis/ [accessed 1 March 2014].

41 Mike Godwin, 'Meme, Counter-Meme', *Wired*, 2 (1994) www.wired. com/wired/archive/2.10/godwin.if_pr.html [accessed 22 May 2012].

42 Dingwall, 'Why Open Access Is Good News for Neo-Nazis'.

43 Small, *The Value of the Humanities*, p. 59.

44 Small, *The Value of the Humanities*, pp. 174–5.

45 Mandler, 'Open Access: A Perspective from the Humanities', p. 169.

46 Erik Möller, 'Creative Commons – NC Licenses Considered Harmful', *kuroshin.org*, 2005 www.kuroshin.org/story/2005/9/11/16331/0655 [accessed 21 January 2013].

47 Huppertz Justizbeschäftigte als Urkundsbeamtin der Geschäftsstelle, 'Urteil Landgericht Köln in Dem Rechtsstreit Klagers Rechtsanwälte Lampmann, Haberkamm & Rosenbaum gegen Die Deutschlandradio K.d.ö.R.', 2014 www.lhr-law.de/wp-content/uploads/2014/03/geschw% C3%A4rztes-Urteil-LG-K%C3%B6ln-2.pdf [accessed 6 April 2014].

48 Adam Crymble, 'Academic Freedom License: An Alternative to CC-BY', *Thoughts on Public & Digital History*, 2013 http://adamcrymble. blogspot.co.uk/2013/10/academic-freedom-license-alternative-to_24. html [accessed 11 July 2014].

49 Andrés Guadamuz, 'Academic Publishers Draft and Release Their Own Open Access Licences', *TechnoLlama* www.technollama.co.uk/ academic-publishers-draft-and-release-their-own-open-access-licences [accessed 18 July 2014].

50 For more on this, see McGettigan, *The Great University Gamble*, p. 86.

51 John Holmwood, 'The Neo-Liberal Knowledge Regime, Inequality and Social Critique', *openDemocracy*, 2013 www.opendemocracy.net/john-holmwood/neo-liberal-knowledge-regime-inequality-and-social-critique [accessed 3 March 2014].

52 John Holmwood, *A Manifesto for the Public University* (London: Bloomsbury Academic, 2011) http://dx.doi.org/10.5040/9781849666459 [accessed 3 March 2014].

4 MONOGRAPHS

1 *The Specialized Scholarly Monograph in Crisis or How Can I Get Tenure If You Won't Publish My Book*, ed. Mary Case (Washington, DC: Association of Research Libraries, 1999).

2 James McPherson, 'A Crisis in Scholarly Publishing', *Perspectives on History*, 2003 www.historians.org/publications-and-directories/perspectives-on-history/october-2003/a-crisis-in-scholarly-publishing [accessed 1 May 2014].

3 See Sanford G. Thatcher, 'The Crisis in Scholarly Communication', *Chronicle of Higher Education*, 3 (1995); Stephen Greenblatt, 'Call for Action on Problems in Scholarly Book Publishing: A Special Letter from Stephen Greenblatt', 2002 www.mla.org/scholarly_pub [accessed 8 May 2014];

Philip Lewis, 'The Publishing Crisis and Tenure Criteria: An Issue for Research Universities?', *Profession*, 2004, 14–24; Judith Ryan, 'Publishing and Purchasing: The Great Paradigm Shift', *Profession*, 2004, 7–13; Domna C. Stanton, 'Working through the Crises: A Plan for Action', *Profession*, 2004, 32–41; Thompson, *Books in the Digital Age*, pp. 103–7; Jerome McGann, 'Information Technology and the Troubled Humanities', *Text Technology*, 14 (2005), 105 if you would really like to read more on this.

4 Judith Ryan and others, 'The Future of Scholarly Publishing: MLA Ad Hoc Committee on the Future of Scholarly Publishing', *Profession*, 2002, 172–86 (p. 176).

5 Peter Suber, 'Open Access to Electronic Theses and Dissertations (ETDs)', *SPARC Open Access Newsletter*, 2006 http://dash.harvard.edu/handle/1/4727443 [accessed 1 May 2014]; Gail McMillan and others, 'An Investigation of ETDs as Prior Publications: Findings from the 2011 NDLTD Publishers' Survey', *University Library Faculty Publications*, 2011 http://scholarworks.gsu.edu/univ_lib_facpub/53.

6 Colin Steele, 'Scholarly Monograph Publishing in the 21st Century: The Future More Than Ever Should Be an Open Book', *Journal of Electronic Publishing*, 11 (2008) http://dx.doi.org/http/10.3998/3336451.0011.201; John Willinsky, 'Toward the Design of an Open Monograph Press', *Journal of Electronic Publishing*, 12 (2009) http://dx.doi.org/http/10.3998/3336451.0012.103.

7 Ellen Collins, 'OAPEN-UK Literature Review V1', 2012 http://oapen-uk.jiscebooks.org/files/2012/06/OAPENUK-Literature-Review-V1-June-2012.doc [accessed 14 March 2014].

8 Higher Education Funding Council for England, 'Policy for Open Access in the Post-2014 Research Excellence Framework'.

9 Nicholson Baker, 'A New Page', *The New Yorker*, 3 August 2009 http://www.newyorker.com/reporting/2009/08/03/090803fa_fact_baker?currentPage=all [accessed 2 May 2014]; Ian Bogost, 'Reading Online Sucks', 2008 www.bogost.com/blog/reading_online_sucks.shtml [accessed 2 May 2014].

10 Janneke Adema and Paul Rutten, 'Digital Monographs in the Humanities and Social Sciences: Report on User Needs' (OAPEN, 2010), pp. 12–14 http://openreflections.files.wordpress.com/2008/10/d315-user-needs-report.pdf.

11 David Nicholas and others, 'E-Journals: Their Use, Value and Impact: Final Report' (Research Information Network, 2009), pp. 20–1 www.rin.ac.uk/our-work/communicating-and-disseminating-research/e-journals-their-use-value-and-impact.

12 Monica Bulger and others, 'Reinventing Research? Information Practices in the Humanities' (Research Information Network, 2011), pp. 72–3 www.rin.ac.uk/our-work/using-and-accessing-information-resources/information-use-case-studies-humanities.

13 Adema and Rutten, 'Digital Monographs in the Humanities and Social Sciences', p. 13.

14 Collins, 'OAPEN-UK Literature Review Vi', p. 2.

15 Adeline Koh and Ken Wissoker, 'On Monographs, Libraries and Blogging: A Conversation with Duke University Press, Part One', *Chronicle of Higher Education*, 2013 http://chronicle.com/blogs/profhacker/what-is-the-future-of-the-monograph-a-conversation-with-duke-university-press-part-one/48263 [accessed 16 March 2014].

16 Hazel Newton, 'Breaking Boundaries in Academic Publishing: Launching a New Format for Scholarly Research', *Insights: The UKSG Journal*, 26 (2013), 70–6 (p. 71) http://dx.doi.org/10.1629/2048–7754.26.1.70.

17 At a risk of a technical digression too far, XML is a markup language in which information is encoded alongside its metadata. For instance, <lastname>Smith<lastname> might be the way in which the word 'Smith' is signalled as an author's last name inside such a document. The most common format for encoding of scholarly documents is the Journal Article Tag Suite (JATS), which, despite its name, can also handle books (although there is also a parallel format). Such a format serves as an intermediary stage in a three-step plan: (1) authors submit in a format of their choice; (2) this is then converted to the intermediate XML; (3) which is then, itself, converted into all the various desired output formats (PDF, EPUB, MOBI, HTML etc.). Stage 2 is difficult (and expensive as this software can often cost tens of thousands of US dollars per year to license), but it then enables a far easier and unified process at stage 3 whereby all the outputs are created from a single, easily readable source. Martin Paul Eve, 'The Means of (Re-)Production: Expertise, Open Tools, Standards and Communication', *Publications*, 2 (2014), 38–43 http://dx.doi.org/10.3390/publications2010038.

18 I.T. Strategies, 'The Evolution of the Book Industry: Implications for U.S. Book Manufacturers and Printers', 2013, p. 21 http://rpp.ricoh-usa.com/images/uploads/Literature/whitepapers/IT-Strategies_FINAL.pdf [accessed 11 July 2014].

19 G. Dean Kortge and Patrick A. Okonkwo, 'Perceived Value Approach to Pricing', *Industrial Marketing Management*, 22 (1993), 133–40 http://dx.doi.org/10.1016/0019–8501(93)90039-A.

20 Kristina Shampanier, Nina Mazar and Dan Ariely, 'Zero as a Special Price: The True Value of Free Products', *Marketing Science*, 26 (2007), 742–57 http://dx.doi.org/10.1287/mksc.1060.0254; Mauricio M. Palmeira and Joydeep Srivastava, 'Free Offer ≠ Cheap Product: A Selective Accessibility Account on the Valuation of Free Offers', *Journal of Consumer Research*, 40 (2013), 644–56 http://dx.doi.org/10.1086/671565.

21 Thompson, *Books in the Digital Age*, p. 46.

22 Jennifer Crewe, 'Scholarly Publishing: Why Our Business Is Your Business Too', *Profession*, 2004, 25–31 (p. 25).

23 By which I mean that the typesetting is done digitally and print is derived from this same source.

24 For more on these costs in the journal sphere, see Brian D. Edgar and John Willinsky, 'A Survey of Scholarly Journals Using Open Journal Systems', *Scholarly and Research Communication*, 1 (2010) http://src-online.ca/index.php/src/article/view/24 [accessed 1 May 2014].

25 Ferwerda, Snijder and Adema, 'OAPEN-NL', p. 3.

26 Ferwerda, Snijder and Adema, 'OAPEN-NL', p. 68.

27 Ferwerda, Snijder and Adema, 'OAPEN-NL', p. 67.

28 Ferwerda, Snijder and Adema, 'OAPEN-NL', pp. 55–7; Swan, 'The Open Access Citation Advantage'.

29 Ferwerda, Snijder and Adema, 'OAPEN-NL', pp. 40–53.

30 Ferwerda, Snijder and Adema, 'OAPEN-NL', p. 83.

31 OAPEN-UK, 'The Pilot', 2013 http://oapen-uk.jiscebooks.org/pilot/ [accessed 25 March 2014]. There is some confusion around the numbers here. Technically, there were 29 original matched pairs (yielding 58 titles), which were then to be joined by a further 18 pairs from Oxford University Press (adding a further 36), making a total of 94. However, four titles remain listed as 'TBC'.

32 Disclosure of interest: I am a member of the OAPEN-UK project's steering group.

33 See Susan Brown and others, 'Published Yet Never Done: The Tension between Projection and Completion in Digital Humanities Research', 3 (2009) http://digitalhumanities.org/dhq/vol/3/2/000040/000040.html [accessed 3 May 2014] for an introduction on the issues of versioning and completion that often inhere in digital humanities projects. Note well, however, that despite the lack of print materiality, this sphere is less delineated from traditional writing than might be supposed; is a piece of writing ever finished, or merely committed as a specific version to the page? I'd suggest the latter.

34 OAPEN-UK, 'Year 1 Focus Group Summary Report', 2012, p. 1 http://oapen-uk.jiscebooks.org/research-findings/y1-initial-focus-groups/ [accessed 25 March 2014].

35 OAPEN-UK, 'Year 1 Focus Group Summary Report', p. 3.

36 Fitzpatrick, *Planned Obsolescence*, pp. 122–3.

37 Fitzpatrick, *Planned Obsolescence*, p. 124.

38 Donald J. Waters, 'Preserving the Knowledge Commons', in *Understanding Knowledge as a Commons: From Theory to Practice*, ed. Charlotte Hess and Elinor Ostrom (Cambridge, MA: MIT Press, 2007), pp. 145–67.

39 OAPEN-UK, 'Researcher Survey', 2012 http://oapen-uk.jiscebooks.org/research-findings/researchersurvey/ [accessed 25 March 2014].

40 OAPEN-UK, 'Royal Historical Society Case Study', 2013 http://oapen-uk.jiscebooks.org/research-findings/learned-society-case-studies/rhs-case-study/ [accessed 26 March 2014].

41 Research Information Network, 'Activities, Costs and Funding Flows in the Scholarly Communications System', 2008, p. 8 www.rin.ac.uk/our-work/communicating-and-disseminating-research/activities-costs-and-funding-flows-scholarly-commu [accessed 21 April 2014].

42 OAPEN-UK, 'Regional Studies Association Case Study', 2013 http://oapen-uk.jiscebooks.org/research-findings/learned-society-case-studies/rsacasestud/ [accessed 26 March 2014].

43 Paul Jump, 'Evolution of the REF', *Times Higher Education*, 17 October 2013 www.timeshighereducation.co.uk/features/evolution-of-the-ref/2008100.fullarticle [accessed 27 March 2014].

44 Higher Education Funding Council for England, 'Policy for Open Access in the Post-2014 Research Excellence Framework', paras. 17–19.

45 Higher Education Funding Council for England, 'Policy for Open Access in the Post-2014 Research Excellence Framework', para. 14.

46 G. R. Evans, 'Questions over Open Books', *Times Higher Education*, 29 May 2014, sec. Letters.

47 Palgrave Macmillan, 'Frequently Asked Questions'.

48 Wellcome Trust, 'Position Statement in Support of Open Access Publishing', *Wellcome Trust*, 2013 www.wellcome.ac.uk/About-us/Policy/Policy-and-position-statements/WTD002766.htm [accessed 28 March 2014].

49 Emily Philippou, 'First Wellcome Trust Open Access Book Charts Serious Fungal Disease', *The Wellcome Trust*, 2013 www.wellcome.ac.uk/News/Media-office/Press-releases/2013/Press-releases/WTP054748.htm [accessed 28 March 2014].

50 Gary Hall, *Digitize This Book! The Politics of New Media, or Why We Need Open Access Now* (Minneapolis: University of Minnesota Press, 2008).

51 Association of American Universities and Association of Research Libraries, 'AAU-ARL Prospectus for an Institutionally Funded First-Book Subvention', 2014 www.arl.org/publications-resources/3280-aau-arl-prospectus-for-an-institutionally-funded-first-book-subvention [accessed 1 July 2014].

52 Gary Hall, 'Towards a New Political Economy: Open Humanities Press and the Open Access Monograph' (presented at the OAPEN 2011: The First OAPEN (Open Access Publishing in European Networks) Conference, Humboldt University Berlin, Germany, 2011) www.garyhall.info/journal/2011/5/30/towards-a-new-political-economy-open-humanities-press-and-th.html [accessed 29 March 2014].

53 Purdue University Scholarship Online, 'Purdue E-Pubs', 2014 http://docs.lib.purdue.edu/ [accessed 29 March 2014].

54 Andrew Albanese, 'Pitt Library and Press Join Forces to Expand Digital Backlist', *Library Journal*, 2007 http://lj.libraryjournal.com/2007/12/academic-libraries/pitt-library-and-press-join-forces-to-expand-digital-backlist/ [accessed 29 March 2014].

55 MediaCommons, 'History', 2014 http://mediacommons.futureofthebook.org/history [accessed 29 March 2014].

56 OpenEdition, 'OpenEdition Freemium' www.openedition.org/8873 [accessed 28 March 2014].

57 Athabasca University Press, 'About', 2014 www.aupress.ca/index.php/about/ [accessed 29 March 2014].

58 Moshe Y. Vardi and Richard Baraniuk, 'A New Model for Publishing Research Monographs', 2012 www.cs.rice.edu/~vardi/newmodel.txt [accessed 29 March 2014].

59 For the costs incurred at various points in the publishing cycle, see Thompson, *Books in the Digital Age*, pp. 16–20.

60 Hugh Look and Frances Pinter, 'Open Access and Humanities and Social Science Monograph Publishing', *New Review of Academic Librarianship*, 16 (2010), 90–7 (p. 95) http://dx.doi.org/10.1080/13614533.2010.512244.

61 Look and Pinter, 'Open Access and Humanities and Social Science Monograph Publishing', p. 91.

62 Lucy Montgomery, 'Knowledge Unlatched Pilot Collection to Become Open Access – Nearly 300 Libraries Globally Pledge Their Support' (Knowledge Unlatched, 2014) www.knowledgeunlatched.org/press-release/ [accessed 30 March 2014].

63 Lucy Montgomery and others, 'Pilot Proof of Concept Progress Summary' (Knowledge Unlatched, 2014) http://collections.knowledge-unlatched.org/wp-content/uploads/2013/09/KU_Pilot_Progress_Summary_Report.pdf [accessed 25 May 2014].

64 Lucy Montgomery, 'Knowledge Unlatched Announces the Launch of Its Pilot Collection' (Knowledge Unlatched, 2013) www.knowledgeun-latched.org/press-release/ [accessed 30 March 2014].

65 Sanford G. Thatcher, 'Back to the Future: Old Models for New Challenges', *Against the Grain*, 2011, 38–43; Adrian Johns, *The Nature of the Book* (Illinois: University of Chicago Press, 1998), p. 450 www.press.uchicago.edu/ucp/books/book/chicago/N/bo3645773.html [accessed 30 March 2014]. Ellipses are Thatcher's.

66 Gluejar, 'Vision', 2014 http://gluejar.com/vision/ [accessed 30 March 2014].

5 INNOVATIONS

1 Suber, *Open Access*, pp. 20–1.

2 Among the more interesting ranks Patrick Bazin, 'Toward Metareading', in *The Future of the Book*, ed. Geoffrey Nunberg (Berkeley: University of California Press, 1996), pp. 153–69.

3 Michel Foucault, 'What Is Enlightenment?', in *Ethics: Subjectivity and Truth: The Essential Works of Michel Foucault, 1954–1984* (London: Penguin, 2000), pp. 303–19 (p. 316).

4 Carlos J. Alonso and others, *Crises and Opportunities: The Futures of Scholarly Publishing*, 57 (American Council of Learned Societies, 2003), p. 2 www.acls.org/uploadedfiles/publications/op/57_crises_and_opportunites.pdf [accessed 2 May 2014].

5 Hall, *Digitize This Book!*, pp. 59–61.

6 Domenic V. Cicchetti, 'The Reliability of Peer Review for Manuscript and Grant Submissions: A Cross-Disciplinary Investigation', *Behavioral and Brain Sciences*, 14 (1991), 119–35.

7 I owe the phrase 'genealogies of validation' to Martin McQuillan.

8 Peter Binfield, 'Open Access MegaJournals – Have They Changed Everything?', *Creative Commons Aotearoa New Zealand*, 2013 http://creativecommons.org.nz/2013/10/open-access-megajournals-have-they-changed-everything/ [accessed 28 November 2013]; Damian Pattinson, 'PLOS ONE Publishes Its 100,000th Article', *EveryONE*, 2014 http://blogs.plos.org/everyone/2014/06/23/plos-one-publishes-100000th-article/ [accessed 24 June 2014].

9 PLOS, 'PLOS ONE Journal Information' www.plosone.org/static/information [accessed 6 May 2013].

10 Clay Shirky, 'It's Not Information Overload. It's Filter Failure' (presented at the Web 2.0 Expo, New York, 2008) http://blip.tv/web2expo/web-2-0-expo-ny-clay-shirky-shirky-com-it-s-not-information-overload-it-s-filter-failure-1283699 [accessed 1 May 2014].

11 Willinsky, *The Access Principle*, p. 203. Note that Biagioli ('From Book Censorship to Academic Peer Review') argues that peer review developed at an earlier stage than the conventionally held point of the Transactions and has roots instead in the seventeenth-century book trade.

12 Fitzpatrick, *Planned Obsolescence*, p. 196.

13 Fitzpatrick, *Planned Obsolescence*, pp. 110–12, 192.

14 Palgrave Macmillan, 'Introduction', *Palgrave Macmillan: Open Peer Review Trial* http://palgraveopenreview.com/introduction/ [accessed 4 April 2014].

15 Fitzpatrick, *Planned Obsolescence*, p. 192.

16 A good example of such pragmatism is evinced in Gordon M. Sayre, 'The Crisis in Scholarly Publishing: Demystifying the Fetishes of Technology and the Market', *Profession*, 2005, 52–8. I do not agree with all that Sayre says but his method of establishing what we need and want, while shying from a fetishisation of technology-for-technology's-sake is worthwhile.

17 Ginsparg, 'Winners and Losers in the Global Research Village'.

18 Peter Suber, 'Guide to the Open Access Movement', 2003 http://legacy.
   earlham.edu/~peters/fos/guide.htm [accessed 10 April 2014].
19 For more on the genesis of this type of logic, see Tim O'Reilly, 'Piracy Is
   Progressive Taxation, and Other Thoughts on the Evolution of Online
   Distribution', *O'Reilly P2P*, 2002 www.openp2p.com/pub/a/p2p/2002/
   12/11/piracy.html [accessed 21 April 2014].

Glossary of open access terms

article processing charge (APC): a supply-side (i.e. author-side, institution-side or funder-side) payment to publishers to cover the business costs of their work in order to achieve gold open access

book processing charge (BPC): an 'article processing charge' for a book

CLOCKSS: a digital preservation initiative. Acronym for Controlled Lots of Copies Keeps Stuff Safe

Creative Commons licenses: a series of licenses designed to allow greater reuse of material than is purely allowed under fair dealing/fair use provisions of copyright law

digital preservation: the practice of ensuring the continued existence and accessibility of digital material. This often takes the form of decentralised, highly distributed and redundant dark-archive systems, such as CLOCKSS and LOCKSS.

disciplinary repository: see 'subject repository'

Document Object Identifier (DOI): an identifier in the form 10.7766/orbit.v2.1.50 or http://dx.doi.org/10.7766/orbit.v2.1.50 that uniquely addresses a scholarly resource. The DOI system is part of the digital preservation infrastructure as, in the event that a journal goes offline or the publisher folds, the DOI is updated to point to the preserved version, ensuring continued access. A DOI is supposed to be an identifier that will always return the resource and it comes with substantial social structures (such as financial penalties if metadata are not kept up-to-date) to ensure this.

double dipping: an instance when a hybrid journal that levies an article processing charge also charges for subscriptions without offsetting the subscription price to reflect revenue claimed from the APC

embargo: a delay period required by some publishers before they will allow open access (green or gold) on a piece of work. The embargo period for journals that allow green OA can be found on the publisher's website or by using the SHERPA/RoMEO tool.

gold open access: scholarly material made open access directly on the publisher's website. NB gold open access does not refer to any specific business model.

gratis open access: open-access material that is free of charge to read but with no additional permissions granted to redistribute, reuse or modify. Some refer to this simply as 'open access'.

green open access: scholarly material made open access by deposit in a repository. NB green open access does not refer to any specific business model.

hybrid journal: a subscription journal that offers an open-access option

institutional repository: an archival space hosted by a higher education institution to facilitate green open access

libre open access: open access that is free of charge and that has lowered permission barriers. Some use simply 'open access' to refer to this.

LOCKSS: a digital preservation initiative, acronym for Lots of Copies Keeps Stuff Safe

mandate: a requirement that work be made open access, usually requested and enforced by a government, funding body or institution

metadata: peripheral information *about* an object, in this case a scholarly resource. For instance, author, affiliation, title, date published, journal name, issue, volume etc. are all pieces of metadata pertaining to a journal article.

open access (OA): the removal of price and permission barriers to research through the use of the internet and more liberal licensing agreements. See also 'green open access' and 'gold open access'. For open access that distinguishes between the types of permission, see 'gratis open access' and 'libre open access'.

platinum open access: a category-error term that supposedly denotes gold open access for which there is no author charge. In reality, this is just gold open access. See also 'article processing charge'.

Portico: a digital preservation initiative

post-print: a manuscript that has passed peer review

pre-print: a manuscript that has not yet been peer-reviewed

repository: an archival space to facilitate green open access. See also 'institutional repository' and 'subject repository'.

self-archiving: the process of an author making his or her work green open access by depositing the work in a repository

subject repository: an archival space hosted by a subject group or learned society to facilitate green open access

toll-access journals: journals that charge a subscription or one-off fee for access

Bibliography

The Ad Hoc Committee on Fair Use and Academic Freedom, *Clipping Our Own Wings: Copyright and Creativity in Communication Research* (The Media and Communication Policy Task Force, 7 May 2010) www.cmsimpact.org/fair-use/related-materials/documents/clipping-our-own-wings-copyright-and-creativity-communication-r [accessed 1 May 2014]

Adema, Janneke, and Paul Rutten, 'Digital Monographs in the Humanities and Social Sciences: Report on User Needs' (OAPEN, 2010) http://openreflections.files.wordpress.com/2008/10/d315-user-needs-report.pdf

Albanese, Andrew, 'Pitt Library and Press Join Forces to Expand Digital Backlist', *Library Journal*, 2007 http://lj.libraryjournal.com/2007/12/academic-libraries/pitt-library-and-press-join-forces-to-expand-digital-backlist/ [accessed 29 March 2014]

Alonso, Carlos J., Cathy N. Davidson, John Unsworth, and Lynne Withey, *Crises and Opportunities: The Futures of Scholarly Publishing*, 57 (American Council of Learned Societies, 2003) http://www.acls.org/uploadedfiles/publications/op/57_crises_and_opportunites.pdf [accessed 2 May 2014]

American Association of University Professors, 'Statement of Principles on Academic Freedom and Tenure', 1940 http://www.aaup.org/report/1940-statement-principles-academic-freedom-and-tenure [accessed 13 February 2014]

Amherst College Press, 'Frequently Asked Questions', 2014 https://www.amherst.edu/library/press/faq [accessed 22 January 2014]

Arendt, Hannah, *The Human Condition* (University of Chicago Press, 1998)

arXiv, 'FAQ', 2013 http://arxiv.org/help/support/faq [accessed 22 December 2013]

Association of American Universities, and Association of Research Libraries, 'AAU-ARL Prospectus for an Institutionally Funded First-Book

Subvention', 2014 www.arl.org/publications-resources/3280-aau-arl-prospectus-for-an-institutionally-funded-first-book-subvention [accessed 1 July 2014]

Association of Learned and Professional Society Publishers, 'ALPSP Survey of Librarians on Factors in Journal Cancellation', 2006

Association of Research Libraries, 'ARL Statistics 2009–2011', 2014 www.arl. org/storage/documents/expenditure-trends.pdf [accessed 1 July 2014]

Athabasca University Press, 'About', 2014 www.aupress.ca/index.php/about/ [accessed 29 March 2014]

Bailey Jr, Charles W., 'Strong Copyright + DRM + Weak Net Neutrality = Digital Dystopia?', *Information Technology and Libraries*, 25 (2013), 116–27, 139 http://dx.doi.org/10.6017/ital.v25i3.3344

Baker, Nicholson, 'A New Page', *The New Yorker*, 3 August 2009 www.newyorker.com/reporting/2009/08/03/090803fa_fact_baker?currentPage=all [accessed 2 May 2014]

Bazin, Patrick, 'Toward Metareading', in *The Future of the Book*, ed. Geoffrey Nunberg (Berkeley: University of California Press, 1996), pp. 153–69

Beall, Jeffrey, 'The Open-Access Movement Is Not Really about Open Access', *tripleC: Communication, Capitalism & Critique. Open Access Journal for a Global Sustainable Information Society*, 11 (2013), 589–97

Beckett, Chris, and Simon Inger, *Self-Archiving and Journal Subscriptions: Co-Existence or Competition?* (Publishing Research Consortium, 2006) http://eprints.ecs.soton.ac.uk/13179 [accessed 9 July 2014]

Belfiore, Eleonora, and Anna Upchurch, eds., *Humanities in the Twenty-First Century Beyond Utility and Markets* (Basingstoke: Palgrave Macmillan, 2013)

Bendix, Henrik, 'Regeringen: Alle Danske Forskningsartikler Skal Være Frit Tilgængelige', *Ingeniøren*, 2014 http://ing.dk/artikel/regeringen-alle-danske-forskningsartikler-skal-vaere-frit-tilgaengelige-169271 [accessed 26 June 2014]

Bergstrom, Theodore C., and Carl T. Bergstrom, 'Can "Author Pays" Journals Compete with "Reader Pays"?', *Nature: Web Focus*, 2004 www.nature. com/nature/focus/accessdebate/22.html [accessed 1 May 2014]

'Berlin Declaration on Open Access to Knowledge in the Sciences and Humanities', 2003 http://oa.mpg.de/lang/en-uk/berlin-prozess/berliner-erklarung

Bérubé, Michael, 'The Futility of the Humanities', in *Humanities in the Twenty-First Century: Beyond Utility and Markets*, ed. Eleonora Belfiore and Anna Upchurch (Basingstoke: Palgrave/Macmillan, 2013), pp. 66–76

Bhaskar, Michael, *The Content Machine: Towards a Theory of Publishing from the Printing Press to the Digital Network* (New York: Anthem Press, 2013)

Binfield, Peter, 'Open Access MegaJournals – Have They Changed Everything?', *Creative Commons Aotearoa New Zealand*, 2013 http://creativecommons.org.nz/2013/10/open-access-megajournals-have-they-changed-everything/ [accessed 28 November 2013]

Bivens-Tatum, Wayne, 'Reactionary Rhetoric against Open Access Publishing', *tripleC: Communication, Capitalism & Critique. Open Access Journal for a Global Sustainable Information Society*, 12 (2014), 441–6

Bliege Bird, Rebecca, and Eric Alden Smith, 'Signaling Theory, Strategic Interaction, and Symbolic Capital 1', *Current Anthropology*, 46 (2005), 221–48

Bloomsbury Group, *Annual Report*, 2012 www.bloomsbury-ir.co.uk/annual_reports/2012/pdf/2012ar.pdf [accessed 22 January 2014]

Blue Ribbon Task Force on Sustainable Digital Preservation and Access, *Sustaining the Digital Investment: Issues and Challenges of Economically Sustainable Digital Preservation*, December 2008 http://brtf.sdsc.edu/biblio/BRTF_Interim_Report.pdf [accessed 2 May 2014]

Bogost, Ian, 'Reading Online Sucks', 2008 www.bogost.com/blog/reading_online_sucks.shtml [accessed 2 May 2014]

Bohannon, John, 'Who's Afraid of Peer Review?', *Science*, 342 (2013), 60–5 http://dx.doi.org/10.1126/science.342.6154.60

Bosch, Stephen, and Kittie Henderson, 'Periodicals Price Survey 2013', *Library Journal*, 2013 http://lj.libraryjournal.com/2013/04/publishing/the-winds-of-change-periodicals-price-survey-2013/ [accessed 6 May 2013]

Bourdieu, Pierre, *Outline of a Theory of Practice* (Cambridge University Press, 1977)

Bradley, Robert L., 'Oil Company Earnings: Reality over Rhetoric', *Forbes*, 2011 www.forbes.com/2011/05/10/oil-company-earnings.html [accessed 21 January 2014]

Brembs, Björn, 'A Fistful of Dollars: Why Corporate Publishers Have No Place in Scholarly Communication', *bjoern.brembs.blog*, 2012 http://bjoern.brembs.net/2013/08/a-fistful-of-dollars-why-corporate-publishers-have-no-place-in-scholarly-communication/ [accessed 27 November 2013]

Brown, Susan, Patricia Clements, Isobel Grundy, Stan Ruecker, Jeffery Antoniuk, and Sharon Balazs, 'Published Yet Never Done: The Tension between Projection and Completion in Digital Humanities Research', 3 (2009) http://digitalhumanities.org/dhq/vol/3/2/000040/000040.html [accessed 3 May 2014]

Buckland, Amy, Martin Paul Eve, Graham Steel, Jennifer Gardy, and Dorothea Salo, 'On the Mark? Responses to a Sting', *Journal of Librarianship and Scholarly Communication*, 2 (2013) http://dx.doi.org/10.7710/2162-3309.1116

Bulger, Monica, Eric T. Meyer, Grace de la Flor, Melissa Terras, Sally Wyatt, Marina Jirotka, and others, 'Reinventing Research? Information Practices in the Humanities' (Research Information Network, 2011) www.rin.ac.uk/our-work/using-and-accessing-information-resources/information-use-case-studies-humanities

Case, Mary, ed., *The Specialized Scholarly Monograph in Crisis or How Can I Get Tenure If You Won't Publish My Book* (Washington, DC: Association of Research Libraries, 1999)

Chan, Leslie, Darius Cuplinskas, Michael Eisen, Fred Friend, Yana Genova, Jean-Claude Guédon, and others, 'Budapest Open Access Initiative', 2002 www.soros.org/openaccess/read.shtml [accessed 18 February 2011]

Chartier, Roger, 'Libraries without Walls', *Representations*, 1993, 38–52 http://dx.doi.org/10.2307/2928617

Cicchetti, Domenic V., 'The Reliability of Peer Review for Manuscript and Grant Submissions: A Cross-Disciplinary Investigation', *Behavioral and Brain Sciences*, 14 (1991), 119–35

Collins, Ellen, 'OAPEN-UK Literature Review V1', 2012 http://oapen-uk.jiscebooks.org/files/2012/06/OAPENUK-Literature-Review-V1-June-2012.doc [accessed 14 March 2014]

Collins, Ellen, Caren Milloy, and Graham Stone, *Guide to Creative Commons for Humanities and Social Science Monograph Authors*, ed. James Baker, Martin Paul Eve, and Ernesto Priego (London: Jisc Collections, 2013) http://eprints.hud.ac.uk/17828 [accessed 23 February 2014]

Cookson, Rod, 'Learned Societies More Confident about Future – and a "new Pragmatism" on Open Access', ALPSP: at the heart of scholarly publishing, 2014 http://blog.alpsp.org/2014/08/learned-societies-more-confident-about.html [accessed 12 August 2014]

Copyright Licensing Agency, 'Comprehensive HE Licence 1 August 2010', 2010 www.cla.co.uk/data/pdfs/he/uuk_basic_he_licence_specimen.pdf [accessed 23 April 2014]

'The Cost of Knowledge' http://thecostofknowledge.com/ [accessed 21 January 2014]

Creative Commons, 'About the Licenses', 2014 https://creativecommons.org/licenses/ [accessed 23 February 2014]

'Attribution 4.0 International Legal Code', 2014 http://creativecommons.org/licenses/by/4.0/legalcode [accessed 28 February 2014]

'Case Law', 2013 http://wiki.creativecommons.org/Case_Law [accessed 6 March 2014]

Creative Commons Aotearoa New Zealand, 'Open Access to Research', 2014 http://creativecommons.org.nz/research/ [accessed 5 August 2014]

Crewe, Jennifer, 'Scholarly Publishing: Why Our Business Is Your Business Too', *Profession*, 2004, 25–31

Crymble, Adam, 'Academic Freedom License: An Alternative to CC-BY', *Thoughts on Public & Digital History*, 2013 http://adamcrymble.blogspot.co.uk/2013/10/academic-freedom-license-alternative-to_24.html [accessed 11 July 2014]

Danish Ministry of Higher Education and Science, 'Denmark 's National Strategy for Open Access', 2014 http://ufm.dk/en/research-and-innovation/cooperation-between-research-and-innovation/open-science/open-access-to-research-publications/engelsk-version-national-strategy-for-open-access.pdf [accessed 24 July 2014]

Darley, Rebecca, Daniel Reynolds, and Chris Wickham, *Open Access Journals in Humanities and Social Science* (London: British Academy, 2014)

Darnton, Robert, *The Business of Enlightenment: A Publishing History of the Encyclopédie, 1775–1800* (Cambridge, MA: Harvard University Press, 1987)

———'What Is the History of Books?', *Daedalus*, 1982, 65–83

Dingwall, Robert, 'Why Open Access Is Good News for Neo-Nazis', *Social Science Space*, 2012 www.socialsciencespace.com/2012/10/why-open-access-is-good-news-for-neo-nazis/ [accessed 1 March 2014]

Directory of Open Access Journals, 'Journals by Publication Charges' www.doaj.org/doaj?func=byPublicationFee&uiLanguage=en [accessed 20 January 2014]

Docherty, Thomas, *For the University: Democracy and the Future of the Institution* (London: Bloomsbury Academic, 2011)

Dolgin, Aleksandr, *The Economics of Symbolic Exchange* (Berlin: Springer, 2009)

Duguid, Paul, 'Material Matters: The Past and Futorology of the Book', in *The Future of the Book*, ed. Geoffrey Nunberg (Berkeley: University of California Press, 1996), pp. 63–101

Durham University, 'Annual Accounts 2013', 2014 www.dur.ac.uk/resources/treasurer/financial_statements/Accounts13.pdf [accessed 4 July 2014]

Ede, Lisa, and Andrea A. Lunsford, 'Collaboration and Concepts of Authorship', *PMLA*, 116 (2001), 354–69

Edgar, Brian D., and John Willinsky, 'A Survey of Scholarly Journals Using Open Journal Systems', *Scholarly and Research Communication*, 1 (2010) http://src-online.ca/index.php/src/article/view/24 [accessed 1 May 2014]

Editors of History Journals, 'Written Evidence', *UK Parliament*, 2013 www.publications.parliament.uk/pa/cm201213/cmselect/cmbis/writev/open-access/m44.htm [accessed 24 January 2014]

'Education Reform Act 1988' www.legislation.gov.uk/ukpga/1988/40/part/IV/crossheading/academic-tenure [accessed 9 July 2014]

Edwards, Lee, Bethany Klein, David Lee, Giles Moss, and Fiona Philip, '"Isn't It Just a Way to Protect Walt Disney's Rights?": Media User Perspectives on Copyright', *New Media & Society*, 2013, http://dx.doi.org/10.1177/1461444813511402

Esposito, Joseph, 'Parting Company with Jeffrey Beall', *The Scholarly Kitchen*, 2013 http://scholarlykitchen.sspnet.org/2013/12/16/parting-company-with-jeffrey-beall/ [accessed 23 January 2014]

Evans, G.R., 'Questions over Open Books', *Times Higher Education*, 29 May 2014

Eve, Martin Paul, 'Flawed Sting Operation Singles out Open Access Journals', *The Conversation*, 2013 http://theconversation.com/flawed-sting-operation-singles-out-open-access-journals-18846 [accessed 23 January 2014]

'Tear It Down, Build It Up: The Research Output Team, or the Library-as-Publisher', *Insights: The UKSG Journal*, 25 (2012), 158–62 http://dx.doi.org/10.1629/2048-7754.25.2.158

'The Means of (Re-)Production: Expertise, Open Tools, Standards and Communication', *Publications*, 2 (2014), 38–43 http://dx.doi.org/10.3390/publications2010038

'Utopia Fading: Taxonomies, Freedom and Dissent in Open Access Publishing', *Journal of Victorian Culture*, 18 (2013), 536–42 http://dx.doi.org/10.1080/13555502.2013.865979

Fernandez, Leila, 'Open Access Initiatives in India – an Evaluation', *Partnership: The Canadian Journal of Library and Information Practice and Research*, 1 (2006) https://journal.lib.uoguelph.ca/index.php/perj/article/view/110 [accessed 19 May 2014]

Ferwerda, Eelco, Ronald Snijder, and Janneke Adema, 'OAPEN-NL: A Project Exploring Open Access Monograph Publishing in the Netherlands Final Report', 2013 www.oapen.nl/images/attachments/article/58/OAPEN-NL-final-report.pdf [accessed 24 March 2014]

Finkelstein, David, and Alistair McCleery, eds., *The Book History Reader*, 2nd edn (Abingdon: Routledge, 2006)

Fitzpatrick, Kathleen, 'On Open Access Publishing', *Society for Critical Exchange*, 2010 http://societyforcriticalexchange.org/blog/blog3.php/2010/01/15/on-open-access-publishing [accessed 3 May 2014]

Planned Obsolescence: Publishing, Technology, and the Future of the Academy (New York: New York University Press, 2011)

Foucault, Michel, 'What Is an Author?', in *The Essential Works of Michel Foucault, 1954–1984*, 3 vols. (London: Penguin, 2000), II, pp. 205–22

'What Is Enlightenment?', in *Ethics: Subjectivity and Truth: The Essential Works of Michel Foucault, 1954–1984* (London: Penguin, 2000), pp. 303–19

Fox Film Corp. v. Doyal (Supreme Court of the United States, 1932)

Friedman, Milton, 'The Social Responsibility of Business Is to Increase Its Profits', *The New York Times Magazine*, 13 September 1970, pp. 32–3, 122–4

Ginsberg, Benjamin, *The Fall of the Faculty: The Rise of the All-Administrative University and Why It Matters* (Oxford University Press, 2013)

Ginsparg, Paul, *'Winners and Losers in the Global Research Village'* (presented at the Electronic Publishing in Science, UNESCO HQ, Paris, 1996) www.cs.cornell.edu/~ginsparg/physics/blurb/pg96unesco.html [accessed 10 April 2014]

Global Research Council, 'About Us', 2014 www.globalresearchcouncil.org/about-us [accessed 17 May 2014]

——— 'Action Plan towards Open Access to Publications', 2013 www.dfg.de/download/pdf/dfg_magazin/internationales/130528_grc_annual_meeting/grc_action_plan_open_access.pdf [accessed 17 May 2014]

Gluejar, 'Vision', 2014 http://gluejar.com/vision/ [accessed 30 March 2014]

Godwin, Mike, 'Meme, Counter-Meme', *Wired*, 2 (1994) www.wired.com/wired/archive/2.10/godwin.if_pr.html [accessed 22 May 2012]

Google, 'Ngram Viewer', 2013 https://books.google.com/ngrams/ [accessed 5 March 2014]

Gowers, Tim, 'Elsevier Journals – Some Facts', *Gowers's Weblog*, 2014 http://gowers.wordpress.com/2014/04/24/elsevier-journals-some-facts/ [accessed 17 May 2014]

Graf, Klaus, and Sanford Thatcher, 'Point & Counterpoint: Is CC BY the Best Open Access License?', *Journal of Librarianship and Scholarly Communication*, 1 (2012) http://dx.doi.org/10.7710/2162-3309.1043

Grafton, Anthony, *The Footnote: A Curious History* (Cambridge, MA:Harvard University Press, 1999)

Grant, Bob, 'Elsevier Abandons Anti-Open Access Bill', *The Scientist*, 2012 www.the-scientist.com/?articles.view/articleNo/31798/title/Elsevier-Abandons-Anti-Open-Access-Bill/ [accessed 21 January 2014]

Greenblatt, Stephen, 'Call for Action on Problems in Scholarly Book Publishing: A Special Letter from Stephen Greenblatt', 2002 www.mla.org/scholarly_pub [accessed 8 May 2014]

Guadamuz, Andrés, 'Academic Publishers Draft and Release Their Own Open Access Licences', *TechnoLlama* www.technollama.co.uk/academic-publishers-draft-and-release-their-own-open-access-licences [accessed 18 July 2014]

Guthrie, Kevin, Rebecca Griffiths, and Nancy Maron, *Sustainability and Revenue Models for Online Academic Resources* (New York: Ithaka,

2008) www.jisc.ac.uk/media/documents/events/2010/04/ithakasus-tainabilityreport.pdf [accessed 4 May 2014]

Hall, Gary, *Digitize This Book! The Politics of New Media, or Why We Need Open Access Now* (Minneapolis: University of Minnesota Press, 2008)

'Towards a New Political Economy: Open Humanities Press and the Open Access Monograph' (presented at the OAPEN 2011: The First OAPEN (Open Access Publishing in European Networks) Conference, Humboldt University Berlin, Germany, 2011) www.garyhall.info/journal/2011/5/30/towards-a-new-political-economy-open-*humanities-press-and-th.html [accessed 29 March 2014]*

Hall, Richard, 'On the Context and Use-Value of Academic Labour', *Richard Hall's Space*, 2014 www.richard-hall.org/2014/02/02/on-the-context-and-use-value-of-academic-labour/ [accessed 4 February 2014]

Harnad, Stevan, 'Overture: A Subversive Proposal', in *Scholarly Journals at the Crossroads: A Subversive Proposal for Electronic Publishing*, ed. Shumelda Okerson and James J. O'Donnell (Washington, DC: Association of Research Libraries, 1994), pp. 11–12 http://hdl.handle.net/2027/mdp.39015034923758 [accessed 8 May 2014]

'Pre Green-OA Fool's Gold vs. Post Green-OA Fair Gold', *Open Access Archivangelism*, 2013 http://openaccess.eprints.org/index.php?/archives/1007-Pre-Green-OA-Fools-Gold-vs.-Post-Green-OA-Fair-Gold.html [accessed 17 May 2014]

'ROARMAP' http://roarmap.eprints.org/ [accessed 25 July 2014]

'Self-Archiving and Journal Subscriptions: Critique of PRC Study' http://users.ecs.soton.ac.uk/harnad/Hypermail/Amsci/5792.html [accessed 9 July 2014]

Henri, Agnès, 'EDP Open Survey Reveals Learned Society Attitudes towards Open Access', 2014 www.edp-open.org/index.php?option=com_content&view=article&id=273&lang=en_GB.utf8%2C+en_GB.UT [accessed 28 May 2014]

Higher Education Funding Council for England, 'Independent Review of the Role of Metrics in Research Assessment', 2014 www.hefce.ac.uk/whatwedo/rsrch/howfundr/metrics/ [accessed 21 June 2014]

'Policy for Open Access in the Post-2014 Research Excellence Framework', 2014 www.hefce.ac.uk/media/hefce/content/pubs/2014/201407/HEFCE2014_07.pdf

Hitchcock, Steve, 'The Effect of Open Access and Downloads ('Hits') on Citation Impact: A Bibliography of Studies', 2013 http://opcit.eprints.org/oacitation-biblio.html [accessed 21 April 2014]

Hoeller, Keith, 'The Academic Labor System of Faculty Apartheid', in *Equality for Contingent Faculty: Overcoming the Two-Tier System*, ed. Keith Hoeller (Nashville: Vanderbilt University Press, 2014), pp. 116–55

Hogler, Raymond, and Michael A. Gross, 'Journal Rankings and Academic Research: Two Discourses about the Quality of Faculty Work', *Management Communication Quarterly*, 23 (2009), 107–26 http://dx.doi.org/10.1177/0893318909335419

Holmwood, John, *A Manifesto for the Public University* (London: Bloomsbury Academic, 2011) http://dx.doi.org/10.5040/9781849666459 [accessed 3 March 2014]

―― 'Markets versus Dialogue: The Debate over Open Access Ignores Competing Philosophies of Openness.', *Impact of Social Sciences*, 2013 http://blogs.lse.ac.uk/impactofsocialsciences/2013/10/21/markets-versus-dialogue/ [accessed 24 January 2014]

―― 'The Neo-Liberal Knowledge Regime, Inequality and Social Critique', *openDemocracy*, 2013 www.opendemocracy.net/john-holmwood/neo-liberal-knowledge-regime-inequality-and-social-critique [accessed 3 March 2014]

House of Commons Business, Innovation and Skills Committee, 'Open Access: Fifth Report of Session 2013–14', *UK Parliament*, 2013 www.publications.parliament.uk/pa/cm201314/cmselect/cmbis/99/99.pdf [accessed 9 July 2014]

House of Commons Science and Technology Committee, 'Supplementary Evidence from Nature Publishing Group', *UK Parliament*, 2004 www.publications.parliament.uk/pa/cm200304/cmselect/cmsctech/399/399we163.htm [accessed 7 January 2013]

Hu, Dehua, Aijing Luo, and Haixia Liu, 'Open Access in China and Its Effect on Academic Libraries', *Journal of Academic Librarianship*, 39 (2013), 110–12 http://dx.doi.org/10.1016/j.acalib.2012.11.009

Huppertz Justizbeschäftigte alsUrkundsbeamtin der Geschäftsstelle, 'Urteil-Landgericht Köln in Dem Rechtsstreit Klagers Rechtsanwälte Lampmann, Haberkamm & Rosenbaum gegen Die DeutschlandradioK.d.ö.R.', 2014 www.lhr-law.de/wp-content/uploads/2014/03/geschw%C3%A4rztes-Urteil-LG-K%C3%B6ln-2.pdf [accessed 6 April 2014]

Informa, *Annual Report*, 2012 www.informa.com/Documents/Investor%20Relations/Corporate%20Governance/Informa%20Annual%20Report%202012-web.pdf [accessed 22 January 2014]

Intellectual Property Office of the United Kingdom, 'Copyright: Essential Reading', 2011 https://ipo.gov.uk/c-essential.pdf [accessed 21 February 2014]

―― 'Permitted Uses of Copyright Works: Teaching in Educational Establishments', 2006 https://ipo.gov.uk/types/copy/c-other/c-exception/c-exception-teaching.htm [accessed 4 March 2014]

I.T. Strategies, 'The Evolution of the Book Industry: Implications for U.S. Book Manufacturers and Printers', 2013 http://rpp.ricoh-usa.

com/images/uploads/Literature/whitepapers/IT-Strategies_FINAL.
pdf [accessed 11 July 2014]

Jakubowska, Dr Longina, *Patrons of History: Nobility, Capital and Political Transitions in Poland*, Google Books (Aldershot: Ashgate Publishing, 2012)

Jensen, Michael, 'Authority 3.0: Friend or Foe to Scholars?', *Journal of Scholarly Publishing*, 39 (2007), 297–307 http://dx.doi.org/10.1353/scp.2007.0027

Jisc, 'Publisher Copyright Policies & Self-Archiving', *SHERPA/RoMEO* www.sherpa.ac.uk/romeo/ [accessed 20 January 2014]

'Research Funders' Open Access Policies', *SHERPA/JULIET*, 2014 www.sherpa.ac.uk/juliet/index.php [accessed 26 February 2014]

Johns, Adrian, *The Nature of the Book* (University of Chicago Press, 1998) www.press.uchicago.edu/ucp/books/book/chicago/N/bo3645773.html [accessed 30 March 2014]

Jump, Paul, 'Evolution of the REF', *Times Higher Education*, 17 October 2013 www.timeshighereducation.co.uk/features/evolution-of-the-ref/2008100.fullarticle [accessed 27 March 2014]

'Open Access Will Cause Problems for Learned Societies' Journals, Accepts Finch', *Times Higher Education*, 15 January 2013 www.timeshighereducation.co.uk/open-access-will-cause-problems-for-learned-societies-journals-accepts-finch/422395.article [accessed 22 January 2014]

Kelty, Christopher M, *Two Bits: The Cultural Significance of Free Software* (Durham, NC: Duke University Press, 2008)

Kennison, Rebecca, and Lisa Norberg, *A Scalable and Sustainable Approach to Open Access Publishing and Archiving for Humanities and Social Sciences* (K|N Consultants, 11 April 2014) http://knconsultants.org/wp-content/uploads/2014/01/OA_Proposal_White_Paper_Final.pdf [accessed 5 May 2014]

Key Perspectives Ltd, *A Comparative Review of Research Assessment Regimes in Five Countries and the Role of Libraries in the Research Assessment Process: A Pilot Study Commissioned by OCLC Research* (Dublin, OH: OCLC, 2009) www.oclc.org/content/dam/research/publications/library/2009/2009-09.pdf?urlm=162926 [accessed 19 January 2014]

Keyt, Aaron, 'An Improved Framework for Music Plagiarism Litigation', *California Law Review*, 76 (1988), 421–64

Koh, Adeline, 'Is Open Access a Moral or a Business Issue? A Conversation with the Pennsylvania State University Press', *The Chronicle of Higher Education*, 2012 http://chronicle.com/blogs/profhacker/is-open-access-a-moral-or-a-business-issue-a-conversation-with-the-pennsylvania-state-university-press/41267 [accessed 22 January 2014]

Koh, Adeline, and Ken Wissoker, 'On Monographs, Libraries and Blogging: A Conversation with Duke University Press, Part One', *Chronicle of Higher Education*, 2013 http://chronicle.com/blogs/profhacker/what-is-the-future-of-the-monograph-a-conversation-with-duke-university-press-part-one/48263 [accessed 16 March 2014]

Kortge, G. Dean, and Patrick A. Okonkwo, 'Perceived Value Approach to Pricing', *Industrial Marketing Management*, 22 (1993), 133–40 http://dx.doi.org/10.1016/0019-8501(93)90039-A

Kranich, Nancy, 'From Collecting to Connecting: Engaging the Academic Community' (presented at The Library in the Digital Age: Communities, Collections, Opportunities, Temple University, 2013)

Lawson, Stuart, 'APC Pricing', 2014 http://dx.doi.org/10.6084/m9.figshare.1056280 [accessed 13 June 2014]

Lessig, Lawrence, *Remix: Making Art and Commerce Thrive in the Hybrid Economy* (New York: Penguin Press, 2008)

Lewis, Philip, 'The Publishing Crisis and Tenure Criteria: An Issue for Research Universities?', *Profession*, 2004, 14–24

Lillis, Theresa, 'Economies of Signs in Writing for Academic Publication: The Case of English Medium "National" Journals', *Journal of Advanced Composition*, 32 (2012), 695–722

Linguistic Society of America, 'Journal Sponsorship', *Semantics and Pragmatics*, 2014 http://semprag.org/about/journalSponsorship [accessed 22 January 2014]

Look, Hugh, and Frances Pinter, 'Open Access and Humanities and Social Science Monograph Publishing', *New Review of Academic Librarianship*, 16 (2010), 90–7 http://dx.doi.org/10.1080/13614533.2010.512244

Mallison, Heinrich, 'Taylor &Francis Misrepresents DFG Guidelines on Open Access – an Innocent Error?', *dinosaurpalaeo*, 2014 https://dinosaurpalaeo.wordpress.com/2014/04/20/taylor-franics-misrepresents-dfg-guidelines-on-open-access-an-innocent-error/ [accessed 20 April 2014]

Mandler, Peter, 'Open Access: A Perspective from the Humanities', *Insights: The UKSG Journal*, 27 (2014), 166–70 http://dx.doi.org/10.1629/2048-7754.89

——— 'Open Access for the Humanities: Not for Funders, Scientists or Publishers', *Journal of Victorian Culture*, 18 (2013), 551–7 http://dx.doi.org/10.1080/13555502.2013.865981

Markovits, Elizabeth, *The Politics of Sincerity: Plato, Frank Speech, and Democratic Judgment* (University Park, PA: Penn State Press, 2008)

McGann, Jerome, *A New Republic of Letters* (Cambridge, MA: Harvard University Press, 2014)

——— 'Information Technology and the Troubled Humanities', *Text Technology*, 14 (2005), 105–21

McGettigan, Andrew, *The Great University Gamble: Money, Markets and the Future of Higher Education* (London: Pluto Press, 2013)

McMillan, Gail, Marisa Ramirez, Joan Dalton, Max Read, and Nancy Seamans, 'An Investigation of ETDs as Prior Publications: Findings from the 2011 NDLTD Publishers' Survey', *University Library Faculty Publications*, 2011 http://scholarworks.gsu.edu/univ_lib_facpub/53

McPherson, James, 'A Crisis in Scholarly Publishing', *Perspectives on History*, 2003 www.historians.org/publications-and-directories/perspectives-on-history/october-2003/a-crisis-in-scholarly-publishing [accessed 1 May 2014]

Meadows, Alice, and David Sweeney, 'Meet David Sweeney of HEFCE – the Higher Education Funding Council of the UK', *Wiley Exchanges*, 2014 http://exchanges.wiley.com/blog/2014/05/06/meet-david-sweeney-of-hefce-the-higher-education-funding-council-of-the-uk/ [accessed 17 May 2014]

MediaCommons, 'History', 2014 http://mediacommons.futureofthebook.org/history [accessed 29 March 2014]

MLA Task Force on Doctoral Study in Modern Language and Literature, *Report of the MLA Task Force on Doctoral Study in Modern Language and Literature* (Modern Language Association of America, 2014) www.mla.org/pdf/taskforcedocstudy2014.pdf [accessed 16 July 2014]

Möller, Erik, 'Creative Commons – NC Licenses Considered Harmful', *kuro5hin.org*, 2005 www.kuro5hin.org/story/2005/9/11/16331/0655 [accessed 21 January 2013]

Montgomery, Lucy, 'Knowledge Unlatched Announces the Launch of Its Pilot Collection' (Knowledge Unlatched, 2013) www.knowledgeunlatched.org/press-release/ [accessed 30 March 2014]

'Knowledge Unlatched Pilot Collection to Become Open Access – Nearly 300 Libraries Globally Pledge Their Support' (Knowledge Unlatched, 2014) www.knowledgeunlatched.org/press-release/ [accessed 30 March 2014]

Montgomery, Lucy, Christina Emery, Frances Pinter, and Leon Loberman, 'Pilot Proof of Concept Progress Summary' (Knowledge Unlatched, 2014) http://collections.knowledgeunlatched.org/wp-content/uploads/2013/09/KU_Pilot_Progress_Summary_Report.pdf [accessed 25 May 2014]

Morrison, Heather, 'Taylor & Francis Open Access Survey: Critique', *The Imaginary Journal of Poetic Economics*, 2013 http://poeticeconomics.blogspot.co.uk/2013/03/taylor-francis-open-access-survey.html [accessed 21 January 2014]

Mukherjee, Bhaskar, and Bidyut Kumar Mal, 'India's Efforts in Open Access Publishing', *Library Philosophy and Practice*, 2012 http://unllib.unl.edu/LPP/mukherjee-mal.htm [accessed 19 May 2014]

Nature, 'Pricing', 2014 www.nature.com/nmat/pricing/index.html#site_li-cence [accessed 17 May 2014]

Newton, Hazel, 'Breaking Boundaries in Academic Publishing: Launching a New Format for Scholarly Research', *Insights: The UKSG Journal*, 26 (2013), 70–6 http://dx.doi.org/10.1629/2048-7754.26.1.70

Neylon, Cameron, '@d_mainwaring . . .I've Also Been Described as "Neo Liberal" (alongside Uber Capitalist) and "Marxist" in the Past Year Which Is Fun. . .', *@CameronNeylon*, 2013 https://twitter.com/CameronNeylon/status/410035300388597760 [accessed 18 January 2014]

Nicholas, David, Ian Rowlands, Peter Williams, David Brown, and David Clark, 'E-Journals: Their Use, Value and Impact: Final Report' (Research Information Network, 2009) www.rin.ac.uk/our-work/communicating-and-disseminating-research/e-journals-their-use-value-and-impact

Nieto, Enrique Peña, 'Open Access in the Knowledge Society', 2014 http://en.presidencia.gob.mx/open-access-in-the-knowledge-society/ [accessed 25 May 2014]

Nietzsche Source, 'Digital Critical Edition of Nietzsche's Works and Letters', 2009 www.nietzschesource.org/documentation/en/eKGWB.html [accessed 18 July 2014]

Nye, Joseph S., *Bound to Lead: The Changing Nature of American Power* (New York: Basic Books, 1991)

OAPEN-UK, 'Regional Studies Assocation Case Study', 2013 http://oapen-uk.jiscebooks.org/research-findings/learned-society-case-studies/rsaca-sestud/ [accessed 26 March 2014]

'Researcher Survey', 2012 http://oapen-uk.jiscebooks.org/research-findings/researchersurvey/ [accessed 25 March 2014]

'Royal Historical Society Case Study', 2013 http://oapen-uk.jiscebooks.org/research-findings/learned-society-case-studies/rhs-case-study/ [accessed 26 March 2014]

'The Pilot', 2013 http://oapen-uk.jiscebooks.org/pilot/ [accessed 25 March 2014]

'Year 1 Focus Group Summary Report', 2012 http://oapen-uk.jiscebooks.org/research-findings/y1-initial-focus-groups/ [accessed 25 March 2014]

Open Access Directory, 'Early OA Journals' http://oad.simmons.edu/oad-wiki/Early_OA_journals [accessed 21 April 2014]

OpenEdition, 'OpenEdition Freemium' www.openedition.org/8873 [accessed 28 March 2014]

O'Reilly, Tim, 'Piracy Is Progressive Taxation, and Other Thoughts on the Evolution of Online Distribution', *O'Reilly P2P*, 2002 www.openp2p.com/pub/a/p2p/2002/12/11/piracy.html [accessed 21 April 2014]

Osborne, Robin, 'Why Open Access Makes No Sense', in *Debating Open Access* (London: British Academy, 2013), pp. 96–105

Palgrave Macmillan, 'Frequently Asked Questions', *Palgrave Open*, 2013 www.palgrave.com/open/faq.asp#section2 [accessed 21 December 2013]

    'Introduction', *Palgrave Macmillan: Open Peer Review Trial* http://palgraveopenreview.com/introduction/ [accessed 4 April 2014]

Palgrave Macmillan Journals, 'Copyright FAQs', 2014 www.palgrave-journals.com/pal/authors/copyright_faqs.html [accessed 22 February 2014]

Palmeira, Mauricio M., and Joydeep Srivastava, 'Free Offer ≠ Cheap Product: A Selective Accessibility Account on the Valuation of Free Offers', *Journal of Consumer Research*, 40 (2013), 644–56 http://dx.doi.org/10.1086/671565

Park, Jane, 'An Interview with Frances Pinter of Bloomsbury Academic', 2008 http://creativecommons.org/weblog/entry/10100 [accessed 22 January 2014]

Pattinson, Damian, 'PLOS ONE Publishes Its 100,000th Article', *Every-ONE*, 2014 http://blogs.plos.org/everyone/2014/06/23/plos-one-publishes-100000th-article/ [accessed 24 June 2014]

Philippou, Emily, 'First Wellcome Trust Open Access Book Charts Serious Fungal Disease', *The Wellcome Trust*, 2013 www.wellcome.ac.uk/News/Media-office/Press-releases/2013/Press-releases/WTP054748.htm [accessed 28 March 2014]

Philp, Mark, 'Foucault on Power: A Problem in Radical Translation?', *Political Theory*, 11 (1983), 29–52

Pinter, Frances, and Christopher Kenneally, 'Publishing Pioneer Seeks Knowledge Unlatched', 2013 http://beyondthebookcast.com/transcripts/publishing-pioneer-seeks-knowledge-unlatched/

PLOS, 'PLOS ONE Journal Information' www.plosone.org/static/information [accessed 6 May 2013]

    'Written Evidence to House of Commons Select Committee Inquiry', in *Inquiry into Open Access. Fifth Report of Session 2013–2014*, by House of Commons Business, Innovation and Skills Committee (London: House of Commons, 2013), pp. Ev80–Ev87

Poynder, Richard, 'Open Access Mandates: Ensuring Compliance', *Open and Shut?*, 2012 http://poynder.blogspot.co.uk/2012/05/open-access-mandates-ensuring.html [accessed 17 May 2014]

Purdue University Scholarship Online, 'Purdue E-Pubs', 2014 http://docs.lib.purdue.edu/ [accessed 29 March 2014]

Readings, Bill, *The University in Ruins* (Cambridge, MA: Harvard University Press, 1996)

Research Councils UK, 'RCUK Policy on Open Access and Supporting Guidance', 2013 www.rcuk.ac.uk/RCUK-prod/assets/documents/documents/RCUKOpenAccessPolicy.pdf [accessed 10 July 2014]

Research Information Network, 'Activities, Costs and Funding Flows in the Scholarly Communications System', 2008 www.rin.ac.uk/our-work/communicating-and-disseminating-research/activities-costs-and-funding-flows-scholarly-commu [accessed 21 April 2014]

Reyes-Galindo, Luis, 'Mexican Policy-Making on OA: A Bitter-Tweet State of Affairs', *Sociology of Science and Open Access* http://blogs.cardiff.ac.uk/luisreyes/121/ [accessed 3 June 2014]

Rizor, Sara L., and Robert P. Holley, 'Open Access Goals Revisited: How Green and Gold Open Access Are Meeting (or Not) Their Original Goals', *Journal of Scholarly Publishing*, 45 (2014), 321–35 http://dx.doi.org/10.3138/jsp.45.4.01

ROAPE Editors, 'Yes to Egalitarian "Open Access", No to "Pay to Publish": A *ROAPE* Position Statement on Open Access', *Review of African Political Economy*, 40 (2013), 177–8 http://dx.doi.org/10.1080/03056244.2013.797757

Ryan, Judith, 'Publishing and Purchasing: The Great Paradigm Shift', *Profession*, 2004, 7–13

Ryan, Judith, Idelber Avelar, Jennifer Fleissner, David E. Lashmet, J. Hillis Miller, Karen H. Pike, and others, 'The Future of Scholarly Publishing: MLA Ad Hoc Committee on the Future of Scholarly Publishing', *Profession*, 2002, 172–86

Sabaratnam, Meera, and Paul Kirby, 'Open Access: HEFCE, REF2020 and the Threat to Academic Freedom', *The Disorder of Things*, 2012 http://thedisorderofthings.com/2012/12/04/open-access-hefce-ref2020-and-the-threat-to-academic-freedom/ [accessed 27 November 2013]

Sample, Ian, 'Harvard University Says It Can't Afford Journal Publishers' Prices', *The Guardian*, 2012 www.theguardian.com/science/2012/apr/24/harvard-university-journal-publishers-prices [accessed 31 May 2014]

Sayre, Gordon M., 'The Crisis in Scholarly Publishing: Demystifying the Fetishes of Technology and the Market', *Profession*, 2005, 52–8

Science Europe, 'Principles for the Transition to Open Access to Research Publications', 2013 www.scienceeurope.org/uploads/PublicDocumentsAndSpeeches/SE_OA_Pos_Statement.pdf [accessed 17 May 2014]

SCOAP3, 'Frequently Asked Questions and Answers', *SPARC*, 2014 www.sparc.arl.org/resources/papers-guides/scoap3-faq [accessed 20 May 2014]

Selwyn, Neil, 'Editorial: In Praise of Pessimism – The Need for Negativity in Educational Technology', *British Journal of Educational Technology*, 42 (2011), 713–18 http://dx.doi.org/10.1111/j.1467-8535.2011.01215.x

Shampanier, Kristina, Nina Mazar, and Dan Ariely, 'Zero as a Special Price: The True Value of Free Products', *Marketing Science*, 26 (2007), 742–57 http://dx.doi.org/10.1287/mksc.1060.0254

Shirky, Clay, 'It's Not Information Overload. It's Filter Failure' (presented at the Web 2.0 Expo, New York, 2008) http://blip.tv/web2expo/web-2-0-expo-ny-clay-shirky-shirky-com-it-s-not-information-over-load-it-s-filter-failure-1283699 [accessed 1 May 2014]

Small, Helen, *The Value of the Humanities* (Oxford University Press, 2013)

Smith, Richard, 'The Irrationality of the REF', *BMJ*, 2013 http://blogs.bmj.com/bmj/2013/05/07/richard-smith-the-irrationality-of-the-ref/ [accessed 11 February 2014]

Snow, C. P., *The Two Cultures*, Canto edn (Cambridge University Press, 1993)

Solomon, David J., and Bo-ChristerBjörk, 'A Study of Open Access Journals Using Article Processing Charges', *Journal of the American Society for Information Science and Technology*, 63 (2012), 1485–95 http://dx.doi.org/10.1002/asi.22673

Spiro, Lisa, '"This Is Why We Fight": Defining the Values of the Digital Humanities', in *Debates in the Digital Humanities*, ed. Matthew K. Gold (Minneapolis: University of Minnesota Press, 2012), pp. 16–35

Stallman, Richard, 'Misinterpreting Copyright: A Series of Errors', in *Free Software, Free Society: Selected Essays of Richard Stallman* (Boston, MA: Free Software Foundation, 2010), pp. 111–20

'Why Open Source Misses the Point of Free Software', in *Free Software, Free Society: Selected Essays of Richard Stallman* (Boston, MA: Free Software Foundation, 2010), pp. 83–8

'Why Software Should Not Have Owners', in *Free Software, Free Society: Selected Essays of Richard Stallman* (Boston, MA: Free Software Foundation, 2010), pp. 37–41

Stanton, Domna C., 'Working through the Crises: A Plan for Action', *Profession*, 2004, 32–41

Steele, Colin, 'Scholarly Monograph Publishing in the 21st Century: The Future More Than Ever Should Be an Open Book', *Journal of Electronic Publishing*, 11 (2008) http://dx.doi.org/10.3998/3336451.0011.201

'Steering Group' http://oapen-uk.jiscebooks.org/overview/steering-group/ [accessed 22 January 2014]

Suber, Peter, 'Creating an Intellectual Commons through Open Access', in *Understanding Knowledge as a Commons: From Theory to Practice*, ed. Charlotte Hess and Elinor Ostrom (Cambridge, MA: MIT Press, 2007), pp. 171–208 http://dash.harvard.edu/handle/1/4552055

'Guide to the Open Access Movement', 2003 http://legacy.earlham.edu/~peters/fos/guide.htm [accessed 10 April 2014]

'Helping Scholars and Helping Libraries', *SPARC Open Access Newsletter*, 2005 http://dash.harvard.edu/handle/1/4552051 [accessed 1 May 2014]

'Open Access and Quality', *SPARC Open Access Newsletter*, 2006 http://dash.harvard.edu/handle/1/4552042 [accessed 1 May 2014]

Open Access, Essential Knowledge Series (Cambridge, MA: MIT Press, 2012) http://bit.ly/oa-book

'Open Access, Markets, and Missions', *SPARC Open Access Newsletter*, 2010 http://dash.harvard.edu/handle/1/4322590 [accessed 21 April 2014]

'Open Access to Electronic Theses and Dissertations (ETDs)', *SPARC Open Access Newsletter*, 2006 http://dash.harvard.edu/handle/1/4727443 [accessed 1 May 2014]

'The Taxpayer Argument for Open Access', *SPARC Open Access Newsletter*, 2003 http://dash.harvard.edu/handle/1/4725013 [accessed 1 May 2014]

'Thinking about Prestige, Quality, and Open Access', 2008 http://dash.harvard.edu/handle/1/4322577 [accessed 21 April 2014]

Suber, Peter, Patrick O. Brown, Diane Cabell, Aravinda Chakravarti, Barbara Cohen, Tony Delamothe, and others, 'Bethesda Statement on Open Access Publishing', 2003 http://dash.harvard.edu/handle/1/4725199 [accessed 4 May 2014]

Sutton, Caroline, Peter Suber, and Amanda Page, 'Societies and Open Access Research', *Harvard Open Access Project*, 2014 bit.ly/hoap-soar [accessed 26 June 2014]

Swan, Alma, 'The Open Access Citation Advantage: Studies and Results to Date', 2010 http://eprints.soton.ac.uk/268516/ [accessed 24 March 2014]

Taylor & Francis, 'Information for Funders & Institutions', 2014 www.tandfonline.com/page/openaccess/funders [accessed 11 May 2014]

'Open Access Survey', 2013 www.tandfonline.com/page/openaccess/opensurvey [accessed 21 January 2014]

'Open Access Survey', 2014 www.tandfonline.com/page/openaccess/opensurvey/2014 [accessed 21 January 2014]

Text Encoding Initiative, 'Projects Using the TEI', 2014 www.tei-c.org/Activities/Projects/ [accessed 5 August 2014]

Thatcher, Sanford G., 'Back to the Future: Old Models for New Challenges', *Against the Grain*, 2011, 38–43

'The Crisis in Scholarly Communication', *Chronicle of Higher Education*, 3 (1995)

Thiede, Malina, 'On Open Access Evangelism', *Serials Librarian*, 67 (2014), 21–6 http://dx.doi.org/10.1080/0361526X.2014.915608

Thompson, John B., *Books in the Digital Age: The Transformation of Academic and Higher Education Publishing in Britain and the United States* (Cambridge: Polity Press, 2005)

Thomson Reuters, 'SciELO Citation Index', 2014 http://thomsonreuters.com/scielo-citation-index/ [accessed 19 May 2014]

Tubbs, Nigel, 'The Importance of Being Useless', *Times Higher Education*, 11 October 2012 www.timeshighereducation.co.uk/features/the-importance-of-being-useless/421413.article [accessed 4 February 2014]

UCU, 'Over Half of Universities and Colleges Use Lecturers on Zero-Hour Contracts', 2013 www.ucu.org.uk/6749 [accessed 6 September 2013]

United States of America, 'U.S. Constitution: Article 1 Section 8', *The U.S. Constitution Online*, 2010 www.usconstitution.net/xconst_A1Sec8.html?ModPagespeed=noscript [accessed 21 February 2014]

University of Illinois Library at Urbana-Champaign, 'The Cost of Journals', *University of Illinois Library at Urbana-Champaign*, 2009 www.library.illinois.edu/scholcomm/journalcosts.html [accessed 25 November 2013]

Van Noorden, Richard, 'Chinese Agencies Announce Open-Access Policies', *Nature*, 2014 http://dx.doi.org/10.1038/nature.2014.15255

Vardi, Moshe Y., and Richard Baraniuk, 'A New Model for Publishing Research Monographs', 2012 www.cs.rice.edu/~vardi/newmodel.txt [accessed 29 March 2014]

Veletsianos, George, and Royce Kimmons, 'Assumptions and Challenges of Open Scholarship', *International Review of Research in Open and Distance Learning*, 13 (2012), 166–89

Vincent, Nigel, and Chris Wickham, 'Debating Open Access: Introduction', in *Debating Open Access*, ed. Nigel Vincent and Chris Wickham (London: British Academy, 2013), pp. 4–12

Wade, Martyn, 'Thriving or Surviving? National Libraries in the Future' (presented at the RLUK Conference, Edinburgh, 2010) www.rluk.ac.uk/files/Martyn%20Wade%20-%202010%20Conf.pdf

Waltham, Mary, *Learned Society Open Access Business Models* (Jisc, June 2005) www.jisc.ac.uk/whatwedo/topics/opentechnologies/openaccess/reports/learnedsociety.aspx [accessed 22 January 2014]

Warne, Verity, 'To CC-BY or Not to CC-BY? A Vignette on Author Choice', *Exchanges*, 2014 http://exchanges.wiley.com/blog/2014/04/14/to-cc-by-or-not-to-cc-by-a-vignette-on-author-choice/ [accessed 23 April 2014]

Waters, Donald J., 'Preserving the Knowledge Commons', in *Understanding Knowledge as a Commons: From Theory to Practice*, ed. Charlotte Hess and Elinor Ostrom (Cambridge, MA: MIT Press, 2007), pp. 145–67

Waters, Lindsay, 'Rescue Tenure from the Tyranny of the Monograph', *Chronicle of Higher Education*, 20 April 2001 https://chronicle.com/article/Rescue-Tenure-From-the-Tyranny/9623 [accessed 18 May 2014]

Weber, Samuel, *Institution and Interpretation*, Cultural Memory in the Present, expanded edn (Stanford, CA: Stanford University Press, 2001)

Wellcome Trust, 'Position Statement in Support of Open Access Publishing', *Wellcome Trust*, 2013 www.wellcome.ac.uk/About-us/Policy/Policy-and-position-statements/WTD002766.htm [accessed 28 March 2014]

Wendling, Amy E., *Karl Marx on Technology and Alienation* (Basingstoke: Palgrave Macmillan, 2009)

Willinsky, John, *The Access Principle: The Case for Open Access to Research and Scholarship*, Digital Libraries and Electronic Publishing (Cambridge, MA: MIT Press, 2006)

'The Unacknowledged Convergence of Open Source, Open Access, and Open Science', *First Monday*, 10 (2005) http://firstmonday.org/ojs/index.php/fm/article/view/1265 [accessed 9 July 2014]

'Toward the Design of an Open Monograph Press', *Journal of Electronic Publishing*, 12 (2009) http://dx.doi.org/10.3998/3336451.0012.103

Winn, Joss, 'Helplessness', *Joss Winn*, 2013 http://josswinn.org/2013/07/helplessness/ [accessed 29 January 2014]

'Is an Open Access Journal Article a Commodity?', *Joss Winn*, 2014 http://josswinn.org/2014/02/is-an-open-access-journal-article-a-commodity/ [accessed 15 February 2014]

Wise, Alicia, 'Evidence to House of Commons Select Committee Inquiry', in *Inquiry into Open Access. Fifth Report of Session 2013–2014*, by House of Commons Business, Innovation and Skills Committee (London: House of Commons, 2013), pp. Ev1–Ev11

Xia, Jingfeng, Sarah B. Gilchrist, Nathaniel X. P. Smith, Justin A. Kingery, Jennifer R. Radecki, Marcia L. Wilhelm, and others, 'A Review of Open Access Self-Archiving Mandate Policies', *portal: Libraries and the Academy*, 12 (2012), 85–102

Index

Lightning Source UK Ltd.
Milton Keynes UK
UKOW06f0753080715

254796UK00008B/187/P